THE
lecturer's
TOOLKIT

A Practical Guide to
Learning, Teaching & Assessment

Second Edition

Phil Race

First published in 1998
Second edition 2001

Kogan Page Limited
120 Pentonville Road
London
N1 9JN
UK

Stylus Publishing Inc.
22883 Quicksilver Drive
Sterling
VA 20166–2012
USA

British Library Cataloguing in Publication Data

A CIP record for this book is available from the British Library.

ISBN 0 7494 3540 2

Typeset by Saxon Graphics Ltd, Derby
Printed and bound in Great Britain by Thanet Press Ltd, Margate

Contents

Preface

This toolkit aims to help you to underpin and develop further your professional practice as a teacher in higher education. Although the contents are intended to be useful to new lecturers, I found with the earlier edition that many old hands found the book a source of practical suggestions, as well as food for thought and reflection.

There is unprecedented pressure on university lecturers to be not just excellent researchers, but also professionally qualified at supporting students' learning, delivering teaching, giving useful feedback to students, and designing and implementing assessment. This pressure comes from all sides: from students, from colleagues, from funding agencies and from institutional managers. With students in the UK and elsewhere increasingly paying towards their own higher education, they are becoming much more aware of their role as consumers, and their right to demand high quality in the ways that their learning, teaching and assessment are delivered.

In 1997 in the UK, an important turning point for higher education was the publication of *Higher Education in the Learning Society* (the 'Dearing Report'), which was the Report of the National Committee of Enquiry on Higher Education, chaired by Sir Ron Dearing (HMSO, 1997). This report made far-reaching recommendations regarding the quality of provision of higher education, not least recommending that all new teaching staff in higher education should be properly trained and accredited in matters relating to learning, teaching and assessment. Furthermore, the report emphasized the importance of students' development of key skills (such as communication, self-organization and independence of thought), and the powerful role to be played in higher education by communications and information technologies. This toolkit is intended to help you to develop your professional practice relating to all these areas, and to serve as a practical reader for programmes for new lecturers, as well as to augment continuing professional development of experienced staff. A direct result of the Dearing Report was the establishment of the Institute for Learning and Teaching in Higher Education (ILT) in 1999.

With the move towards higher education systems where lecturers are trained and accredited in matters relating to learning, teaching and assessment, an increasing amount of attention is focused on *evidence* of good professional practice. In the UK, most universities have in place (or are working towards) programmes for lecturers which link their institutional missions to teaching and learning by means of some identified core knowledge and professional values, such as those adopted by the Institute for Learning and Teaching. These followed on from a series of outcomes and values, developed internationally during the 1990s by the Staff and Educational Development Association (SEDA).

The core knowledge areas and professional values adopted by the ILT are reproduced below (with my comments in brackets showing where in this book the knowledge areas have been addressed directly).

Core knowledge

Members of the ILT will be expected to have knowledge and understanding of:

- the subject material that they will be teaching (I take this for granted);
- appropriate methods for teaching and learning in the subject area and at the level of the academic programme (addressed particularly by Chapters 1, 3 and 4);
- models of how students learn, both generically and in their subject (generic models are addressed by Chapter 1, group-based learning is addressed by Chapter 4, and resource-based learning is addressed by Chapter 6);
- the use of learning technologies appropriate to the context in which they teach (addressed in Chapter 2 relating to giving feedback, Chapter 3 for large-group teaching, and Chapter 5 for resource-based learning);
- methods for monitoring and evaluating their own teaching (included in Chapter 6);
- the implications of quality assurance for practice (included in various parts of the book, particularly parts of Chapter 6).

Professional values

Members of the Institute will be expected to adhere to the following professional values:

- a commitment to scholarship in teaching, both generally and within their own discipline;
- a respect for individual learners and for their development and empowerment;
- a commitment to the development of learning communities, including students, teachers and all those engaged in learning support;
- a commitment to encouraging participation in higher education and to equality of educational opportunity;
- a commitment to continued reflection and evaluation and consequent improvement of their own practice.

As can be seen above, this book has been written to relate directly to the core knowledge on teaching, learning and assessment which is the basis of most of the accredited programmes for lecturers in the UK and beyond. Furthermore, I trust that readers will find that the professional values underpin the ways in which the core knowledge areas have been addressed.

At the time of writing this edition, the quality of teaching is being systematically measured in universities by the Quality Assurance Agency for Higher Education (QAA) on behalf of the respective funding councils. While the processes and procedures for implementing quality assurance are continuing to evolve, it seems certain that there will continue to be some form of systematic assessment or review of a variety of aspects of teaching, learning and assessment. Many universities also undertake such assessment and observation as part of their own staff-development, training and appraisal programmes for staff. I have included in various parts of the book checklists and activities derived from the kinds of agenda that those observing or reviewing teaching quality are presently using. These are intended to help you both to prepare for those aspects of your own appraisal which relate to teaching, learning and assessment, and to be ready for any external reviews of your own work in these areas.

What this edition covers, and why

There are six chapters in the new edition. Each chapter is written to be relatively complete in itself. References and suggestions for further reading are collected at the end of the book. Most of the book links to the central agenda of the quality of student learning introduced in Chapter 1, and I hope that you will find this a useful start to whichever parts of your professional practice you decide to review and develop first. Each chapter is prefaced by some intended outcomes, which tell more about the particular purposes the chapters are intended to serve.

Chapter 1, 'Learning – a natural human process', aims to get you thinking about the fundamental processes which underpin your students' learning. In this chapter, I ask you to interrogate your own learning (past or present), and draw out five key factors which need to be catered for in making learning truly learner-centred. All these factors are things that you can take into account in any of the learning, teaching and assessment contexts your students are likely to encounter. This chapter also now includes some suggestions on expressing and using learning outcomes, and developing students' competencies.

Chapter 2, 'Designing assessment and feedback to enhance learning', is in some ways the most crucial part of this book. Of all the things that lecturers do, I believe it is assessment, and feedback from lecturers, that most profoundly influence the ways in which students go about their learning. My intention in this chapter is to alert you to some of the tensions between effective learning and assessment, and to encourage you to diversify your approaches to assessment, so that as many as possible of your students will be able to use a range of assessment formats to show themselves at their best. I am also aware of the fact that lecturers in higher education are often severely overloaded with marking, and offer suggestions about ways of making this a more manageable part of your professional life, without prejudicing the quality and relevance of assessment. The chapter ends with a section on involving students in their own assessment, to deepen their learning and make them more aware of how assessment works in other contexts.

Chapter 3, 'Refreshing your lecturing', explores ways to design large-group teaching situations so that students' learning during them is optimized. Especially for those new to lecturing, the thought of standing up before a large group of students can be somewhat intimidating. The thrust of the chapter is about thinking through what your *students* will be doing during a large-group session, planning ways in which they can be involved, and making the most of the opportunities in large groups for students to get feedback on how their learning is progressing. I have added to this chapter a range of suggestions aiming to help you make large-group teaching work for your students, and tips about using technology in lecture rooms.

Chapter 4, 'Making small-group teaching work', explores ways of getting students to participate effectively. Small-group learning situations can be deep learning experiences for students, but need skilful facilitation to get the most out of the opportunities they provide. This chapter focuses on the processes which can be used to help all students to engage in small-group learning situations. The chapter also looks at the place of academic tutorials in higher education, at a time when it is increasingly difficult to provide the ideal quality or quantity of such student–staff encounters.

Chapter 5, 'Resource-based learning', reviews briefly the fields of open, distance and flexible learning, and aims to encourage you to make the most of the wide range of learning resource materials that are available to support learning. With larger numbers of students at university, and lecturers increasingly under higher workloads, the role of resource-based learning pathways or elements in higher education continues to grow in significance. In this chapter, I offer particular advice for those wishing to adapt existing resources to optimize their usefulness to their own students, and to those setting out to design new learning resource materials for their students. The chapter continues by helping you to interrogate how effectively students learn from both print-based and electronic resources using the widening range of communication and information technologies available.

Chapter 6 is to help *you* to survive! I have chosen the most relevant of the suggestions from *2000 Tips for Lecturers* (Race 1999) to help you take control of your time, workload, paperwork, meetings and so on, and added more detailed suggestions about preparing for appraisal, subject review, and (for experienced higher education colleagues working in the UK) how to go about applying (should you choose to do so) for Membership of the Institute for Learning and Teaching in Higher Education (ILT). The chapter ends with some suggestions on how to go about gathering feedback from your students about their experience of higher education in general, and your teaching in particular. Several feedback methods are illustrated, each with their own advantages and drawbacks.

Most chapters in the 1998 edition contained extracts from the *500 Tips* series I have written or co-authored for Kogan Page. In this new edition, the tips have been expanded and updated, and are mostly taken from the revised versions I used in *2000 Tips for Lecturers* (Race, 1999) or *500 Tips on Group Learning* (Race, 2000). I hope that the increased focus on learning, teaching and assessment will make the new edition all the more relevant to colleagues working their way through institutional accredited programmes leading to awards such as a Postgraduate Certificate in Academic Practice.

Perhaps the most visible change is that there are now two versions of this toolkit. The bound version is intended to be used by individual lecturers as their own personal copy. To make this of a manageable size, I have taken out most of the tasks and activities that interspersed the discussion in the 1998 edition. The 'institutional' version is still a ring-bound, photocopiable resource, and contains at the end of each chapter new versions of what turned out to be the most useful of the tasks and activities, as photocopiable pro formas.

Acknowledgements

I am grateful to thousands of lecturers at the workshops I run, in the UK and abroad, for their feedback, which continues to help me develop the ideas and suggestions throughout this book. I am also indebted to large numbers of students with whom I continue to run interactive sessions on developing their learning skills. Alongside my work with lecturers, I need to keep working with students, as they continually remind me of their needs, problems, aspirations and expectations, and their feelings relating to what it is like to be learning in higher education today.

I am particularly grateful to Sally Brown, with whom I wrote the first edition of this toolkit, and Steve McDowell, with whom I wrote several of the sets of tips included in this book, who have continued to give me invaluable feedback on the adjustments I have made, and on the new material I have introduced.

1: Learning – a natural human process

Intended outcomes of this chapter

The exercises and discussion points in this chapter are intended to help you to:

- remind yourself of factors involved in your own successful learning;
- consider some of the things which can go wrong when learning;
- review some of the literature on theories of learning;
- further develop your thinking about how your own students learn effectively in your own discipline;
- recognize and accommodate students' individual differences in approaches to learning;
- identify factors which can help you to make your students' learning as effective as possible.
- express the intended learning outcomes of your own curriculum elements in ways which will help your students to achieve them well, and also serve you yourself well when your intended outcomes are interrogated in quality review processes.

Never mind the teaching – feel the learning!

Whatever sort of training we think about, or whatever sort of educational experience we consider, the one thing they all need to have in common is that they lead to effective learning. There is no single ideal way to teach. Learning would be very boring if all teachers used exactly the same approaches. However, whatever teaching approaches we choose to use, it is worth stopping to think about exactly how our choices impact on our students' learning.

The human species is unique in its capacity for learning – that is why our species has evolved as much as it has. The record of human beings engaging in learning goes back to the dawn of civilization (and for quite some time before either of the words 'education' and 'training' were invented). Yet much that has been written about *how* we learn tends to have language that is unfamiliar and sometimes even alienating to most of the people who want to learn, or indeed to those who wish to cause learning to happen. In the first part of this chapter, my intention is to lead you through your own responses to four straightforward questions about learning, and to propose a simple yet powerful model of learning. It is further proposed that this model of learning can be of direct use to trainers and educators in ways that have eluded some of the more complex models of learning. The models of learning I shall explore in the next few pages of this chapter prove to be a very tangible basis upon which to build a strategy for designing lectures, tutorials and student assignments, and also for developing open-learning materials, computer-based and electronically-transmitted learning resources. However, before the chapter takes the practical look at learning described above, there follows a short review of some of the most significant ideas in the related literature.

Theories of learning

A number of models have been put forward to explain the processes of learning, or the ways that people acquire skills. There have been two main schools of thought on how learning happens. The behaviourist school takes as its starting point a view that learning happens through stimulus, response and reward: in other words a conditioning process. The stimulus is referred to as an 'input', and the learnt behaviours as 'outputs'. It can be argued that the present emphasis on expressing intended learning outcomes derives from the behaviourist school of thinking, and that clearly-articulated assessment criteria are an attempt to define the learning outputs.

The other main approach is the cognitive view, which focuses on perception, memory and concept formation, and on the development of people's ability to demonstrate their understanding of what they have learnt by solving problems. In the paragraphs below, some of the main contributors to both models are mentioned.

One of the most popular theories of the 'cognitive' school arises from the work of Lewin (1952) in 'Field theory in social science', which is part *of Selected Theoretical Papers* edited by Cartwright. This was extended by Kolb (1983) in his book *Experiential Learning: Experience as the source of learning and development*. Kolb's model identifies the fact that most of what we know we learn from experience of one kind or another, and he breaks this down into four stages, turning them into a learning cycle. Another important approach is that of Ausubel (1968), who in his book *Educational Psychology: A cognitive view* put particular emphasis on starting-points, and asserts, 'The most important single factor influencing learning is what the learner already knows. Ascertain this and teach him accordingly.' Many practices now common in training can be matched to the cognitive-psychology approach of Ausubel (1968), and his ideas of the need for 'anchoring' concepts, advance organizers (such as what we now commonly refer to as learning objectives or statements of intended learning outcomes), and clearly-broken-down learning material. This can be regarded as bringing together useful elements of the cognitive and behaviourist ways of thinking about learning.

Cognitive psychology has also made use of clinical, experimental and survey-type researches, linking personality factors of learners to their successes or failures at learning. Such research has included the ways in which learning can depend on individuals' learning skills, their approaches to learning and their learning styles; see for example the work of Pask (1976), who in an article entitled 'Styles and strategies of learning' compares serialist (basically step-by-step) and holist (meaning whole-subject, broad) approaches, respectively using operational learning (in other words, learning to do one thing at a time) and comprehension learning (in other words, gaining a deeper understanding) strategies, which tend to divide people into knowledge-seekers and understanding-seekers.

Skinner (1954), in a journal article entitled 'The science of learning and the art of teaching', presented one of the seminal papers for the behavioural school, and paid particular attention to the importance of repeated practice, and the use of rewards to help appropriate responses to be retained. Another way of looking at learning is to try to define it in terms of learning outcomes. In the 1950s and 1960s behavioural objectives ruled, and one of the most influential publications was the Bloom *et al Taxonomy of Educational Objectives, volume 1 The Cognitive Domain*, published in 1956. This approach to learning outcomes has had many forms, and can be said to have led to much of the competence-based philosophy now underpinning National Vocational Qualifications in Britain.

A useful comparison of the theories of learning is presented by Brown and Atkins (1988), in their book *Effective Teaching in Higher Education*. Ramsden (1992), in his book *Learning to Teach in Higher Education*, gives an alternative review of some of the models of learning, and mentions, for example, some of the differences between surface approaches to learning and deep approaches. He quotes an article by Biggs (1989), entitled 'Approaches to the advancement of tertiary teaching', which explains:

> Knowing facts and how to carry out operations may well be part of the means for under-standing and interpreting the world, but the quantitative conception stops at the facts and skills. A quantitative change in knowledge does not in itself change understanding. Rote-learning scientific formulae may be one of the things scientists do, but it is not the way that scientists think.

More recently, Biggs (1999) has brought together a comprehensive survey of the links between teaching and learning in higher education in his book *Teaching for Quality Learning at University*. A wide range of thinking on learning can be gained from the work of 28 practitioners from a range of disciplines and perspectives included in the collection edited by Fry, Ketteridge and Marshall (1999). The profound influence of assessment design on approaches to learning is brought into sharp relief by Gibbs (1999) in his chapter in *Assessment Matters in Higher Education* edited by Brown and Glasner. Race (1999, 2000) offers to students themselves advice on how to tune their learning in to the assessment processes, practices and instruments they will meet.

Meanwhile, Ramsden and Entwistle (1981 and subsequently) devised question-naires and interview questions with which to study how students approach learning. Various authors have taken similar approaches, and there is a substantial literature on learning styles. However, such approaches can be criticized on the grounds that they can result in students feeling labelled or stuck in a particular approach to learning, depending on their responses to the questions. Furthermore, it is desirable to try to help students gain control of their learning styles, rather than be trapped by them.

Many of the sources referred to above inform the view of learning that this chapter will now propose. However, it can be argued that some of the literature on learning uses language and concepts that most learners and teachers find different from their everyday experience, and in this chapter a more pragmatic approach is sought, to inform appropriately teaching, learning and assessment practices throughout the rest of this book. The approach outlined in this chapter is based on asking students (and others) questions about their own learning, and then analysing their responses (to date from many thousands of people from a wide range of disciplines, professions and vocations) to identify primary factors which influence the quality of learning. These factors, as you will see in this book, can be addressed consciously and directly both by students and teachers. Students can be helped to gain control over the factors, and teachers can plan their teaching to maximize the learning payoff associated with each factor.

Factors underpinning successful learning

One of the problems common to some, if not most, of the theories of learning referred to above is that they tend to be written using educational or psychological terminology. This does not mean that they are wrong, but it does mean that they are not particularly valuable when we try to use them to help our students to learn more effectively, or to help ourselves to teach more successfully. The remainder of this chapter is intended to provide you with a jargon-free, practical approach to enquiring into how learning happens best, which you can share with your students, and which you can use to inform all parts of your own work in supporting students' learning.

Getting people to think of something they have learnt successfully is a positive start to alerting them to the ways in which they learn. It does not matter what they think of as the successful learning experience of their choice – it can be work-related, or a sporting achievement, or any practical or intellectual skill. Try it for yourself: answer the pair of questions which follow now before reading on.

Question 1

(a) Think of something you are good at – something that you know you do well. Jot it down in the space below.

(b) Write below a few words about *how* you became good at this.

Now please turn to the end of this chapter, and look at *Response 1* and compare your answers to typical ones given by other people.

How did your answers compare with the typical ones included in *Response 1*? Did you feel when you read the response that you were able to put your own answers in perspective? As you will have seen from other people's answers to Question 1, relatively few people give answers such as 'by being trained' or 'by being taught' or 'by listening to experts' or 'by reading about it'. So one key to learning is *doing*. There is nothing new about this – it has already been called experiential learning for long enough – but let us stay with short words like *doing* for the present. 'Trial and error' are also important. Learning through one's mistakes is one of the most natural and productive ways to learn almost anything. Sadly, our educational culture – and particularly our assessment culture – leaves little room for learning from mistakes. Too often, mistakes are added up and used against learners!

Next, another question, to probe another dimension of successful learning.

Feeling the learning

The matter of *feelings* is something that has not been sufficiently explored by the developers of theories of learning. Feelings are as much about what it is to be human as any other aspect of humanity. There is a lot of discussion about student motivation (particularly when there is a *lack of* motivation – I shall return to this later in the chapter), but perhaps too little energy has been invested in exploring the *emotions* upon which motivation depends. A relatively simple question yields a wealth of information about the connection between feelings, emotions and successful learning. Try it for yourself.

Question 2

(a) Think of something about yourself that you feel good about – a personal attribute or quality perhaps. Jot it down in the space below.

(b) Write below a few words about how you *know* that you can feel good about whatever it is. In other words, what is the *evidence* for your positive feeling?

When you have jotted down your own notes, please turn to *Response 2* at the end of the chapter.

Receiving positive feedback

It is useful to follow up our exploration of the importance of positive feelings with some thoughts about how students can be helped to *receive* positive feedback. In some cultures, including that of the UK, there is quite a strong tendency to shrug off compliments and praise, or to resort to the defence strategy of laughter! The effects of this behaviour detract from the value of the positive feedback in the following ways:

- the positive feedback is often not really taken on board;
- the person giving the feedback may feel rejected, snubbed or embarrassed;
- the ease of giving further praise may be reduced.

Helping students (and others) to confront these possibilities can be useful in developing their skills to derive the maximum benefit from positive feedback. For example, simply replying along the lines, 'I'm glad you liked that', can make all the difference between embarrassment, and feedback effectively delivered and received.

When this is extended to the domain of negative feedback, further dividends are available. It can be very useful to train students (and ourselves!) to thank people for negative feedback, while weighing up the validity and value of it. This is much better than resorting to defensive stances, which tend in any case to stem the flow of negative feedback, usually before the most important messages have even been said.

Doing + feedback = successful learning?

Though these two elements are essential ingredients of successful learning, there are some further factors that need to be in place. These are easier to tease out by asking a question about *unsuccessful learning*. Try it for yourself now, then read on.

Question 3

(a) Think, this time, of something that you *do not* do well! This could have been the result of an unsatisfactory learning experience. Jot down something you are *not* good at in the space below.

(b) Now reflect on your choice in two ways. First, write a few words indicating what went wrong when you tried to learn whatever it was.

(c) Next, try to decide whose fault it was (if anyone's, of course). Does any blame rest with you, or with someone else (and if so, whom?).

Now please turn to *Response 3*, at the end of this chapter.

Wanting *to learn*

If there is something wrong with one's motivation, it is unlikely that successful learning will happen. However, motivation (despite being very close to 'emotion') is a rather cold word; *wanting* is a much more human word. Everyone knows what 'want' means. Also, *wanting* implies more than just motivation. *Wanting* goes right to the heart of human urges, emotions and feelings. When there is such a powerful factor at work helping learning to happen, little wonder that the results can be spectacular. We have all been pleasantly surprised at how well people who really *want* to do something usually manage to do it. If people want to learn, all is well. Unfortunately, the *want* is not automatically there. When subject matter gets tough, the *want* can evaporate quickly. When learners do not warm to their teachers, or their learning environments, their *want* can be damaged.

Making sense of what one has learnt – digesting – realizing

This is about making sense of the learning experience – and also making sense of feedback received from other people. *Digesting* is about sorting out what is important in what has been learnt. *Digesting* is about extracting the fundamental principles from the background information. *Digesting* is also about discarding what is not important. It is about putting things into perspective. *Digesting*, above all else, is about establishing a sense of *ownership* of what has been learned. It is about *far more* than just reflection. Students often describe digesting as 'getting my head around it'. They sometimes explain it as 'realizing'. When one has just *realized* something, one is then able to communicate the idea to other people – tangible evidence that learning has been successful.

Thousands of people have answered the three questions we have looked at, and even written their answers down. The people asked have covered all age ranges, occupations and professions. It is not surprising to discover that very different people still manage to learn in broadly similar ways. After all, learning is a *human* process – it matters little whether you are a human trainer, a human student, or a human manager. In face-to-face training, or large-group-based education, learners are already surrounded by people who can help with the *digesting* stage – most importantly, each other. When learners put their heads together informally to try to make sense of a difficult idea or problem, a lot of digesting and realizing occurs.

One more question!

For the final question, let us return to successful learning, but this time without that vital 'want'.

Question 4

(a) Think of something that you did in fact learn successfully, but at the time you did not *want* to learn it. Probably it is something that you are *now* glad you learnt. Jot something of this sort below.

(b) Write down a few words about 'what kept you at it' – in other words the alternatives that worked even when your *want* to learn was low or absent.

Once more, please turn to *Response 4* at the end of the chapter before reading on.

Needing to learn – a substitute for motivation?

Responses to Question 4 often highlight the fact that a successful driving force for learning is necessity. There are some subjects where it can be very difficult to generate in students a strong *want* to learn, but where it may be quite possible for us to explain to them convincingly why they really do *need* to learn them. For example, for many years I taught students chemical thermodynamics. Few (normal!) students *want* to get to grips with the Second Law of Thermodynamics, but many *need* to get their heads round it. When students have ownership of a *want* to learn, there is little that we need to do to help them maintain their motivation. However, helping students to gain ownership of the *need* to learn something is a reasonable fallback position, and can still help students to learn successfully.

Five factors underpinning successful learning

From my analysis of thousands of people's answers to the four straightforward questions we have explored so far in this chapter, the principal factors underpinning successful learning can be summarized as follows.

Wanting	motivation, interest, enthusiasm
Needing	necessity, survival, saving face
Doing	practice, trial and error
Feedback	other people's reactions seeing the results
Digesting	making sense of what has been learnt, realizing, gaining ownership

Learning cycles

Probably the best known learning cycle is that involving the stages of active experimentation, reflective observation, concrete experience and abstract conceptualization. One problem with this cycle is that it is not too clear where on the cycle one should best start, or indeed which way round to go, or even in which order the four steps should be connected. You will notice I have not included any arrows. Another problem is the vocabulary chosen for the steps in such cycles. It can of course be argued that active experimentation, reflective observation, concrete experience and abstract conceptualization collectively mean the same as *wanting* or *needing, doing, feedback* and *digesting* – but try asking some of your own non-specialist students to explain what the terms in the former list mean! (Asking people to define concrete experience for you may produce more than one reference to sand, cement and paths!)

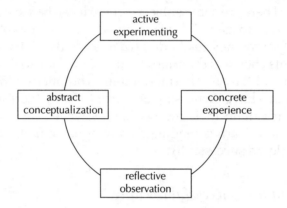

Figure 1.1   Traditional representation of stages of learning after Kolb

In fact, there are times when one needs to be in two places at once in the cycle. Also, the terminology in the cycle may mean a lot to those who think they know what it all means, but it leaves most other people quite cold. It is tempting to try drawing a cycle with *wanting, doing, feedback* and *digesting*. At least there seems to be an obvious logical order.

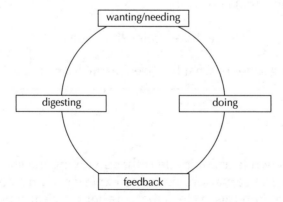

Figure 1.2   A cyclic order for factors underpinning successful learning?

But are we really going round in circles?

Although it is useful to consider learning as a combination of processes, imposing a cyclic order on learning processes is – to say the least – a gross oversimplification. In fact, the more that the processes can be made to overlap, the better. For example:

- It is important to keep on *wanting* while *doing*.
- It is useful to be seeking *feedback* while *doing* as well as after *doing*.
- It is useful to be continuing to seek *feedback* while *digesting*.
- It is useful to be continuing the *doing* while receiving *feedback* and while *digesting*.
- It is important to *digest* both the experience of *doing* and the *feedback* that is received.

'Ripples on a pond'…

The human brain is not a computer that works in a linear or pre-programmed way all the time. Our brains often work at various overlapping levels when, for example, solving problems or making sense of ideas. The *wanting* stage needs to pervade throughout, so that *doing* is wanted, *feedback* is positively sought, opportunities for *digesting* are seized, and so on. Perhaps a more sensible model would have *wanting* at the heart, and *feedback* coming from the outside, and *doing* and *digesting* occurring in an overlapping way as pictured below.

One can imagine this as a spreading-ripples model, fired by the *wanting*, where the bounced-back ripples from the external world constitute the *feedback* and continue to influence the *doing*. The effects of the *feedback* on the *doing* could be thought of as *digesting*. The main benefit of such a model is that it removes the need to think about learning as a unidirectional sequence. The model has about it both a simplicity and a complexity – in a way mirroring the simultaneous simplicity and complexity in the ways in which people actually learn.

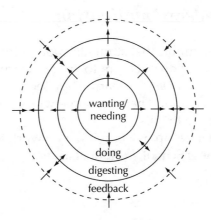

Figure 1.3   'Ripples on a pond' model of learning processes

Using the model

Probably the greatest strength of the *wanting/needing, doing, feedback, digesting* model of learning is that it lends itself to providing a solid foundation upon which to design educational and training programmes. If you look at any successful form of education and training, you will find that one way or another, all of these factors underpinning effective learning are addressed. Different situations and processes attend to each of the factors in different ways.

For example, *wanting* is catered for by the effective face-to-face lecturer who generates enthusiasm. *Wanting* can be catered for by carefully-worded statements showing the intended learning outcomes, which capture the learners' wishes to proceed with their learning. The wanting can be enhanced by the stimulation provided by attractive colours and graphics in computer-based packages or on the Internet. What if there is no *wanting* or *needing* there in the first place? Perhaps feedback can, when coupled with learning by doing and digesting, cause the ripple to move back into the centre, and create some motivation.

Learning by *doing* is equally at the heart of any good course, and equally in any well-designed flexible learning package or computer-based learning package.

Feedback is provided by tutors, or by the printed responses to exercises or self-assessment questions in flexible learning materials, or by feedback responses on-screen in computer assisted learning programmes, or simply by fellow learners giving feedback to each other. Feedback can be regarded as the process that prevents the whole 'ripple' simply dying away, as feedback interacts with the *digesting and doing* stages, and keeps the learning moving.

The one that is all too easy to miss out is *digesting*. However, all experienced tutors know how important it is to give learners the time and space to make sense of their learning and to put it into perspective. Similarly, the best learning packages cater for the fact that learners need to be given some opportunity to practise with what they have already learnt, before moving on to further learning.

Ways to increase students' motivation

In many universities, staff grumble that students' motivation is not what it used to be. There are students who simply do not seem to *want* to learn. There are students who do not seem to see why they may *need* to learn. They seem less willing to sit at our feet and imbibe of our infinite wisdom. There are some who even seem to believe that we are paid to do their learning to them!

With a small international group of lecturers, who work with students from many cultures at European Business School, London, I asked:

- Why is motivation often low?
- What symptoms can we observe?
- How can we address the situation?

Why is motivation often low?

There are many reasons for increased incidence of low levels of student motivation, including the following:

- **There are many more students in our higher education system.** We still have those students who are keen to learn, but they are diluted by students whose motivation is much less, and who would not have come into our system some years ago. The proportion of students who know exactly *why* they are in higher education has decreased.
- **More students enter higher education to satisfy other people's expectations of them, rather than through their own motivation to succeed.** Some are coaxed, cajoled or pressed by parents and others, and come in as a duty rather than as a mission.
- **There is a greater culture shock on moving from school to higher education – all those distracting temptations, and scary unprecedented freedom.** Many students are unprepared for the increased responsibility for their own learning which higher education places upon them.
- **Students are much more grown-up than they used to be.** Their lifestyle expectations have increased. This means that problems with finances and difficulties with relationships take a greater toll on the energies of more students than used to be the case.
- **The rigours of our academic systems can mean that there may be no chance of remediation for poor assessed work,** and failure can breed irrecoverably low motivation.

The symptoms of low motivation

Some symptoms of failing motivation appear to us as in-class behaviours, others we see evidence of as out-of-class behaviours, with yet more symptoms reflecting students' perceptions about ourselves.

Some in-class symptoms of low motivation:

- Coming to class late and/or leaving early, or indeed not turning up at all.
- Talking to friends in class about other things.

- Looking out of the window, scribbling, drawing, doodling, writing letters to friends, sending text messages on mobile phones.
- Lack of engagement, not asking questions, not being willing to answer questions, nor volunteering responses when invited.
- Diverting lecturers from the main issues.
- Not coming in equipped with pens, paper, books, calculators, and so on.
- Taking a longer break than is intended during long sessions, or failing to return at all.
- Yawning, looking uninterested, and avoiding eye contact.
- Inappropriate social interactions in class (compare back row of cinema!).

Some out-of-class symptoms of low motivation

- Consistent absence without reason.
- Inadequate preparation for class work.
- Handing in scribbled last-minute work – botched, or not handing in any work.
- Low-quality individual and/or group work.
- Damaging each other's attitude.
- Work-avoidance strategies – giving in too easily to doing only unimportant tasks and putting off doing important ones.
- Ignoring lecturers out of class.
- Being found not to have contributed to group tasks – doing only what is necessary for coursework marks, but not doing other things.
- Not buying books or using library resources.
- Maintaining poor folders and disorganized collections of handouts.

Is some of it our fault?

Some explanations of low student motivation are directed in our direction! The charges against us include:

- Our seeming indifference to time of day factors – Friday afternoon classes, students' need for an early afternoon snooze after lunch.
- Students' experiences of the unevenness of the pressure of work – for example, weeks go by with nothing to hand in, then there is a deluge of hand-in dates.
- Some students feeling that they have been labelled by us already as low achievers, and taking all slightly-critical feedback as reinforcement of their lowered self-esteem.
- Seating plans too rigid and predictable, room quality, the overall learning environment being scruffy or unenthusing.

- The teachers they meet – our own looks, sounds, level of enthusiasm, perceived lack of understanding about learning styles or the effects of the learning environment.
- More able students feeling that they are undervalued and under-challenged, and that we spend too long catering for the lower-fliers.
- Insufficient acceptance on our part of a basic human need for students (like children) to win at least some of the battles.

How to tackle low motivation

The following suggestions are tactics, rather than solutions. However, choosing tactics can be our first steps towards building a strategy to counter the malaise of poor student motivation. You will already have your own tactics to add to (or supersede) the ones suggested below:

1 **Accept that it is a real problem.** Pretending that low motivation does not exist does not make it disappear. Treating it as an issue to be addressed jointly with students increases the chance that they will recognize it themselves, and (as only they can) make adjustments to their rationale for being students in higher education.

2 **Recognize the boundary conditions of the problem.** Low motivation is essentially a problem with full-time students, rarely with part-timers. Low motivation is essentially a problem with younger students, rather than mature returners. When we have large mixed-ability, mixed-age classes containing full-timers and part-timers together, the range of motivation is even more of a problem to all concerned.

3 **Remember that students have difficult lives.** First-year students may be far from home, family, friends, familiar streets, for the first extended time so far. For some, it is like being on remand – they have been sent there by other people. Some delight in their new environment, others are homesick, but all are expending a lot of their energy adjusting their lives. The differences between school and university are more profound than perhaps they were when we were new students.

4 **Many young people are rebels.** It is a natural enough stage of growing up. But this means that they are not so keen to please us, and may be more willing to be sullen, uncooperative and passive. In our consumer-led society (and students are consumers) they are less likely to try to hide their dissatisfaction. None of this means that they are not intelligent, or that they lack potential.

5 **Seek different kinds of feedback from students.** We already seek lots

of feedback, but often with repetitive, boring devices such as tick-box questionnaires, where students do not really tell us anything other than their surface responses to too-often-asked structured questions about our teaching. Ask students how they feel about topics, rooms, assignments, and us! Ask for words, not just rankings.

6 **Make it OK to be demotivated.** Students sometimes feel that their low morale is yet another failure, and it becomes a self-fulfilling prophecy. All human beings (ourselves included) have peaks and troughs in motivation, and students need to see that (for example) success can breed more success.

7 **Do not expect students to be passionately interested in things they do not yet understand.** The passion often comes with understanding, and the understanding often comes with experience and interaction, so concentrate on learning by doing, peer feedback and in-class involvement. Do not lecture to a group that is supposed to be entirely switched-on, when we know all too well that it is not.

8 **Do not presuppose that your own topic is the light in the life of all the students you see.** A few may end up researching in this topic, but for most it is just another stepping-stone to the degree that they are going to use for something quite different from your own particular field. Make it an interesting stepping-stone, but do not expect all the students to take it as seriously as you perhaps do.

9 **Concentrate on their learning, rather than your teaching.** Think more carefully when you are teaching about what will be going on in their minds, rather than the information in your mind that you would love to transfuse to your students. Knowledge is not infectious, and is much more than mere information. Enthusiasm is, however, infectious – we can try to transmit this.

10 **Get assessment into perspective.** The assessments students do for you are done alongside all the other assessed tasks they do for all their other teachers. Do not let students' lives be dominated by assessed work, to the exclusion of the natural joy of learning.

11 **Spend more time helping all students to become better learners.** Do not regard it as someone else's business. Do not assume that students should already be skilled learners. Help students to gain more control over how they learn, so that they have a greater ownership over what they learn. Above all, continue to help them to address why they are learning.

12 **Spend more energy on praising.** Students (like ourselves) respond well to positive feedback. Ticks are not enough. It is all too easy for us to spend our limited time on giving constructive critical feedback, but if there is not enough praise there, this just seems like condemnation to demotivated students.

13 **Continue being a student.** Perhaps a requirement for employment as a teacher in higher education should be that we too should always be enrolled on an academic programme as students, and that we should see our studies through to assessment. And we should have the opportunity to fail or succeed, just like our students. Therein lies the essence of understanding students' motivations.

Developing students' competencies

Let us stand back from what we have already thought about in this chapter, and go back to the central purposes of everything we do when teaching, or designing learning resources for students. We intend to help students become more competent. The competencies we are addressing are not just those relating to skills which students will be able to demonstrate to us, nor are they all amenable to our usual assessment processes and practices. The competencies include those connected with thinking, creativity, originality, problem-solving and so on, as well as those linked to mastery of defined areas of knowledge.

What is the opposite of competence? 'Incompetence' is the word that immediately comes to mind. Unfortunately, incompetence is a word with negative associations, so some time ago I coined the word 'uncompetence' to mean not-yet-competent, a concept less threatening than incompetence.

It is useful to add to our thinking about learning by exploring how we can help our students to gain competence, and how we can help them to be aware of what is happening as they learn. This is why I developed a model of conscious versus unconscious competence and uncompetence.

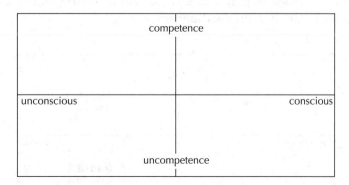

Figure 1.4 Conscious–unconscious competence–uncompetence

The 'target' box

We want to help our students to become consciously competent. This can be regarded as the target box on the competence–uncompetence matrix. The more we can help students to be *aware* of their competencies, the better their motivation. In other words, conscious competence links to the *wanting* to learn factor. It breeds confidence. We can address this by expressing intended learning outcomes as clearly as we can, so that students are aware when they have reached the position of achieving these outcomes, and know that they are able to demonstrate their achievement of them to us when we assess their performance.

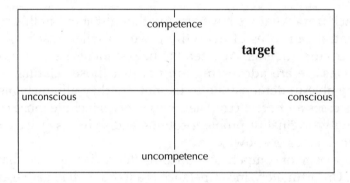

Figure 1.5   Conscious competence: the 'target' box

The 'transit' box

There is nothing wrong with 'conscious uncompetence'. Indeed, knowing what one cannot yet do is usually an essential step towards becoming able to do it. Of course, many unconscious uncompetencies do not even need to be addressed, including all the things one does not need to become able to do, and so on. It is only those conscious uncompetencies which relate to the topics to be learnt that need to be moved towards the target box on the diagram.

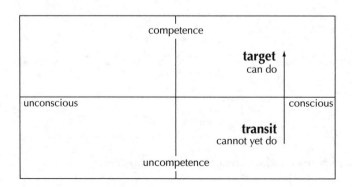

Figure 1.6   Conscious uncompetence: the 'transit' box

When the intended learning outcomes are clear, it is easier for students themselves to work out what they cannot yet do, and they can often turn their conscious uncompetencies into competencies without further help. However, as teachers we can often help students to gain feedback which gives them a lot more detail of exactly how they should go about moving out of the transit position. Similarly, students can gain a great deal of feedback from each other about how best to make the move.

Unconscious uncompetence: the 'danger' box

This is about not knowing what one cannot yet do. For most learners (students, but also ourselves), it is the things we do not know we are not yet good at which pose the greatest threat. It could be argued that the art of teaching is about helping students to find out what lies hidden in their 'danger' boxes on this diagram! Clear expressions of intended learning outcomes can help students to see that there are things they had not yet identified that they needed to become able to achieve. However, even more help can be brought to bear by assessment and feedback, where we (and indeed fellow students) contribute to giving students information about what they did not know that they could not yet do.

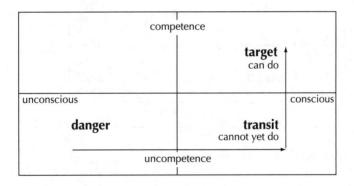

Figure 1.7   Unconscious uncompetence: the 'danger' box

It is of course possible for students to jump straight from the 'danger' position to the 'target' one, but then it can be argued that their learning is not nearly as deep as it would have been if they had been alerted to the detail of exactly what it was that they did not know they could not yet do, then had tackled the situation consciously and addressed the problem.

It is increasingly recognized that an important function of higher education is to help students to develop their key transferable skills. Some of the most important of these are those connected with becoming self-sufficient, autonomous learners.

Ideally, we need to be training students to become able to probe for themselves what might lie in the danger box in their learning.

Unconscious competence: the 'magic' box

Fortunately, we all have unconscious competencies as well as conscious ones. Many skilful teachers do not actually *need* to be aware of exactly wherein lies the success of their teaching. Students who can already achieve learning outcomes do not necessarily have to *know* that they are already in a position to do so. However, it can be argued that the transition from the 'magic' box to the 'target' one is a useful part of the learning process. For example, the excellent teacher who finds out *why* his or her teaching is successful is in a much better position to help others emulate that success. Similarly, students who find out about their unconscious competencies are in a better position to build up their confidence, and to draw from that gain in self-understanding reflective processes which they can use in their conscious learning.

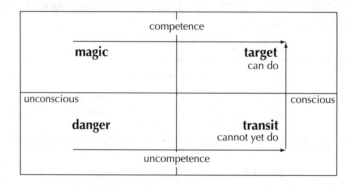

Figure 1.8 Unconscious competence: the 'magic' box

It can be a little unsettling to translate unconscious competencies into conscious ones. It can be compared to being able to ride a bike, and wobbling when becoming aware of the processes involved. However, the learning which accompanies this sort of transition can be of value when it is applied to new learning scenarios.

More importantly, most students find that when they are alerted to the things they did not realize that they could already do well, they gain confidence and self-esteem. As teachers, we need to remind ourselves that our work is not just about telling students what they need to do, but equally about alerting students to strengths they already have. Positive feedback is a powerful aid to motivation, and where better to direct our positive feedback than to the things that students may not have realized deserved our praise.

Positioning the goalposts – designing and using learning outcomes

So far, this chapter has been about *how* learning can be caused to happen. All of this is academic unless we also link it to *what* is intended to be learnt, including thinking about why, when and where. That is where learning outcomes come in.

Learning outcomes represent the modern way of defining the content of a syllabus. The old-fashioned way was simply to list topic headings, and leave it to the imagination of the lecturer exactly what each heading would mean in practice, and how (or indeed if) each part of the content would be assessed in due course. Nowadays, expressions of learning outcomes are taken to define the content, level and standard of any course, module or programme. External scrutiny interrogates assessment criteria against learning outcomes to ensure that the assessment is appropriate in level and standard to the course or module. Even more importantly, however, learning outcomes can be vitally useful to students themselves, who (with a little guidance) can be trained to use the expressed learning outcomes as the targets for their own achievement.

The intended learning outcomes are the most important starting point for any new teaching–learning programme. Learning outcomes give details of syllabus content. They can be expressed in terms of the objectives that students should be able to *show* that they have achieved, in terms of knowledge, understanding, skills and even attitudes. They are written as descriptors of ways in which students will be expected to demonstrate the results of their learning. The links between learning outcomes and assessment criteria need to be clear and direct. Learning outcomes indicate the standards of courses and modules, and are spotlighted in quality review procedures.

Why learning outcomes should be used

Well-expressed statements of intended learning outcomes help students to identify their own targets, and work systematically towards demonstrating their achievement of these targets.

Learning outcomes are now required, in the higher education sector in the UK, for subject review by the Quality Assurance Agency, and will be increasingly cross-referenced by academic reviewers against assessment processes, instruments and standards.

In the context of benchmarking, learning outcomes can provide one of the most direct indicators of the intended level and depth of any programme of learning.

Where learning outcomes can be useful to students

Learning outcomes should not just reside in course validation documentation (though they need to be there in any case). They should also underpin everyday teaching–learning situations. They can be put to good use in the following places and occasions:

- in student handbooks, so that students can see the way in which the whole course or module is broken down into manageable elements of intended achievement, and set their own targets accordingly;
- at the start of each lecture, for example on a slide or transparency, so that students are informed of the particular purposes of the occasion;
- at the end of each lecture, so that students can estimate the distance they have travelled towards being able to achieve the intended outcomes associated with the lecture;
- at suitable points in the briefing of students for longer elements of their learning, including projects, group tasks, practical work and field work;
- on each element of handout material issued before, during or after lectures, to reinforce the links between the content of the handout and students' intended learning;
- on tasks and exercises, and briefings to further reading, so that students can see the purpose of the work they are intended to do;
- on the first few screens of each computer-based learning programme that students study independently (or in groups);
- at the beginning of self-study or flexible learning packages, so that students can estimate their own achievement as they work through the materials.

Tips on designing and using learning outcomes

It is natural enough that professional people such as lecturers may feel some resistance to having the content of their teaching 'pinned down' by pre-expressed statements of intended learning outcomes. However, the rationale for using learning outcomes is so strong that we need to look at some practical pointers which will help even those who do not believe in them to be able to write them reasonably success-fully. It is in the particular public context of linking learning-expressed outcomes to assessment criteria that most care needs to be taken. The following suggestions (opposite) are based on many workshops I have run helping lecturers to put into clear, everyday words the gist of their intentions regarding the learning they intend to be derived from a particular lecture, or a practical exercise, or a tutorial, or students' study of a journal paper and so on – *each and every* element which makes up a programme of study.

1 **Work out exactly what you want students to be able to do by the end of each defined learning element.** Even when you are working with syllabus content that is already expressed in terms of learning outcomes, it is often worth thinking again about your exact intentions, and working out how these connect together for different parts of students' learning.

2 **Do not use the word 'students' in your outcomes** – except in dry course documentation. It is much better to use the word 'you' when addressing students. 'When we've completed this lecture, you should be able to compare and contrast particle and wave models of radiation' is better than stating, 'The expected learning outcome of this lecture is that students will… . Similarly, use the word 'you' when expressing learning outcomes in student handbooks, handouts, laboratory briefing sheets, and so on. Students need to feel that learning outcomes belong to them, not just to other people.

3 **Work imaginatively with existing learning outcomes.** There may already be externally-defined learning outcomes, or they may have been prescribed some time ago when the course or programme was validated. These may, however, be written in language which is not user-friendly or clear to students, and which is connected more with the teaching of the subject than the learning process. You should be able to translate these outcomes, so that they will be more useful to your students.

4 **Match your wording to your students.** The learning outcomes as expressed in course documentation may be off-putting and jargonistic, and may not match the intellectual or language skills of your students. By developing the skills to translate learning outcomes precisely into plain English, you will help the outcomes to be more useful to them, and at the same time it will be easier for you to design your teaching strategy.

5 **Your intended learning outcomes should serve as a map to your teaching programme.** Students and others will look at the outcomes to see if the programme is going to be relevant to their needs or intentions. The level and standards associated with your course will be judged by reference to the stated learning outcomes.

   Remember that many students will have achieved at least some of your intended outcomes already. When introducing the intended learning outcomes, give credit for existing experience, and confirm that it is useful if some members of the group already have some experience and expertise which they can share with others.

6 **Be ready for the question 'why?'** It is only natural for students to want to know why a particular learning outcome is being addressed. Be prepared to illustrate each outcome with some words about the purpose of including it.

7 **Be ready for the reaction 'so what?'** When students, colleagues, or external reviewers still cannot see the point of a learning outcome, they are likely to need some further explanation before they will be ready to take it seriously.

8 **Work out your answers to 'what's in this for me?'** When students can see the short-term and long-term benefits of gaining a particular skill or competence, they are much more likely to try to achieve it.

9 **Do not promise what you cannot deliver.** It is tempting to design learning outcomes that seem to be the answers to everyone's dreams. However, the real test for your teaching will be whether it is seen to enable students to achieve the outcomes. It is important to be able to link each learning outcome to an assessable activity or assignment.

10 **Do not use words such as 'understand' or 'know'.** While it is easy to write (or say), 'When you have completed this module successfully, you will understand the Third Law of Thermodynamics', it is much more helpful to step back and address the questions, how will we know that they have understood it, how will they themselves know they have understood it, and what will they be able to do to *show* that they have understood it? Replies to the last of these questions lead to much more useful ways of expressing the relevant learning outcomes.

11 **Do not start at the beginning.** It is often much harder to write the outcomes that will be associated with the beginning of a course, and it is best to leave attempting this until you have got into your stride regarding writing outcomes. In addition, it is often much easier to work out what the 'early' outcomes actually should be once you have established where these outcomes are leading students towards.

12 **Think ahead to assessment.** A well-designed set of learning outcomes should automatically become the framework for the design of assessed tasks. It is worth asking yourself, 'How can I measure this?' for each draft learning outcome. If it is easy to think of how it will be measured, you can normally go ahead and design the outcome. If it is much harder to think of how it could be measured, it is usually a signal that you may need to think further about the outcome, and try to relate it more firmly to tangible evidence that could be assessed.

13 **Keep sentences short.** It is important that your students should be able to get the gist of each learning outcome without having to reread it several times, or ponder on what it really means.

14 **Consider illustrating your outcomes with 'for example...' descriptions.** If necessary, such extra details could be added in smaller print, or in brackets. Such additional detail can be invaluable to students

in giving them a better idea what their achievement of the outcomes may actually amount to in practice.

15 **Test-run your learning outcome statements.** Ask target-audience students, 'What do you think this really means?' to check that your intentions are being communicated clearly. Also test your outcome statements out on colleagues, and ask them whether you have missed anything important, or whether they can suggest any changes to your wording.

16 **Aim to provide students with the whole picture.** Put the student-centred language descriptions of learning outcomes and assessment criteria into student handbooks, or turn them into a short self-contained leaflet to give to students at the beginning of the course. Ensure that students do not feel swamped by the enormity of the whole picture. Students need to be guided carefully through the picture in ways that allow them to feel confident that they will be able to succeed a step at a time.

17 **Do not get hung up too much on performance, standards and conditions when expressing learning outcomes.** For example, do not feel that such phrases as 'on your own', or 'without recourse to a calculator or computer' or 'under exam conditions' or 'with the aid of a list of standard integrals' need to be included in every well-expressed learning outcome. Such clarifications

are extremely valuable elsewhere, in published assessment criteria. Do not dilute the primary purpose of a learning outcome with administrative detail.

18 **Do not be trivial.** Trivial learning outcomes support criticisms of reductionism. One of the main objections to the use of learning outcomes is that there can be far too many of them, only some of which are really important.

19 **Do not try to teach something if you cannot think of any intended learning outcome associated with it.** This seems obvious, but it can be surprising how often a teaching agenda can be streamlined and focused by checking that there is some important learning content associated with each element in it, and removing or shortening the rest.

20 **Do not confuse learning outcomes and assessment criteria.** It is best not to cloud the learning outcomes with the detail of performance criteria and standards until students know enough about the subject to understand the language of such criteria. In other words, the assessment criteria are best read by students *after* they have started to learn the topic, rather than at the outset (but make sure that the links will be clear in due course).

21 **Do not write any learning outcomes that cannot (or will not) be assessed.** If it is important enough to propose as an intended learning outcome, it should be worthy of

being measured in some way, and it should be *possible* to measure it.

22 **Do not design any assessment task or question that is not related to the stated learning outcomes.** If it is important enough to measure, it is only fair to let students know that it is on their learning agenda.

23 **Do not state learning outcomes at the beginning, and fail to return to them.** It is important to come back to them at the end of each teaching–learning element, such as lecture, self-study package, element of practical work and so on. Turn them into checklists for students, for example along the lines 'Check now that you feel able to…' or 'Now you should be in a position to…'.

Conclusions about learning

For too long, learning has been considered as a special kind of human activity, requiring its own jargon and vocabulary. It is not! To learn is to be human. My main point is that *wanting/needing, doing, feedback* and *digesting* are so close to the essence of being human that it is possible to keep these processes firmly in mind when designing educational courses, training programmes, learning resources and open learning materials. In addition, it is worth thinking about the conscious and unconscious sides of developing students' competencies, to become better equipped to help students to develop their own learning skills. Even more important, it is useful to be able to relate the fundamental factors explored in this chapter to something that is usually inextricably linked to learning: assessment.

Furthermore, we need to remember that learning is done *by* people – not *to* them. In other words, it is useful to use a model of learning which learners themselves can understand. Moreover, it is important to use a model of learning which learners themselves *believe in*. The *wanting/needing, doing, feedback, digesting* model can easily be introduced to learners by asking them the questions used earlier in this chapter, and they then gain a sense of ownership of the model. Similarly, students themselves readily identify with the competence–uncompetence model illustrated in this chapter, and find it helpful in taking more control of their own learning. It often comes as a pleasant surprise and a welcome relief that there is not something mystical or magical about how people learn.

Finally, having paid due regard to *how* students (and of course we ourselves) learn, you will find it vital to become very skilled at putting into clear, unambiguous words your descriptions of *what* is to be learnt. Writing learning outcomes is not an activity that can be done off the cuff. Expressions of intended learning outcome, need to be drafted, edited, discussed, refined and continuously reviewed, if we are to define our curriculum in ways which will stand up to the increasing levels of external scrutiny of our professional practice.

Many people returning to study later in life have hang-ups about things that went wrong in their previous experience of education or training. Straightforward approaches to how they learn, and clarification of what they are intended to learn, give them renewed confidence in their own abilities to apply everyday, common-sense approaches to the business of studying.

Responses

Near the beginning of this chapter were four questions about your own learning. Below are some responses other people have made to these questions. Check out whether your own thoughts about the questions are spanned by those summarized below.

Response to Question 1

It does not seem to matter at all what people choose for the thing they are good at. It also does not seem to matter what sort of people they are. I would like you to scan through the typical answers I get, and see whether your thoughts are matched by those of others. This set of responses is typical of those from large groups of students, this time from an occasion when the students were asked to write down not only how they became good at things, but also what exactly they claimed to be good at. Not surprisingly, the answers included some which make one smile.

driving	lessons, test, practice
playing the piano	practice, lessons
dancing	practice, lessons, experience
gardening	experience, reading about it, talking and listening to gardeners
painting	taught techniques, then practice and experimentation
essays	practice
table tennis	taught, practice, time, experience, sticking with it, endeavour
cooking	practice, necessity, interest

acting	practice, taught techniques by tutor, involving myself in pantomimes
playing clarinet	practice, making mistakes, help from others, books, threats
swimming	practice, enjoyment
drinking beer	extended practice, socializing
sex	practice, pain, pleasure and struggle and hard work
mix concrete	by trial and error after being shown how to do it
sewing	being taught, practice, enjoying doing it so practising more

A further common thread which can be inferred from many of the students' responses above is that there is a strong connection between their developing confidence and developing competence (whatever the variety).

To sum up, in general the most frequent answers to this question are along the following lines:

- practice, repetition;
- by doing it;
- by trial and error;
- by getting it wrong at first and learning from mistakes.

Now please return to the main text and try the next question.

Response to Question 2

Below are typical responses to the second part of Question 2 – are these similar to yours?

- other people's responses;
- reactions of others – feedback from others;
- fun, I enjoy it, it feels good, it feels right;
- good feedback, seeing results, helping others to achieve things;
- compliments – reinforcement from others;
- quality of finished task;
- measuring self against others.

By far the most frequent answers are reactions of other people, feedback, compliments and seeing the results.

All of these amount to *feedback* of one sort or another. Relatively few people claim that the origin of their positive feelings comes from within. Most people need to have approval from fellow human beings to develop a really positive feeling about something. Positive feelings are a crucial stepping-stone along the way towards successful learning. Indeed, two of the most common things that can prevent successful learning are the absence of positive feedback and the reception of *negative* feedback. Criticism or disapproval can be powerful contributors to unsuccessful learning.

From the two responses so far, we have seen that *learning by doing* and *getting feedback* are vital ingredients for successful learning. However, there are still some things missing from a complete recipe for successful learning, so please return to the main text and try another question.

Response to Question 3

Here are some answers which the second part of Question 3 yields:

The causes of some unsuccessful learning experiences are as follows:

- No chance to practise; sheer lack of ability.
- My inability to fathom technical information; no human help given?
- I never learnt how to 'get on the wavelength' of those who do it well.
- I was warned by my father not to become competent at this activity.
- Did not make sense; felt bad. Could not get to grips with it. Social pressure.
- Insufficient commitment by teacher.
- Never knew when I was doing well/badly. Didn't practise sufficiently. Began too late.
- The explanation was given at too rapid a speed without any acknowledgement of need to reflect and digest.
- Failure of confidence. Possibly I didn't really need to do it? Motivation problem?
- Insufficient practice.
- Unrealistic explanations; damning feedback (or none).
- Not allowing enough extra time to make good choices.

The answers which emerge from these questions are often quite complex, but the general trends hardly vary at all between very different groups in terms of age, experience, profession or vocation. It has to be said that a not infrequent response is for people to write down the name of their best-remembered mathematics teacher!

However, apart from this, a pattern emerges quite readily. For a start, there are usually some answers which relate to something having gone wrong with the two essentials we have already looked at. For example:

> - lack of opportunity to practise, or to learn safely from mistakes;
> - 'bad' feedback – critical feedback given in a hostile or negative way.

Looking for further factors, the following are often found in people's answers:

> - no motivation;
> - lack of time to make sense of it;
> - fear of failure;
> - couldn't see why it was worth doing;
> - unable to understand it before moving on.

These boil down to two further essentials for successful learning: *wanting* and *digesting*. Let us next look at each of these in turn in a little more detail. Please return once again to the main text, and one final question.

Response to Question 4

It is fascinating to see the things that people learnt successfully, even when they did not want to learn them! People's replies to Question 4 include just about everything, but favourites seem to be driving, swimming, using computers and cooking! However, all sorts of theoretical and conceptual agendas also crop up in people's answers. There are two main factors which account for 'what kept you at it'. These are **need** and **pressure**.

The 'need' factors come in many forms, ranging from needing to learn it for one's job, to needing to learn it for survival. The 'pressure' factors come in various kinds, ranging from strong supportive encouragement from family, friends and teachers, to threats and jibes. From these answers, however, the principal additional factor to emerge is needing to learn, as the encouragement-type (or less positive exhortations) are already covered by the feedback dimension that I discussed in Question 2. Please return now to the main text of the chapter.

2: Designing assessment and feedback to enhance learning

Intended outcomes of this chapter

When you have explored the ideas in this chapter, and tried out the most appropriate ones in the context of your own teaching and assessment, you should be better able to:

- design assessment processes and instruments which will be integral to your students' learning;
- reduce the assessment burden on yourself and on your students;
- interrogate your assessment processes, practices and instruments to ensure that they are valid, reliable and transparent;
- give more and better feedback to more students in less time;
- diversify the assessment processes and instruments you use, so that the same students are not repeatedly disadvantaged by a few of these;
- involve students in appropriate elements of their own assessment, to deepen further their learning.

Putting assessment and feedback into perspective

Whether we think of ourselves as lecturers, or teachers, or facilitators of learning, the most important thing we do for our students is to assess their work. This is why, in this book, I have gone straight into assessment after thinking about learning. It is in the final analysis the assessment we do that determines our students' diplomas, degrees and future careers. One of the most significant problems with assessment is that just about all the people who do it have already survived having had it done to them. This can make us somewhat resistant to confronting whether it was, when we experienced it at the receiving end, valid, fair and transparent, and explains why so many outdated forms of assessment still permeate higher education practice today.

Over the last decade many of us have seen our assessment workload grow dramatically, as we work with increasing numbers of students who are ever more diverse. Consequently, the time we have available to devote to assessing each student has fallen. Even those methods and approaches which used to work satisfactorily with relatively small numbers of students are now labouring as we try to extend them to a mass higher education context. It is therefore more important than ever to review the way we design and implement our assessment.

Sally Brown and Angela Glasner (1999) began the conclusion of their edited collection *Assessment Matters in Higher Education* with the words:

> Assessment does matter. It matters to students whose awards are defined by the outcomes of the assessment process; it matters to those who employ the graduates of degree and diploma programmes; and it matters to those who do assessing. Ensuring that assessment is fair, accurate and comprehensive – and yet manageable for those doing it – is a major challenge. It is a challenge which has been grappled with by many…. Despite the fact that there is a considerable body of international research about assessment and related issues, we experiment largely in ignorance of the way others have effected positive change, and we have limited opportunity to learn from the lessons of others.

Their book makes an excellent starting place from which to work backwards through the literature on innovative assessment during the last years of the 20th century.

In Chapter 1 of this book, I looked at feedback as a fundamental process underpinning successful learning. Indeed, feedback on not-yet-successful learning can be even more important, as learning by trial and error is a perfectly valid way to learn. Unfortunately, the assessment culture within which higher education systems currently work tends to reward successful learning with credit, and to equate not-yet-successful learning with failure. The accompanying feedback culture tends all too often to take the form of giving students critical feedback when things go wrong, and precious little comment when things go right. In this situation, the feedback which students receive can be almost as damaging to their motivation as the label of failure that we pin on their not-yet-successful learning.

My overall aim in this chapter is to challenge your thinking on how best to assess students' learning, and how to optimize the impact of our feedback on students' learning – whether that learning has proved successful or not. I hope too to provide food for thought to enable you to confront the difficulties in order to move towards making assessment demonstrably fair, valid and reliable. As a prelude to this chapter, I would like to share some overarching thoughts and questions about teaching, learning and assessment, and the relationships between these processes. Then I will outline some 'concerns' about unseen written examinations, and about continuous assessment. The remainder of this chapter is intended to offer some thoughts about 15 particular forms of assessment, each with its pros and cons, and with some suggestions for making each work better, to improve student learning.

In this chapter, I offer various practical suggestions regarding how assessment can be improved, particularly so that assessment can be:

- more valid, measuring that which we really intend to measure, rather than 'ghosts' of students' real learning;

- more reliable and consistent, moving away from the subjectivity that can cause assessment to be unfair;
- more diverse, so that individual students are not disadvantaged unduly by particular forms of assessment;
- more transparent, so that students know where the goalposts are, and so that external reviewers can see clear links between intended learning outcomes as spelt out in course documentation, and assessment criteria applied to students' work;
- more useful in terms of feedback, so that students' learning is enhanced;
- more successful in promoting deep learning, so that students get a firmer grasp of the important theories and concepts underpinning their learning.

Values for an assessment code of practice

Recently in the UK, the Quality Assurance Agency for Higher Education (QAA) has published 'Codes of Practice' for each of a range of aspects of professional practice in higher education, with the expectation that these codes will be used as a measure of the quality of higher education provision, with links to the continued funding of our institutions. The Code of Practice for Assessment is probably one of the most important of these. It sets out an assessment charter. Let us begin by identifying some values as a starting point on our mission to optimize assessment in terms of validity, reliability and transparency. For a start, let us try to define these terms, and add some further values to work towards in our assessment:

- **Assessment should be valid.** It should assess what it is that you really want to measure. For example, when attempting to assess problem-solving skills, the assessment should be dependent not on the quality and style of written reports on problem solving, but on the quality of the solutions devised.
- **Assessment should be reliable.** If we can get the task briefings, assessment criteria and marking schemes right, there should be good inter-tutor reliability when more than one lecturer marks the work, as well as good intra-lecturer reliability (lecturers should come up with the same results when marking the same work on different occasions). All assignments in a batch should be marked to the same standard. (This is not the same as the strange notion of benchmarking, which implies that assignments should hit the same standards in every comparable course in existence – an interesting but quite unachievable idea.)
- **Assessment should be transparent.** There should be no hidden agendas. There should be no nasty surprises for students. Assessment should be in line with the intended learning outcomes as published in student handbooks and syllabus documentation, and the links between these outcomes and the

assessment criteria we use should be plain to see (not just by external scruti-neers such as QAA subject reviewers, but by students themselves).

- **Assessment should be fair.** Students should have equivalence of opportunities to succeed even if their experiences are not identical. This is particularly important when assessing work based in individual learning contracts. It is also important that all assessment instruments and processes should be *seen to be fair* by all students.

- **Assessment should be equitable.** Assessment practices should not discriminate between students, and should disadvantage no individual or group. Obviously, students may prefer and do better at different kinds of assessment (some love exams and do well in them, while others are better at giving presentations, for example) so a balanced diet of different means of assessment within a course will set out to ensure that no particular group is favoured over any other group.

- **Assessment should be formative, even when it is also intended to be summative.** Assessment is a time-consuming process for all concerned, so it seems like a wasted opportunity if it is not used as a means of letting students know how they are doing, and how they can improve. Assessment that is primarily summative in its function (for example, when only a number or grade is given) gives students very little information, other than frequently to confirm their own prejudices about themselves.

- **Assessment should be timely.** Assessment that occurs only at the end of a learning programme is not much use in providing feedback, and also leads to the 'sudden death' syndrome, where students have no chance to practise before they pass or fail. Even where there is only end-point formal assessment, earlier opportunities should be provided for rehearsal and feedback.

- **Assessment should be incremental.** Ideally, feedback to students should be continuous. There is sense therefore in enabling small units of assessment to build up into a final mark or grade. This avoids surprises, and can be much less stressful than systems when the whole programme rests on performance during a single time-constrained occasion.

- **Assessment should be redeemable.** Most universities insist that all assessment systems contain within them opportunities for the redemption of failure when things go wrong. This is not only just, but avoids high attrition rates.

- **Assessment should be demanding.** Assessment systems should not be a pushover, and the assurance of quality is impossible when students are not stretched by assessment methods. That is not to say that systems should only permit a fixed proportion of students to achieve each grade: a good assessment system should permit all students considered capable of undertaking a course of study to have a chance of succeeding in the assessment, provided they learn effectively and work hard.

- **Assessment should be efficient and manageable.** Brilliant systems of assessment can be designed, but they may be completely unmanageable because of ineffective use of staff time and resources. The burden on staff should not be excessive, nor should be the demands on students undertaking the assessment tasks.

Reasons to assess

If we think clearly about our reasons for assessment, this helps to clarify which particular methods are best suited for our purposes, as well as helping to identify who is best placed to carry out the assessment, and when and where to do it. Some of the most common reasons for assessing students are listed below. You might find it useful to look at these, deciding which are the most important ones in the context of your own discipline, with your own students, at their particular level of study:

- **To classify or grade students.** There are frequently good reasons for us to classify the level of achievements of students individually and comparatively within a cohort. Assessment methods to achieve this will normally be summative, and involve working out numerical marks or letter grades for students' work of one kind or another.
- **To enable student progression.** Students often cannot undertake a course of study unless they have a sound foundation of prior knowledge or skills. Assessment methods to enable student progression therefore need to give a clear idea of students' current levels of achievement, so they – and we – can know if they are ready to move onwards.
- **To guide improvement.** The feedback students receive helps them to improve. Assessment that is primarily formative need not necessarily count towards any final award and can therefore be ungraded in some instances. The more detailed the feedback we provide, the greater is the likelihood that students will have opportunities for further development.
- **To facilitate students' choice of options.** If students have to select electives within a programme, an understanding of how well (or otherwise) they are doing in foundation studies will enable them to have a firmer understanding of their current abilities in different subject areas. This can provide them with guidance on which options to select next.
- **To diagnose faults and enable students to rectify mistakes.** Nothing is more demotivating than struggling on, getting bad marks and not knowing what is going wrong. Effective assessment lets students know where their problems lie, and provides them with information to help them put things right.
- **To give us feedback on how our teaching is going.** If there are generally significant gaps in student knowledge, this often indicates faults in the teaching of the areas concerned. Excellent achievement by a high proportion of students is often due to high quality facilitation of student learning.

- **To motivate students.** As students find themselves under increasing pressure, they tend to become more and more strategic in their approaches to learning, only putting their energies into work that counts. Assessment methods can be designed to maximize student motivation, and prompt their efforts towards important achievements.
- **To provide statistics for the course, or for the institution.** Universities need to provide funding bodies and quality assurance agencies with data about student performance, and assessment systems need to take account of the need for appropriate statistical information.
- **To enable grading and final degree classification.** Unlike some overseas universities, UK universities still maintain the degree classification system. However, some universities are continuing to ponder the introduction of a no-classifications system coupled with the production of student portfolios.
- **To add variety to students' learning experience, and add direction to our teaching.** Utilizing a range of different assessment methods spurs students to develop different skills and processes. This can provide more effective and enjoyable teaching and learning.

Concerns about assessment

Before it is possible to persuade people to review what they are presently doing, and to consider implementing changes, it is useful to take a critical look at whether current practices actually work as well as we think they do. Therefore I continue this chapter with a critical review of the two principal areas of assessment which most students encounter: traditional unseen written exams and assessed coursework. In each case I will list several general concerns, starting with concerns about the links between these kinds of assessment and the factors underpinning successful learning drawn from Chapter 1 of this book: wanting to learn, needing to learn, learning by doing, learning through feedback and making sense of or digesting what has been learnt. For most of the concerns, I will add hints at how the repercussions they cause can be ameliorated, or at least confronted. Later in the chapter I offer a range of practical pointers suggesting how even the traditional methods of assessment can be put to good use.

Concerns about exams

Much has been written about the weaknesses of traditional examinations – in particular time-constrained unseen written exams. In many subject disciplines, this assessment format seems to be at odds with the most important factors underpinning successful learning. Moreover, there is abundant evidence that even in discipline areas where the subject matter is well defined, and answers to questions are either correct or incorrect, assessors still struggle sometimes to make exams valid, reliable and transparent to students. In disciplines where the subject matter is more discursive, and flexibility exists in how particular questions can be answered well, it can be even harder demonstrably to achieve reliability in assessment, even when validity is well achieved.

Overall in higher education at present, with larger numbers of students, and staff-time under more pressure, there is evidence of a drift back to reliance on exams, which can be argued to be one of the more time-efficient and cost-effective methods of assessment, where it is fairly easy to achieve fairness and reliability, and with the added bonus that plagiarism and cheating cause fewer headaches to markers than many other forms of assessment.

Some of the principal concerns that can be expressed about unseen written exams are summarized below:

- **Exams do not do much to increase students' desire to learn.** Students often make choices in modular schemes strategically, so that they avoid this kind of assessment if they can. This can lead them to choose subjects in which they are less interested rather than those which they fear to select because they will be subjected to exams.
- **Exams are not often a good way of alerting students to what they really need to learn.** Admittedly, students will often only get down to serious learning when an impending exam causes them to revise actively, but the fact that in unseen exams the actual assessment agenda has to be guessed at rather than worked towards systematically means that the resultant learning can be unfocused, and the assessment judgement becomes too dependent upon the success of the agenda-guessing.
- **Exams are not ideal occasions for learning by doing.** Though students may do a lot of learning *before* formal unseen written examinations, their actual experiences of learning *in* such situations is very limited. In other words, a note could be placed on the door of the exam room stating 'Exam cancelled; you've already done all the learning that this exam could have caused'! The learning payoff during an assessment element should be considered more. It is therefore worth our while revisiting our testing processes to search for forms of assessment which are in themselves better learning experiences.
- **The amount of feedback that students receive about exams is not optimal.** Most systems require marked exam scripts to be regarded as secret documents, not to be shown to students on any account. It is worth asking what reasons underlie this philosophy. It is useful to reconsider the value that students can derive from seeing their marked examinations papers, where it should be possible to be able to demonstrate to students that the examination marking has indeed been reliable, fair and valid. Moreover, the natural process of

learning from mistakes should always be accommodated, even when the assessment judgements have already been taken down to be used in evidence against the candidates.

- **Exams tend not to do much to help students make sense of what they have learnt.** While there may be a significant amount of 'digesting' concepts and theories during the time leading up to exams, the assessment experience itself does little to help students further to deepen their grasp of these. One of the consequences of modularizing the curriculum can be that some subject matter is introduced too close to an impending exam for the content to be satisfactorily digested.

- **We mark exam scripts in a rush.** Most staff who mark exams agree that the task usually has to be completed in haste, in preparation for timetabled exam boards. The situation has been worsened by modularization and semesterization developments in most institutions, which give tighter turn-round intervals between examinations and progression to the next element of study. While our marking may still be fair and reliable, it can be shocking to students who have spent a great deal of time preparing for unseen written exams to find out that their scripts are marked so quickly.

- **Unseen written exams can lead to us placing too much emphasis on unimportant factors in candidates' answers.** For example, factors such as quality of handwriting and neatness of overall presentation of scripts can influence examiners, consciously or subconsciously. Many students nowadays are much more comfortable composing essays or reports using a keyboard, and adjusting their writing on-screen, cutting and pasting to bring their writing to a logical or coherent whole; this is much harder to do well with pen and paper, against the clock, in a threateningly silent environment.

- **We are often tired and bored when we mark exam scripts.** Because of the speed with which exam scripts need to be marked, and the pressure to do the task well, we may not be functioning at our best while undertaking the task.

- **We are not good at marking objectively.** There is abundant data on the problems of both inter-assessor reliability and intra-assessor reliability, particularly with the more qualitative or discursive kinds of exam question.

- **Unseen written exams tend to favour candidates who happen to be skilled at doing exams.** If we look at exactly what skills are measured by unseen written exams, the most important of these from students' points of view turn out unsurprisingly to be the techniques needed to do unseen written exams, and the same students can get rewarded time after time. This skill may have little to do with the competencies we need to help students to develop to become professionals in the subject disciplines they are learning.

- **Unseen written exams force students into surface learning, and into rapidly clearing their minds of previous knowledge when preparing for the next exam.** Students are encouraged to clear their brains of the knowledge they have stored for each exam in turn. This of course is quite contrary to our real intentions to help students to achieve deep learning.

■ **There are many important qualities which are not tested well by traditional exams.** For example, unseen written exams are limited or useless for measuring teamwork, leadership, and even creativity and lateral thinking, all of which have their parts to play in heading towards graduate status.

Concerns about continuous assessment

Having made a broadside about the limitations of unseen written exams, I have to admit that such exams have advantages as well, particularly that in their own way they are fair to candidates, and they are not subject to most of the problems of plagiarism, unwanted collaboration and so on which can affect the assessment of coursework. Let me proceed further to balance the picture by expressing some parallel concerns about continuous assessment – including that of essays and reports:

■ **If students are under too much coursework-related pressure, their 'want' to learn is damaged.** When almost everything that students do, as part of their learning, is measured, they naturally adopt strategic approaches to their learning, and only concentrate on those things that are going to be assessed. In many disciplines, we need to ensure that students' practical work is focused on quality learning, and is not unnecessarily burdensome regarding quantity.

■ **Continuous assessment does not always alert students to important aspects of their need to learn.** For example, when continuous assessment is repetitive in format (too many essays or too many reports), students may indeed become better able to deliver in these formats, but their overall learning is not deepened in ways that could be achieved by matching each assessment format to the nature of the intended learning outcome that is to be assessed.

■ **The range of learning by doing may be too narrow.** For example, repetitive use of formats such as essays and reports narrow the scope of students' learning, and tend to favour inordinately those students who happen to master the skills associated with the format at the expense of other students who have been more successful at learning the subject itself.

■ **Coursework feedback may be eclipsed by marks or grades.** Students pay most attention to their scores or grades when they get back marked work, and often are quite blind to valuable feedback which may accompany their returned work. A way out of this problem is to return students' work with feedback but without grades in the first instance, then get them to self-assess their own grades. Most students' self-assessments (when they are primed with clear assessment criteria, linked to clear statements defining the intended learning outcomes) are within 5 per cent or one grade point, and it is possible to allow students' own grades or scores to count. It is well worth talking to the few students whose self-assessment is at odds with our own assessment, and alerting them to the blind spots which could have caused them to overestimate the worth of their work, or (this happens more often) to boost their self-esteem by reassuring them that their work was worth more than they believed it to be.

■ **Students may not have the opportunity to make sense of the feedback they receive.** Particularly when there is a delay in getting feedback to students, they may already have moved on to learning other topics, and they do not then make learning from the feedback available to them a priority. Modularization and semesterization have both in their own ways contributed to making delays in receiving feedback more significant, related to the overall learning timescales involved.

■ **It is getting harder to detect unwanted collaboration.** Particularly with assignments submitted in word-processed formats, it is difficult if not impossible to detect every instance of plagiarism or copying. Whether the task is marking essays or practical reports, if there are several lecturers or demonstrators involved in marking them, students who have copied can be quite skilled at making sure that different people mark their respective work, minimizing the chance that the collaboration is detected. The most skilful plagiarists will always evade our detection!

■ **Too much of our time may be involved in fairly routine kinds of marking.** In many courses, lecturers continue to try to use the same continuous assessment processes that worked quite well when student numbers were much smaller. With large numbers of students, it is essential that human assessment and feedback should be reserved for higher-level agendas, and that computer-delivered assessment formats (in those curriculum areas where they can be designed well) should be exploited to provide assessment and feedback on relatively routine matters. There has already been a significant growth in the use of computer-aided assessment in many subject disciplines, saving a great deal of assessor time, while (when used well) providing a great deal of feedback to students, often very quickly.

■ **Students may not be aware of the criteria used to assess their work.** When students are practised in interpreting and making use of assessment criteria, the standard of their assessed work rises dramatically. Alerting students to the detail of the assessment agenda is regarded by some staff as a move towards 'spoonfeeding'. However, it can be argued that enabling students to demonstrate their full potential is a desirable goal. Involving students in self-assessment of suitable elements of their own work, and in peer assessment of appropriate assignments, can help students to gain a substantial understanding of the way that their work is assessed by tutors. Moreover, there is an increased level of expectation that assessment criteria can closely be linked to the achievement of expressed learning outcomes, and students themselves can make good use of these ways of clarifying the assessment agenda.

- **Students often get the balance wrong between continuous assessment and exams.** Students feel the pressure to submit coursework by stated deadlines, and may still be working on such work at a late stage in their studies on a particular module, when they would be better advised to cut their losses regarding that coursework and prepare for important exams. This particularly happens when students who fall behind in writing up practical work continue to try to get this work finished and handed in, when they may be better advised to spend their remaining time making sure that they are well prepared for forthcoming formal exams.

- **Learning may become driven by assessment, and students may only do those things that are assessed.** Earlier in these concerns, it was mentioned that students tend to adopt strategic approaches to their learning. Such approaches can be made beneficial if the nature and range of the assessed tasks are adjusted to make *all* the learning that students do in their assessed work as relevant as possible to the intended learning outcomes. In particular, it can help to reduce the size of many of the assessments. A well-designed essay plan (for example a mind-map, alongside a short written introduction, and a concise summary or conclusion) can present (say) 90 per cent of the thinking that would have taken ten times as long to write (and to mark) in a full essay.

- **Too little use may be made of the learning that can be achieved when students assess their own, and each others', work.** Involving students in self-assessment and peer assessment (when well facilitated) can deepen students' learning, and help them to develop awareness of the nature of assessment criteria, and of the overall assessment culture surrounding their studies.

Pros and cons of fifteen assessment techniques

Assessment can take many forms, and it can be argued that the greater the diversity in the methods of assessment, the fairer assessment is to students. Each and every one of the forms of assessment I consider in this chapter can be claimed to disadvantage those students who do not give of their best in the particular circumstances in which it is used. Therefore, diversifying assessment so that students experience a range of assessment methods evens out the situation, and increases the chance that all students will be able to demonstrate their best performance in at least some of the formats. The art of assessing therefore needs to embrace several different kinds of activity. I would like to encourage colleagues to broaden the range of assessment processes, and I have tried to provide practical suggestions how to maximize the benefits of each of a number of methods I have addressed overleaf.

In the next part of this chapter, I will look systematically at each of 15 forms of assessment, listing a few advantages and some disadvantages, and offering some suggestions (sometimes a few, sometimes a lot) for making the particular assessment device work better. None of these lists should be considered as anything more than a starting point. Nor should the 15 kinds of assessment I happen to have chosen be taken as representative of a sufficiently diverse range of assessment processes.

1 Traditional unseen, time-constrained written exams

Traditional unseen written exams still make up the lion's share of assessment in higher education, though in some disciplines, for example mathematics, engineering and sciences courses, this situation is considerably balanced by the inclusion of practical work, projects and other contributions to the evidence on the basis of which we grade and classify students. Despite growing concern about the validity and fairness of traditional exams, for all sorts of reasons they will continue to play a large part in the overall assessment picture. Despite many concerns about exams, I have tried in the following discussion to suggest a number of ways in which the use of exams can be improved. I have given more suggestions about setting exam questions than for setting any of the other types of assessment explored in this chapter, as in general, good practice in writing exam questions overlaps with, or extends across, many of the other types.

Advantages

- **Relatively economical.** Exams can be more cost-effective than many of the alternatives (though this depends on economies of scale when large numbers of students are examined, and also on how much time and money needs to be spent to ensure appropriate moderation of assessors' performance). However, any form of assessment can only truly be said to be cost-effective if it is actually *effective* in its contribution to students' learning.
- **Equality of opportunity.** Exams are demonstrably fair in that students have all the same tasks to do in the same way and within the same timescale. (However, not all things are equal in exams – ask any hay-fever sufferer, or candidate with menstrual problems.)
- **We know whose work it is.** It is easier to be sure that the work being assessed was done by the candidate, and not by other people. For this reason, exams can be considered to be an 'anti-plagiarism assessment' device, and although there are instances of attempting to cheat in exam rooms, good invigilation practice and well-planned design of the room (and the questions themselves) can eliminate most cheating.
- **Teaching staff are familiar with exams.** Familiarity does not always equate with validity, but the base of experience that teaching staff already have with traditional

unseen exams means that at least some of the problems arising from them are well known, and sometimes well addressed.

- **Exams cause students to get down to learning.** Even if the assessment method has problems, it certainly causes students to engage deliberately with the subject matter being covered by exams, and this can be worthwhile particularly for those 'harder' discipline areas where students may not otherwise spend the time and energy that is needed to make sense of the subject matter.

Disadvantages

- **Students get little or no feedback** about the detail of their performance. Though it can be argued that the purpose of exams is measurement rather than feedback, the counter-argument is that most exams, to some extent, represent lost learning opportunities because of this lack of feedback. Where students are given the opportunity to see their marked scripts (even with no more feedback than seeing the sub-totals and total marks awarded along the way), they learn a great deal about exactly what went wrong with some of their answers, as well as having the chance to receive confirmation regarding the questions they answered well.
- **Badly-set exams encourage surface learning**, with students consciously clearing their minds of one subject as they prepare for exams in the next subject. In many discipline areas, it is inappropriate to encourage students to put out of their minds important subject matter, where they will need to retain their mastery for later stages in their studies.
- **Technique is too important.** Exams tend to measure how good students are at answering exam questions, rather than how well they have learnt. The consequence is that those students who become skilled at exam technique are rewarded time after time, while other students who may have mastered the subject material to a greater degree may not get due credit for their learning if their exam technique repeatedly lets them down.
- **Exams only represent a snapshot of student performance, rather than a reliable indicator of it.** How students perform in traditional exams depends on so many factors other than their grasp of the subject being tested. Students' state of mind on the day, their luck or otherwise in tackling a good question first, their state of health, and many other irrelevant factors creep in.

Setting unseen written exam questions

Many experienced lecturers remember with some horror the first time they put pen to paper to write exam questions. Sometimes they felt well equipped to do so, as they had been involved in exams as candidates for most of their lives, and thought that it was quite straightforward to write good questions. But then the realization dawned that the words and tasks used in exam questions could determine students' future careers, prospects, incomes and lifestyles. Often, only when marking the exam scripts do lecturers first become aware of just how sensitively the questions need to be designed, and how clearly the assessment criteria and marking schemes need to be laid out to anticipate as many as possible of the different ways in which even the most unambiguous looking question can be answered. The suggestions below can help to spare you from some of the headaches which can result from hastily-written exam questions.

- **Do not do it on your own.** Make sure you get feedback on each of your questions from colleagues. They can spot whether your question is at the right level more easily than you can. Having someone else look at one's draft exam questions is extremely useful. It is better still when all questions are discussed and moderated by teams of staff. Where possible, draft questions *with* your colleagues. This allows the team to pick the best questions from a range of possibilities, rather than use every idea each member has.
- **Ask colleagues, 'What would you say this question really means?'** If they tell you anything you had not thought of, you may need to adjust your wording a little.
- **Get one or two colleagues to *do* your questions**. Sometimes even sketch answers can be helpful. This may be asking a lot of busy colleagues, but the rewards can be significant. You will often find that they answered a particular question in a rather different way than you had in mind when you designed the question. Being alerted in advance to the ways in which different students might approach a question gives you the opportunity to accommodate alternative approaches in your marking scheme, or to adjust the wording of your question so that your intended or preferred approach is made clear to students.
- **Have your intended learning outcomes in front of you as your draft your questions.** It is all too easy to dream up interesting questions which turn out to be tangential to the learning outcomes. Furthermore, it is possible to write too many questions addressing particular learning outcomes, leaving other outcomes unrepresented in the exam.
- **Keep your sentences short.** You are less likely to write something that can be interpreted in more than one way if you write plain English in short sentences. This also helps reduce any discrimination against those students whose second or third language is English.
- **Work out what you are really testing.** Is each question measuring decision making, strategic planning, problem solving, data processing (and so on), or is it too much dependent on memory? Most exam questions measure a number of things at the same time. Be up-front about all the things each question is likely to measure. In any case, external scrutiny of assessment may interrogate whether your questions (and your assessment criteria) link appropriately with the published learning outcomes for your course or module.

- **Do not measure the same things again and again.** For example, it is all too easy in essay-type exam questions repeatedly to measure students' skills at writing good introductions, firm conclusions, and well-structured arguments. Valuable as such skills are, we need to be measuring other important things too.
- **Include data or information in questions to reduce the emphasis on memory.** In some subjects, case-study information is a good way of doing this. Science exams often tend to be much better than other subjects in this respect, and it is appropriate to be testing what candidates can *do* with data rather than how well they remember facts and figures.
- **Make the question layout easy to follow.** A question with bullet points or separate parts can be much easier for (tense) candidates to interpret correctly than one which is just several lines of continuous prose.
- **Do not overdo the standards.** When you are close to a subject, it is easily possible for your questions to get gradually harder year by year. For example, in exams including quantitative questions, there is the danger that numerical problems become more difficult in each successive exam, partly because of the wish to stretch students a little further than did the worked examples they may have seen in lectures, or the problems students tackled in tutorials.
- **Write out an answer to your own question.** This will be handy when you come to mark answers, but also you will sometimes find that it takes *you* an hour to answer a question for which candidates have only half-an-hour. Lecturers setting problem-type questions for students often forget that familiarity with the type of problem profoundly influences the time it takes to solve it. Students who get stuck on such a question may end up failing the exam more through time mismanagement than through lack of subject-related competence.
- **Decide what the assessment criteria will be.** Check that these criteria relate clearly to the syllabus objectives or the intended learning outcomes. Make it your business to ensure that students themselves are clear about these objectives or intended outcomes, and emphasize the links between these and assessment. When students are aware that the expressed learning outcomes are a template for the design of assessment tasks, it is possible for them to make their learning much more focused.
- **Work out a tight marking scheme.** Imagine that you are going to delegate the marking to a new colleague. Write it all down. You will find such schemes an invaluable aid to share with future classes of students, as well as colleagues actually co-marking with you, helping them to see how assessment works.
- **Use the question itself to show how marks are to be allocated.** For example, put numbers in brackets to show how many marks are attached to various parts of the question (or alternatively, give suggested timings such as 'Spend about ten minutes on Part 2').

- **Try out your questions.** Use coursework and student assignments to do pilot runs of potential components of your future exam questions, and use or adapt the ones that work best for exams.
- **Proofread your exam questions carefully.** Be aware of the danger of seeing what you *meant*, rather than what you actually *wrote*! Even if you are very busy when asked to check your questions, a little extra time spent editing your questions at this time may save you many hours sorting out how to handle matters arising from any ambiguities or errors which could have otherwise slipped through the proofreading process.

Designing marking schemes

Making a good marking scheme can save you hours when it comes to marking a pile of scripts. It can also help you to know (and show) that you are doing everything possible to be uniformly fair to all students. As your marking schemes will normally be shown to people including external examiners and quality reviewers, it is important to design schemes in the first place so that they will stand up to such scrutiny. The following suggestions should help:

- **Write a model answer for each question.** This can be a useful first step towards identifying the mark-bearing ingredients of a good answer. It also helps you see when what you thought was going to be a 30-minute question turns out to take an hour. If you have difficulties answering the questions, the chances are that your students will too. Making model answers and marking schemes for coursework assignments can give you good practice for writing exam schemes.
- **Make each decision as straightforward as possible.** Try to allocate each mark so that it is associated with something that is either present or absent, or right or wrong, in students' answers.
- **Aim to make your marking scheme usable by a non-expert in the subject.** This can help your marking schemes be useful resources for students themselves, perhaps in next year's course.
- **Aim to make it so that anyone can mark given answers, and agree on the scores within a mark or two.** It is best to involve colleagues in your piloting of first-draft marking schemes. They will soon help you to identify areas where the marking criteria may need clarifying or tightening up.
- **Allow for 'consequential' marks.** For example, when a candidate makes an early mistake, but then proceeds correctly thereafter (especially in problems and calculations), allow for some marks to be given for the ensuing correct steps even when the final answer is quite wrong.
- **Pilot your marking scheme by showing it to others.** It is worth even showing marking schemes to people who are not closely associated with your subject

area. If they cannot see exactly what you are looking for, it may be that the scheme is not yet sufficiently self-explanatory. Extra detail you add at this stage may help you to clarify your own thinking, and will certainly assist fellow markers.

- **Make yourself think about honourable exceptions.** Ask yourself whether your marking scheme is sufficiently flexible to accommodate a brilliant student who has not conformed strictly to your original idea of what should be achieved. There are sometimes candidates who write exceptionally good answers which are off-beam and idiosyncratic, and they deserve credit for these.
- **Consider having more than 20 marks for a 20-mark question.** Especially in essay-type answers, you cannot expect students to include all the things you may think of yourself. It may be worth having up to 30 or more 'available' marks, so that students approaching the question in different ways still have the opportunity to score well.
- **Look at what others have done in the past.** If it is your first time writing a marking scheme, looking at other people's ways of doing them will help you to focus your efforts. Choose to look at marking schemes from other subjects that your students may be studying, to help you tune in to the assessment culture of the overall course.
- **Learn from your own mistakes.** No marking scheme is perfect. When you start applying a scheme to a pile of scripts, you will soon start adjusting it. Keep a note of any difficulties you experience in adhering to your scheme, and take account of these next time you have to make one.

Marking examination scripts

The following suggestions may help you approach the task of marking exam scripts efficiently, while still being fair and helpful to students.

- **Be realistic about what you can do.** Marking scripts can be boring, exhausting and stressful. As far as constraints allow, do not attempt to mark large numbers of scripts in short periods of time. Put scripts for marking into manageable bundles. It is less awesome to have ten scripts on your desk and the rest out of sight than to have the whole pile threatening you as you work.
- **Avoid halo effects.** If you have just marked a brilliant answer on a script, it can be easy to go into the *same* student's next answer seeing only the good points and passing over the weaknesses. Try to ensure that you mark each answer dispassionately. Conversely, when you look at the *next* student's answer, you may be over-critical if you have just marked a brilliant one.
- **Watch out for prejudices.** There will be all sorts of things which you like and dislike about the style and layout of scripts, not to mention handwriting quality.

Make sure that each time there is a 'benefit of the doubt' decision to be made, it is not influenced by such factors.

- **Recognize that your mood will change.** Every now and then, check back to scripts you marked earlier, and see whether your generosity has increased or decreased. Be aware of the middle-mark-bunching syndrome. As you get tired, it feels safe and easy to give a middle-range mark. Try as far as possible to look at each script afresh.

- **Remind yourself of the importance of what you are doing.** You may be marking a whole pile of scripts, but each individual script may be a crucial landmark in the life of the student concerned. Your verdict may affect students for the rest of their careers.

- **Take account of the needs of second markers.** Many universities use a blind double-marking system, in which case you should not make any written comments or numbers on the scripts themselves, to avoid prejudicing the judgement of a second marker (unless of course photocopies have already been made of each script for double marking). You may find it useful to use post-it notes or assessment pro formas for each script, so you are able to justify the marks you give at any later stage. Such aide-memoires can save you having to read the whole scripts again, rethinking how you arrived at your numbers or grades.

- **Write feedback for students.** In most exams, the system may not allow you to write on the scripts the sort of feedback you would have given if the questions had been set as assessed coursework. However, students still need feedback, and making notes for yourself of the things you would have explained about common mistakes can help you prepare some discussion notes to issue to students after the exam, or can remind you of things to mention next time you teach the same subjects.

- **Devise your own system of tackling the marking load.** You may prefer to mark a whole script at a time, or just Question 1 of every script first. Do what you feel comfortable with, and see what works best for you.

- **Provide feedback for yourself and for the course team.** As you work through the scripts, note how many students answered each question, and how well they performed. You may begin to realize that some questions turned out to have been very well written, while others could have been framed better. You will find out which questions proved to be the hardest for students to answer well, even when all questions were intended to be of an equal standard. Such feedback and reflection should prove very useful when designing questions next time round.

- **Set aside time for a review.** Having marked all the scripts, you may wish to capture your thoughts, such as suggestions about changes for part of the course or module, or the processes used to teach it. It is really useful, however tired you feel, to write a short draft report on the marking as soon as you have completed it. Otherwise, important things which are still fresh in your tired mind will all too quickly evaporate.

Using exam questions as class exercises

Answering exam questions well is still one of the principal skills which students need to develop to succeed in their studies in most subjects. In our attempts to increase the learning payoff of taught sessions, we can help students to develop their exam skills by making use of past exam questions. The following suggestions may help you to build related activities into your lectures and tutorials, but do not try to implement more than two or three of these suggestions with any one cohort – you have not got time!

- **Let a class have a try at an exam question under exam conditions.** Then ask students to exchange their answers, and lead them through marking their work using a typical marking scheme. This helps students to learn quickly how examiners' minds work. It is well worth using the whole of at least one lecture slot for such an exercise; the learning payoff for students is likely to be considerably more than if you had just spent an extra hour with one small element of their curriculum.
- **Issue two or three old exam questions for students to try in preparation for a tutorial.** Then lead them through assessing their work using a marking scheme during the tutorial. Ask them to prepare lists of questions on matters arising from the exercise, both on subject content and requirements for exams, and use their questions to focus tutorial discussion.
- **Display an exam question on-screen in a large group lecture.** Ask students in groups to brainstorm the principal steps they would take in approaching the question. Then give out a model answer to the question as a handout, and talk the class through the points in the model answer where marks would be earned. All this can be achieved in less than half of the overall time of a typical lecture, and you may be surprised at the levels of interest and attention which students pay to such elements in a lecture slot.
- **In a lecture or a tutorial, get students in groups to think up exam questions themselves.** You can base this on work they have already covered, or on work currently in progress. Ask the groups to transcribe their questions onto overhead transparencies. Display each of these in turn, giving feedback on how appropriate or otherwise each question is in terms of standard, wording, length and structure. (You will get many questions this way which you can later use or adapt for next year's exams or future coursework assignments!)
- **Use exam questions to help students to create an agenda.** In a lecture or tutorial, give out two or three related exam questions as a handout. Ask students

in groups to make lists of short questions to which they do not yet know the answers. Then allow the groups to use you as a resource, quizzing you with these questions. You do not have to answer them all at once – for some your reply will be along the lines, 'We'll come to this in a week or two', and for others, 'You won't actually be required to know this'.

- **Get students to make marking schemes.** Give them a typical exam question, and ask groups of students to prepare a breakdown of how they think the marks should be allocated. Ask them to transcribe the marking schemes to overhead transparencies. Discuss each of these in turn with the whole group, and give guidance on how closely the marking schemes resemble those used in practice.
- **Get students to surf the net.** Ask them to access the Internet to see if they can find appropriate exam questions on the subjects they are studying. Suggest that they work in twos or threes, and bring the questions they find to the next class session. You can encourage them to download the questions they find, and make an electronic question bank.
- **Ask students in groups to think up a 'dream' question.** Ask the groups to make bullet-point lists of the ten most important things that they would include in answers to these questions. These questions will give you useful information about their favourite topics.
- **Ask students in groups to think up 'nightmare' questions.** With these, you can open up a discussion of the causes of their anxieties and traumas, and can probably do a lot to allay their fears, and point them in the right direction regarding how they might tackle such questions.
- **Ask students to think of way-out, alternative questions.** Suggest that they think of questions that are not just testing their knowledge and skills, but that get them to think laterally and creatively. This encourages deeper reflection about the material they are learning, and will probably give you some interesting ideas to use in future exams.

2   Open-book exams

In many ways these are similar to traditional exams, but with the major difference that students are allowed to take in with them sources of reference material. Alternatively, candidates may be issued with a standard set of resource materials that they can consult during the exam, and are informed in advance about what will be available to them, so that they can prepare themselves by practising to apply the resource materials. Sometimes, in addition, the 'timed' element is relaxed or abandoned, allowing students to answer questions with the aid of their chosen materials, and at their own pace.

Advantages

These have many of the advantages of traditional exams, with the addition that:

- **There is less stress on memory.** The emphasis is taken away from students being required to remember facts, figures, formulae and other such information.
- **They measure retrieval skills.** It is possible to set questions which measure how well students can use and apply information, and how well they can find their way round the contents of books and even databases.
- **Slower writers can be helped.** If coupled with a relaxation in the timed dimension (say, a nominal two-hour paper where students are allowed to spend up to three hours if they wish), some of the pressure is taken away from those students who happen to be slower at writing down their answers (and also students who happen to think more slowly).

Disadvantages

- **There may not be enough books or resources.** It is hard to ensure that all students are equally equipped regarding the books they bring into the exam with them. Limited stocks of library books, and the impossibility of students purchasing their own copies of expensive books, mean that some students may be disadvantaged.
- **There may be a shortage of desk space.** Students necessarily require more desk space for open-book exams if they are able to use several sources of reference as they compose their answers to exam questions. This means fewer students can be accommodated in a given exam room than with traditional unseen exams, and therefore open-book exams are rather less cost-effective in terms of accommodation and invigilation.

Tips on setting open-book exam questions

All of the suggestions regarding traditional exam questions still apply. In addition:

- **Decide whether to prescribe the books students may employ.** This is one way round the problem of availability of books. It may even be possible to arrange supplies of the required books to be available in the exam room.
- **Consider compiling a source-collection for the particular exam.** Check on copyright issues, and see if it is cost-effective to put together a set of papers, extracts, data and other information from which students can find what they need to address the questions in the particular exam.
- **Set questions which require students to do things with the information available to them,** rather than merely summarizing it and giving it back.

- **Make the actual questions particularly clear and straightforward to understand.** The fact that students will be reading a lot during the exam means that care has to be taken that they do not read the actual instructions too rapidly.
- **Focus the assessment criteria on what students will have done with the information,** and not just on them having located the correct information.
- **Plan for shorter answers.** Students doing open-book exams will be spending quite a lot of their time searching for, and making sense of, information and data. They will therefore write less per hour than students who are answering traditional exam questions 'out of their heads'.

3   Open-notes exams

These are similar to open-book exams described above, but this time students are allowed to bring into the examination room any notes that *they* have prepared for the purpose. In other words, we are talking about a situation of 'legitimized crib-notes'. Your first thought may be that this is all very strange, but in fact such exams can work surprisingly well. Many of the advantages and suggestions for open-book exams continue to apply; the following additional matters arise.

Advantages

- **Students can achieve a very significant learning payoff simply making the notes in the first place.** The act of making revision summaries can have a high learning payoff. It is best not to place stringent limits on the amount of materials which students can bring in. Those who bring in everything they have ever written about your topic will be disadvantaging themselves in that it will take them much longer to search for the relevant parts of their notes, compared to students who have been really selective in summarizing the important parts of your topic.
- **The emphasis on memory is reduced, allowing competence to be tested more effectively.** Open-notes exams can also spread candidates' abilities out more fairly, as the better candidates will have made better notes in the first place.
- **You can write shorter questions.** When it is up to the students to ensure that they have with them important information or data, you do not have to put so much into the questions themselves.

Disadvantages

- **Students need rehearsal at preparing for open-notes exams.** They may take two or three practice runs to develop the art of making comprehensive but manageable summaries of the important data or information you intend them to make available to themselves.

- **Candidates whose open notes were not very suitable are penalized quite severely.** Some of these candidates may have been better at answering traditional exam questions with no notes.
- **Extra desk-space is needed, just as for open book exams.**

Tips on designing open-notes exams

- **Think of giving a topic menu in advance.** This can save candidates from trying to prepare open notes on everything they have learnt about your topic. It does, of course, also mean that you are letting them off the hook regarding trying to learn some of the things that you *do not* include in your menu.
- **Consider having an inspection process.** For example, let it be known that you or your colleagues will be keeping an eye on the range and content of the open notes, or even that they may be temporarily retained after the exam.

4 Structured exams

These include multiple-choice exams, and several other types of format where students are not required to write 'full' answers, but are involved in making true/false decisions, or identifying reasons to support assertions, or filling in blanks or complete statements, and so on. It is of course possible to design mixed exams, combining free-response traditional questions with structured ones. In the following discussion, I will concentrate on the benefits and drawbacks of multiple-choice questions. Many of the same points also apply at least in part to other types of structured exam questions, such as true–false, short-answer, and sequencing questions.

Advantages

- **They allow greater syllabus coverage.** It is possible, in a limited time, to test students' understanding of a much greater cross-section of a syllabus than could be done in the same time by getting students to write in detail about a few parts of the syllabus.
- **Multiple choice exams test how fast students think, rather than how fast they write.** The level of their thinking depends on how skilled the question-setters have been.
- **Students waste less time.** For example, questions can already show formulae, definitions, equations or statements (correct and wrong) and students can be asked to select the correct one, without having to provide it for themselves.

- **They save staff time and energy.** With optical mark readers, it is possible to mark paper-based multiple-choice exams very cost-effectively, and avoid the tedium and subjectivity which affect the marking of traditional exams.
- **Computer-based tests can save even more time.** As well as processing all of the scores, computer software can work out how each question performs, calculating the discrimination index and facility value of each question. This allows the questions which work well as testing devices to be identified, and selected for future exams.
- **They can test for higher-level skills.** Multiple-choice exams can move the emphasis away from memory, and towards the ability to interpret information and make good decisions. However, the accusation is often made that such exams seem only to test lower cognitive skills, and there are numerous examples which seem to support this argument. There are, however, examples where high-level skills are being tested effectively, and more attention needs to be given to the design of such testing to build on these.

Disadvantages

- **The guess factor reduces accuracy of results.** Students can often gain marks by lucky guesses rather than correct decisions.
- **Designing structured questions takes time and skill.** It is harder to design good multiple-choice questions than it is to write traditional open-ended questions. In particular, it can be difficult to think of the last distractor or to make it look sufficiently plausible. It is sometimes difficult to prevent the correct answer or best option from standing out as being the one to choose.
- **They tend to be in black and white rather than shades of grey.** While it is straightforward enough to reward students with marks for correct choices (with zero marks for choosing distractors), it is more difficult to handle subjects where there is a 'best' option, and a 'next-best' one, and so on.
- **Where multiple-choice exams are being set on computers, check that the tests are secure.** Students can be ingenious at getting into computer files that are intended to be secret.
- **There can be a danger of impersonators.** The fact that exams composed entirely of multiple-choice questions do not require students to give any evidence of their handwriting increases the risk of substitution of candidates.

Designing multiple-choice exams

- **Continuously try out questions with colleagues and with large groups of students.** Make sure that you select for exam usage questions where people are selecting correct options for the right reasons, and not because in one way or another the question gives away which is the correct option.

- **Make sure that distractors are plausible.** If no one is selecting a given distractor, it is serving no useful purpose. Distractors need to represent anticipated errors in students' knowledge or understanding.
- **Try to avoid overlap between questions.** If one question helps students successfully to answer further questions, the possibility increases of students picking the right options for the wrong reasons.
- **Avoid options such as 'none of the above' or 'all of the above'.** These options are a let-out for students who find it hard to decide between the other alternatives, and are often chosen by weaker students in surface-thinking mode. Also, it is surprisingly rare for such options to be in fact the correct one, and test-wise candidates will already have guessed this. To complicate matters, the best students will sometimes spot weaknesses with the option which is intended to be correct, and select 'none of these' because of this.
- **Pilot questions in formative tests before using them in summative exams.** Ideally, multiple-choice questions that appear in formal exams should be tried and tested ones. It is worth consulting the literature on multiple-choice question design and finding out how to assess the discrimination index and facility value of each question from statistical analysis of the performance of substantial groups of students.
- **Remember that students can still guess.** The marking scheme needs to take into account the fact that all students can score some marks by pure luck. If most of the questions are, for example, four-option ones, the average mark which would be scored by a monkey would be 25 per cent, so the real range lies between this and 100 per cent. It is important that people are indeed allowed to get 100 per cent in such structured exams, and that this does not cause any problems when the marks are blended with more traditional exam formats where written answers in some subjects still attract marks only in the 70s even when they are reckoned to be first-class answers.
- **Write feedback responses to each option.** Where possible, it is useful to be able to explain to students selecting the correct (or best) option exactly *why* their selection is right. It is even more useful to be able to explain to students selecting the wrong (or less good) options exactly what may be wrong with their understanding. When multiple-choice questions are computer-marked, it is a simple further step to get the computer to print out feedback responses to each student. This practice can equally be applied to formative multiple-choice tests, and to formal multiple-choice exams. Furthermore, the availability of feedback responses to each decision students make lends itself to extending the use of such questions in computer-based learning packages, and even computer-managed exams.
- **Ensure that students are well-practised at handling multiple-choice questions.** Answering such questions well is a skill in its own right, just as is writing open

answers well. We need to ensure that students are sufficiently practised, so that multiple-choice exams measure their understanding and not just their technique.

- **Look at a range of published multiple-choice questions.** For example, in the UK several Open University courses have multiple-choice assignment questions, as well as multiple-choice exams. You may be surprised how sophisticated such questions can be, and may gain many ideas that you can build into your own question design.
- **Gradually build up a large bank of questions.** This is best done by collaborating with colleagues, and pooling questions that are found to be working well. It then becomes possible to compose a multiple-choice exam by selecting from the bank of questions. If the bank becomes large enough, it can even be good practice to publish the whole collection, and allow students to practise with it. Any student who has learnt to handle a large bank of questions can normally be said to have learnt the subject well.
- **When you have a large bank of questions, there is the possibility of on-demand exams.** Students can then take a multiple-choice test with a random selection of questions from the bank, at any time during their studies, and 'pass' the component involved as soon as they are able to demonstrate their competence with the questions.

5   Essays

In some subjects, assessment is dominated by essay writing. Traditional (and open-book) exams often require students to write essays. Assessed coursework often takes the form of essays. It is well known that essay answers tend to be harder to mark, and more time-consuming to assess, than quantitative or numerical questions. There are still some useful functions to be served by including some essay questions in exams.

Advantages

- **Essays allow for student individuality and expression.** They are a medium in which the 'best' students can distinguish themselves. This means, however, that the marking criteria for essays must be flexible enough to be able to reward student individuality fairly.
- **Essays can reflect the depth of student learning.** Writing freely about a topic is a process which demonstrates understanding and grasp of the material involved.
- **Essay-writing is a measure of students' written style.** It is useful to include good written communication somewhere in the overall assessment strategy. The danger of students in science disciplines missing out on the development of such skills is becoming increasingly recognized.

Disadvantages

- **Essay writing is very much an art in itself.** Students from some backgrounds are disadvantaged regarding essay-writing skills as they have simply never been coached in how to write essays well. For example, a strong beginning, a coherent and logical middle, and a firm and decisive conclusion combine to make up the hallmarks of a good essay. The danger becomes that when essays are over-used in assessment strategies, the presence of these hallmarks is measured time and time again, and students who happen to have perfected the art of delivering these hallmarks are repeatedly rewarded irrespective of any other strengths and weaknesses they may have.

- **Essays take a great deal of time to mark objectively.** Even with well-thought-out assessment criteria, it is not unusual for markers to need to work back through the first dozen or so of the essays they have already marked, as they become aware of the things that the best students are doing with the questions, and the difficulties experienced by other students.

- **'Halo effects' are significant.** If the last essay answer you marked was an excellent one, you may tend to approach the next one with greater expectations, and be more severe in your assessment decisions based upon it.

- **Essays take time to write (whether as coursework or in exams).** This means that assessment based on essay writing necessarily is restricted regarding the amount of the syllabus that is covered directly. There may remain large untested tracts of syllabus.

- **'Write down the number we first thought of'.** Essays are demonstrably the form of assessment where the dangers of subjective marking are greatest. Essay-marking exercises at workshops on assessment show significant differences between the mark or grade that different assessors award the same essay – even when equipped with clear sets of assessment criteria.

Tips on setting and using essay-type questions

Most of the suggestions given earlier in this chapter about writing traditional exam questions continue to apply, whether essays are to be used as assessed coursework or as exam questions. Some further suggestions are given below

- **Help students to see exactly how essays are marked.** Alert students to the credit they gain from good structure and style. One of the best ways of doing this is to involve classes of students in looking at examples of past (good, bad and indifferent) essays, and applying assessment criteria. This can be followed by involving students in peer assessment of each others' essays.

- **Do not leave students to guess the real agenda.** Some essay questions are so open-ended that it is hard for students to work out exactly what is being sought. The authors of such questions will defend their questions by saying, 'Well, it is important to find the students who know what to do in such circumstances', but the fact remains that it is an aspect of study technique which is being rewarded, rather than mastery of the learning involved in answering the question.

- **Subdivide essay questions into several parts, each with marks publicly allocated.** This helps to prevent students from straying so far off the point that they lose too many of the marks that they could have scored.

- **Give word limits.** Even in exams, it can be useful to suggest to students that an essay-answer should lie between (for example) 800 and 1,200 words for a 30-minute question, and so on. This helps to avoid the quantity-versus-quality issue, which leads some students into simply trying to write a lot, rather than thinking deeply about what they are writing, and it also helps reduce the time it takes to mark the essays.

- **Help students to develop the skills required to plan the content for essays.** This is particularly important in those disciplines where students will be more accustomed to handling structured questions and problems. The danger then is that students tackling essay questions in exams spend far too long on them, and penalize themselves regarding time for the rest of the examination. One of the best – and most time-effective – ways of helping students to become better at handling essay questions is to set class or coursework tasks which require students to prepare essay plans rather than fully-finished masterpieces. A concept-map or diagram can show a great deal about the eventual 'worth' of students' essays, and can avoid distraction from the elements of style and structure. Students can put together maybe half a dozen essay plans in the time it would take them to complete one essay, and making the plans involves far more payoff per unit time in thinking and learning.

- **Do not assess essays too often.** Any assessment form advantages those students who happen to be skilled at delivering what is being measured. This applies to essays too, and there is a significant danger that those students who happen to become good at planning and writing essays continue to be advantaged time and time again.

- **Have a clear, well-structured marking scheme for each essay question.** This can save a lot of time when marking, and can help guarantee that students' answers are assessed fairly and consistently.

- **Do not assume that longer equals better.** It is often harder for students to write succinctly than to just ramble on. However, students need to be briefed on how best we want them to develop their art in writing briefly.

- **Consider involving students in peer assessing some essays or essay plans.** This helps them to put their own efforts into perspective, and to learn things to emulate (and things to avoid!) by seeing how other students go about devising essays.

- **Help students to improve their technique through feedback.** Consider the range of approaches you can use to give students useful feedback on their essays, including statement banks, assignment return sheets, email messages, and try to minimize the time you spend writing similar feedback comments onto different students' essays.

- **Use some class time to get students to brainstorm titles for essays.** This helps them to think about the standard they could anticipate for essay questions in forthcoming exams, and gives them topic areas to base their practice on.

6 Reviews and annotated bibliographies

Anyone who reviews books or articles for journals or magazines will confirm that there is no better way of making oneself look deeply into a book or article than to be charged with the task of writing a review of it. Getting students to write reviews is therefore a logical way of causing them to interact in depth with the information they review. One way of getting students to review a lot of material at once is to ask them to produce annotated bibliographies on a topic area, and to use these as assessment artefacts.

Advantages

- **Reviewing is an active process.** Reviewing material gives students a task to do which focuses their thinking, and helps them avoid reading passively, or writing the content out in 'transcribing' mode.
- **Reviews are useful for revision.** When students have reviewed material, the reviews are useful learning tools in their own right, and may spare students from having to wade through the material on subsequent revision.
- **Reviewing involves important cognitive processes.** When students are required to review material from different sources critically, they are necessarily engaged in higher-level skills of comparing, contrasting and evaluating – far beyond passive reading.
- **Reviewing other papers and articles is useful practice for research writing.** Students who will move on to research can benefit from the training involved in writing reviews, and gain skills in communicating their conclusions coherently.
- **Reviewing helps students to develop critical skills.** Getting students to compare and contrast chosen sources helps them think more deeply about the subject matter involved.
- **Compiling annotated bibliographies is a way of requiring students to survey a considerable amount of material.** It also helps them to reduce a large field to a manageable body of notes and references.

Disadvantages

- **Reviews are necessarily quite individual.** For reviews to lend themselves to assessment, it is important that the task should be delineated quite firmly. This may go against the open-ended approach to reviewing which we may wish students to develop.
- **There may not be enough books.** With large numbers of students and limited library resources, students may find it difficult or impossible to get adequate access to the materials we want them to review.
- **Reviewing individually can be lonely.** Reviewing a range of resources is often best done as a group task rather than an individual one, maximizing the benefits that students derive from discussion and debate. It then becomes more difficult to assess individual contributions to such reviews.

Setting assessed review tasks

- **Promote variety.** Ask students to select their own subject for research, and give them a wide range of topics to choose from.
- **Prompt awareness of audience.** Ask students to write reviews of different kinds of publication (learned journal, subject magazine, next year's students, student newsletter, and so on), so that they become aware of the differences in tone and style of writing which are appropriate for different audiences.
- **Get students to assess existing reviews.** For example, issue students with a selection of existing reviews, and ask them to identify features of the best reviews, and faults of the worst ones.
- **Help students to see that reviewing is not just a matter of summarizing what everyone has said.** You only have to look at book reviews in journals to see how some reviewers make up their contributions by summarizing the 'contents' pages of the material that they are reviewing. This is not a high-level intellectual activity.
- **Decide about credit to be awarded to 'search' tasks.** It is useful to get students both to locate all relevant major resources addressing a field, and to prioritize (for example) the most-important or most-relevant half-dozen sources.
- **Consider limiting the parameters.** Getting students to do a short comparative review of two or three important sources can be easier (and fairer) to assess than when the reviews are done without any restrictions. When such focused review tasks are coupled with a general search, it is possible to measure information retrieval skills as well as the higher-level 'compare and contrast' skills, without the agenda for the latter remaining too wide for objective assessment.
- **Set a tight word-limit for the review.** The art of writing a good, short review is more demanding than writing long reviews. When students' reviews are of equal length, it becomes easier to distinguish the relative quality of their work.

However, brief students on how to draft and redraft their work, to ensure the quality of short reviews. Make sure that students do not adopt the 'stop when you've written a thousand words' approach.

- **Think about combining collaborative and individual work.** For example, suggest that groups of students do a search collaboratively, and identify the most relevant sources together. Then suggest they write individual reviews of different sources. Finally, consider asking them to share their reviews, then write individual comments comparing and contrasting the sources.

- **Ask students to look at the same texts, but give them different foci.** For example, students could look at a series of articles on pollution, and write different reviews of them aimed to be separately useful to conservationists, parents, individualists and general consumers.

- **Encourage qualitative judgement.** Prompt students to write on not only what a book or article is about, but also how effective it is in providing convincing arguments, and how well it is expressed.

- **Involve your library or information services staff.** It is a mean trick to send off large groups of students to rampage through the library, without giving notice to the staff there of what you are doing. Discussing your plans with your faculty librarians, for example, gives them a chance to be prepared, and gives opportunities for them to make suggestions and give advice to you on the nature of the task, before you give it to students.

- **Think hard about resource availability.** Make sure that there will not be severe log-jams with lots of students chasing particular library resources. Widen the range of suggested resources. Consider arranging with library staff that any books which will be in heavy demand are classified as 'reference only' stock for a specified period, so that they can remain in the library rather than disappearing on loan.

- **Consider setting annotated bibliographies as formative group tasks.** This can encourage students to collaborate productively in future information-seeking tasks, and can reduce the drudgery sometimes experienced in tasks such as literature searching. Giving feedback on the reviews can be sufficiently valuable to students to make it unnecessary to couple the task with formal assessment.

- **Consider making the final product 'publishable'.** Aim to compile collections of the best reviews and annotated bibliographies, for example to use in next year's Course Handbook, or as the basis of an assessed task for next year's students.

- **Explore the possibility of involving library staff in the assessment.** Library staff may be willing and able to assess annotated bibliographies and reviews in parallel with yourself, or may be willing to provide additional feedback comments to students.

7 Reports

Assessed reports make up at least part of the coursework component of many courses. Report writing is one of the most problematic study-skills areas in which to work out how and what to advise students to do to develop their approaches. The format, layout, style and nature of an acceptable report vary greatly from one discipline to another, and even from one assessor to another in the same discipline. The most common kinds of report that many students write are those associated with their practical, laboratory or field work. Several of the suggestions offered in this section relate particularly to report writing in science and engineering disciplines, but can readily be extended to other subject areas.

Advantages

- **Report writing is a skill relevant to many jobs.** In many careers and professional areas, the ability to put together a convincing and precise report is useful. Report writing can therefore provide a medium where specific skills relevant to professional activity can be addressed.
- **Reports can be the end-product of useful learning activities.** For example, the task of writing reports can involve students in research, practical work, analysis of data, comparing measured findings with literature values, prioritizing and many other useful processes. Sometimes these processes are hard or impossible to assess directly, and reports provide secondary evidence that these processes have been involved successfully (or not).
- **Report writing can allow students to display their talents.** The fact that students can have more control when they write reports than when they answer exam questions allows students to display their individual strengths.

Disadvantages

- **Collaboration can be difficult to detect.** For example with laboratory work, there may be a black market in old reports. Also, when students are working in pairs or groups in practical work, it can be difficult to set the boundaries between collaborative work and individual interpretation of results.
- **Report writing can take a lot of student time.** When reports are assessed and count towards final grades, there is the danger that students spend too much time writing reports at the expense of getting to grips with their subject matter in a way which will ensure that they succeed in other forms of assessment such as exams.
- **Report marking can take a lot of staff time.** With increased numbers of students, it becomes more difficult to find the time to mark piles of reports and to maintain the quality and quantity of feedback given to students about their work.

Setting assessed report writing

- **Give clear guidance regarding the format of reports.** For example, issue a sheet listing principal generic section headings, with a short description of the purpose and nature of each main section in a typical report. Remind students, when necessary, of the importance of this guidance in your ongoing feedback to their reports.
- **Get students to assess subjectively some past reports.** Issue students with copies of some good, bad and indifferent reports, and ask them to mark them independently, simply giving each example an impression mark. Then facilitate a discussion where students explain why they allocated the marks in the ways they did.
- **Get students to assess objectively some past reports.** Issue groups of students with good, bad and indifferent reports, along with a sheet listing assessment criteria and a mark scheme. Ask each group to assess the reports. Then initiate discussions and comparisons between groups.
- **Make explicit the assessment criteria for reports.** Help students to see the balance between the marks associated with the structure of their reports, and those given to the content and the level of critical thinking and analysis.
- **Ask students for full reports less often.** For example, if during a course students tackle eight pieces of work involving report writing, ask students to write full reports for only two of these, and ask for summary or 'short-form' or 'memorandum' reports for the remaining assignments. These shorter reports can be structured in note form or bullet points, and can still show much of the evidence of the thinking and analysis that students have done.
- **Accommodate collaboration.** One way round the problems of collaboration is to develop approaches where students are required to prepare reports in groups – often closer to real-life than preparing them individually.
- **Involve students in assessing each other's reports.** When marks for reports count significantly, it may be desirable to moderate student peer assessment in one way or another, but probably the greatest benefit of peer assessment is that students get a good deal more feedback about their work than hard-pressed staff are able to provide. It is far quicker to moderate student peer assessment than to mark all the reports from scratch.
- **Consider asking students to write (or word process) some reports onto pre-prepared pro formas.** This can help where there are significant 'given' elements such as equipment and methodology. You can then concentrate on assessing the important parts of their writing, for example interpretation of data.
- **Publish clear deadlines for the submission of successive reports.** For example, in the case of practical work, allow only one or two weeks after the laboratory session. It is kinder to students to get them to write up early, rather than to allow them to accumulate a backlog of report writing, which can interfere (for example) with their revision for exams.

- **Prepare a standard assessment/feedback grid, to return to students with marked reports.** Include criteria and marks associated with (for example) the quality of data, observations, calculations, conclusions, references and verdicts.
- **Start students thinking even before the practical work.** For example, allocate practical work in advance of laboratory sessions, and include some assessed pre-laboratory preparation as a prelude to the eventual report, One way of doing this is to pose half a dozen short-answer questions for students to complete before starting a piece of laboratory work. This helps students know what they are doing, rather than follow instructions blindly. It also avoids wasting time at the start of a laboratory session by working out only then which students are to undertake each experiment.
- **Include some questions linked closely to practical or field work in examinations.** For example, tell students that two exam questions will be based on work they will have done outside the lecture room. This helps to ensure that practical work and associated reports do not get forgotten when students start revising for exams.
- **Get students to design exam questions based on the work covered by their reports.** Set groups of students this task. Allocate some marks for the creativity of their questions. When done over several years, the products could be turned into a bank of questions which could be placed on computer for students to consult as they prepare for exams.
- **Consider the use of computers in the laboratories and other practical work situations.** Where facilities are available, arrange for students to input their experimental data directly onto a computer or network. Many universities now enable students to write up their reports straight into a word processor alongside the laboratory bench, using a report template on disk. Such reports can be handed in immediately at the end of the laboratory session, and marked and returned promptly.

8 Practical work

Many areas of study involve practical work, but it is often much more difficult to assess such work in its own right; assessing reports of practical work may only involve measuring the quality of the end-product of the practical work, and not the work itself. The following discussion attempts to help you to think of ways of addressing the assessment of the practical work itself.

Advantages

- **Practical work is really important in some disciplines.** In many areas of physical sciences, for example, practical skills are just as important as theoretical competencies. Students proceeding to research or industry will be expected to have acquired a wide range of practical skills.
- **Employers may need to know how good students' practical skills are (and not just how good their reports are).** It is therefore useful to reserve part of our overall assessment for practical skills themselves, and not just the final written products of practical work.
- **Practical work is learning by doing.** Increasing the significance of practical work by attaching assessment to it helps students approach such work more earnestly and critically.

Disadvantages

- **It is often difficult to assess practical work in its own right.** It is usually much easier to assess the end-point of practical work, rather than the processes and skills involved in their own right.
- **It can be difficult to agree on assessment criteria for practical skills.** There may be several ways of performing a task well, requiring a range of alternative assessment criteria.
- **Students may be inhibited when someone is observing their performance.** When doing laboratory work, for example, it can be very distracting to be watched. Similar considerations apply to practical exercises such as interviewing, counselling, advising and other 'soft skills' which are part of the agenda of many courses.

Questions and suggestions for assessing practical work

It is important to address a number of questions about the nature and context of practical work, the answers to which help to clarify how best to go about assessing such work. First the questions, then some suggestions.

- **What exactly are the practical skills we wish to assess?** These may include a vast range of important skills, from deftness in assembling complex glassware in a chemistry laboratory to precision and speed in using a scalpel on the operating table. It is important that students know the relative importance of each skill.
- **Why do we need to measure practical skills?** The credibility of our courses sometimes depends on what students can do when they enter employment. It is often said by employers that students are very knowledgeable, but not necessarily competent in practical tasks.

- **Where is the best place to try to measure these skills?** Sometimes practical skills can be measured in places such as laboratories or workshops. For other skills, students may need to be working in real-life situations.
- **When is the best time to measure practical skills?** When practical skills are vitally important, it is probably best to start measuring them very early on in a course, so that any students showing alarming problems with them can be appropriately advised or redirected.
- **Who is in the best position to measure practical skills?** For many practical skills, the only valid way of measuring them involves someone doing detailed observations while students demonstrate the skills involved. This can be very time-consuming if it has to be done by staff, and also can feel very threatening to students.
- **Is it necessary to establish minimum acceptable standards?** In many jobs, it is quite essential that everyone practising does so with a high level of skill (for example, surgery). In other situations, it is possible to agree on a reasonable level of skills, and for this to be safe enough (for example, teaching!).
- **How much should practical skills count for?** In some disciplines, students spend a considerable proportion of their time developing and practising practical skills. It is important to think clearly about what contribution to their overall assessment such skills should make, and to let students know this.
- **May student self-assessment of practical skills be worth using?** Getting students to assess their own practical skills can be one way round the impossible workloads which could be involved if staff were to do all the requisite observations. It is much quicker for staff to moderate student self-assessment of such skills than to undertake the whole task of assessing them.
- **May student peer assessment of practical skills be worth using?** Involving students in peer assessment of practical skills can be much less threatening than using tutor assessment. The act of assessing a peer's practical skills is often very good for the peer assessors, in terms of improving similar skills of their own, and learning from others' triumphs and disasters.
- **Is it necessary to have a practical examination?** In some subjects, some sort of end-point practical test may be deemed essential. Driving tests, for example, could not wholly be replaced by a written examination on the *Highway Code*.
- **Reserve some marks for the processes.** Help students to see that practical work is not just reaching a defined end-point, but is about the processes and skills involved in doing so successfully.
- **Ask students to include in their reports 'Ways I would do the experiment better next time'.** This encourages students to become more self-aware of how well (or otherwise) they are approaching practical tasks.
- **Add some 'supplementary questions' to report briefings.** Make these questions that students can only answer when they have thought through their own prac-

tical work. For example, students can be briefed to compare their findings with a given published source, and comment on any differences in the procedures used in the published work from those they used themselves.

- **Design the right end-products.** Sometimes it is possible to design final outcomes which can only be reached when the practical work itself is of high quality. For example, in chemistry, the skills demonstrated in the preparation and refinement of a compound can often be reflected in the purity and amount of the final product.

9 Portfolios

Building up portfolios of evidence of achievement is becoming much more common, following on from the use of Records of Achievement at school. Typically, portfolios are compilations of evidence of students' achievements, including major pieces of their work, feedback comments from tutors, and reflective analyses by the students themselves. It seems probable that in due course, degree classifications will no longer be regarded as sufficient evidence of students' knowledge, skills and competencies, and that profiles will be used increasingly to augment the indicators of students' achievements, with portfolios to provide in-depth evidence. Probably the most effective way of leading students to generate portfolios is to build them in as an assessed part of a course. Here, the intention is to alert you to some of the more general features to take into account when assessing student portfolios. You may, however, also be thinking about building your own portfolio to evidence your teaching practice, and can build on some of the suggestions below to make this process more effective and efficient.

Advantages

- **Portfolios tell much more about students than exam results.** They can contain evidence reflecting a wide range of skills and attributes, and can reflect students' work at its best, rather than just a cross-section on a particular occasion.
- **Portfolios can reflect development.** Most other forms of assessment are more like 'snapshots' of particular levels of development, but portfolios can illustrate progression. This information reflects how fast students can learn from feedback, and is especially relevant to employers of graduates straight from university.
- **Portfolios can reflect attitudes and values as well as skills and knowledge.** This too makes them particularly useful to employers looking for the 'right kind' of applicants for jobs.

Disadvantages

- **Portfolios take a lot of looking at.** It can take a long time to assess a set of port-folios. The same difficulty extends beyond assessment; even though portfolios may contain material of considerable interest and value to prospective employers, it is still much easier to draw up interview shortlists on the basis of paper qualifications and grades. However, there is increasing recognition that it is not cost-effective to skimp on time spent selecting the best candidate for a post. This is as true for the selection of lecturers as for the selection of students for jobs. Lecturers are increasingly expected to produce hard evidence of the quality of their teaching and research, as well as to demonstrate how they teach to those involved in their appointment.
- **Portfolios are much harder to mark objectively.** Because of the individual nature of portfolios, it is harder to decide on a set of assessment criteria which will be equally valid across a diverse set of portfolios. This problem can, however, be overcome by specifying most of the criteria for assessing portfolios in a relatively generic way, while still leaving room for topic-specific assessment.
- **The ownership of the evidence can sometimes be in doubt.** It may be necessary to couple the assessment of portfolios with some kind of oral assessment or interview, to authenticate or validate the origin of the contents of portfolios, particularly when much of the evidence is genuinely based on the outcomes of collaborative work.

Designing and assessing portfolios

- **Specify or negotiate intended learning outcomes clearly.** Ensure that students have a shared understanding of the level expected of their work.
- **Propose a general format for the portfolio.** This helps students demonstrate their achievement of the learning outcomes in ways which are more easily assembled.
- **Specify or negotiate the nature of the evidence which students should collect.** This makes it easier to assess portfolios fairly, as well as more straightforward for students.
- **Specify or negotiate the range and extent of the evidence expected from students.** This helps students plan the balance of their work effectively, and helps them avoid spending too much time on one part of their portfolio while missing out important details on other parts.
- **Do not underestimate the time it takes to assess portfolios.** Also do not underes-timate their weight and volume if you have a set of them to carry around with you!
- **Prepare a pro forma to help you assess portfolios.** It is helpful to be able to tick off the achievement of each learning outcome, and make decisions about the quality of the evidence as you work through a portfolio.

- **Use post-it notes to identify parts of the portfolio you may want to return to.** This can save a lot of looking backwards and forwards through a portfolio in search of something you know you've seen in it somewhere.
- **Consider using post-its to draft your feedback comments.** You can then compose elements of your feedback as you work through the portfolio, instead of having to try to carry it all forward in your mind until you have completed looking at the portfolio.
- **Put a limit on the physical size of the portfolio.** A single box file is ample for most purposes, or a specified size of ring-binder can provide guidance for the overall size.
- **Give guidance on audio or video elements.** Where students are to include video or audiotapes, it is worth limiting the duration of the elements they can include. Insist that they wind the tapes to the point at which they want you to start viewing or listening, otherwise you can spend ages trying to find the bit that they intend you to assess.
- **Provide interim assessment opportunities.** Give candidates the opportunity to receive advice on whether the evidence they are assembling is appropriate.
- **Quality not quantity counts.** Students should be advised not to submit every piece of paper they have collected over the learning period, otherwise the volume of material can be immense.
- **Get students to provide route-maps.** Portfolios are easier to assess if the material is carefully structured, and accompanied by a reflective account which not only outlines the contents but also asserts which of the criteria each piece of evidence contributes towards.
- **Get students to provide a structure.** Portfolio elements should be clearly labelled and numbered for easy reference. If loose-leaf folders are used, dividers should be labelled to enable easy access to material. All supplementary material such as audiotapes, videos, drawings, computer programs, tables, graphs, and so on should be appropriately marked and cross-referenced.
- **Be clear about what you are assessing.** While detailed mark schemes are not really appropriate for portfolios, it is still necessary to have clear and explicit criteria, both for the students' use and to guide assessment.
- **Structure your feedback.** Students may well have spent many hours assembling portfolios and may have a great deal of personal investment in them. To give their work number marks only (or pass/fail) may seem small reward. Consider using an assessment pro forma so that your notes and comments can be directly relayed to the students, particularly in cases where required elements are incomplete or missing.
- **Encourage creativity.** For some students, this may be the first time they have been given an opportunity to present their strengths in a different way. Hold a brainstorming session about the possible contents of portfolios, for example,

which may include videos, recorded interviews, newspaper articles and so on.
- **Provide opportunities for self-assessment.** Having completed their portfolios, a valuable learning experience in itself is to let the students assess them. A short exercise is to ask them, 'In the light of your experience of producing a portfolio, what do you consider you did especially well, and what would you now do differently?'.
- **Assess in a team.** If possible set aside a day as a team. Write your comments about each portfolio, and then pass them round for others to add to. In this way, students get feedback that is more comprehensive, and assessors get to see a more diverse range of portfolios.
- **Set up an exhibition.** Portfolios take a long time to complete and assess. By displaying them (with students' permission) their valuable experience can be shared.
- **Think about where and when you will mark portfolios.** They are not nearly as portable as scripts, and you may need equipment such as video or audio playback facilities to review evidence. It may be helpful therefore to set aside time when you can book a quiet, well-equipped room where you are able to spread out materials and look at a number of portfolios together. This will help you get an overview, and makes it easier to get a feel for standards.

10   Presentations

Giving presentations to an audience requires substantially different skills from writing answers to exam questions. Also, it can be argued that the communications skills involved in giving good presentations are much more relevant to professional competencies needed in the world of work. It is particularly useful to develop students' presentation skills if they are likely to go on to research, so that they can give effective presentations at conferences. It is therefore increasingly common to have assessed presentations as part of students' overall assessment diet.

Advantages

- **There is no doubt whose performance is being assessed.** When students give individual presentations, the credit they earn can duly be given to them with confidence.
- **Students take presentations quite seriously.** The fact that they are preparing for a public performance usually ensures that their research and preparation are addressed well, and therefore they are likely to engage in deep learning about the topic concerned.

- **Presentations can also be done as collaborative work.** When it is less important to award to students individual credit for presentations, the benefits of students working together as teams, preparing and giving presentations, can be realized.
- **Where presentations are followed by question-and-answer sessions, students can develop some of the skills they may need in oral examinations or interviews.** Perhaps the most significant advantage of developing these skills in this way is that students can learn a great deal from watching each others' performances.

Disadvantages

- **With large classes, a round of presentations takes a long time.** This can be countered by splitting the large class into groups of (say) 20 students, and facilitating peer assessment of the presentations within each group on the basis of a set of assessment criteria agreed and weighted by the whole class.
- **Some students find giving presentations very traumatic.** However, it can be argued that the same is true of most forms of assessment, not least traditional exams.
- **The evidence is transient.** Should an appeal be made, unless the presentations have all been recorded, there may be limited evidence available to reconsider the merit of a particular presentation.
- **Presentations can not be anonymous.** It can prove difficult to eliminate subjective bias.

Assessing presentations

- **Be clear about the purposes of student presentations.** For example, the main purpose could be to develop students' skills at giving presentations, or it could be to cause them to do research and reading and improve their subject knowledge. Usually, several such factors may be involved together.
- **Make the criteria for assessment of presentations clear from the outset.** Students will not then be working in a vacuum and will know what is expected of them.
- **Get students involved in formulating or weighting the assessment criteria.** This can be done either by allowing them to negotiate the criteria themselves or by giving them plenty of opportunities to interrogate criteria you share with them.
- **Ensure that students understand the weighting of the criteria.** Help them to know whether the most important aspects of their presentations are to do with the *way* they deliver their contributions (voice, clarity of expression, articulation, body language, use of audio-visual aids and so on) or the *content* of their presentations (evidence of research, originality of ideas, effectiveness of argument, ability to answer questions and so on).
- **Give students some prior practice at assessing presentations.** It is useful, for example, to give students a dry run at applying the assessment criteria they have

devised to one or two presentations on video. The discussion which this produces usually helps to clarify or improve the assessment criteria.

- **Let the students have a mark-free rehearsal.** This gives students the chance to become more confident and to make some of the more basic mistakes at a point where they do not count against them. Constructive feedback is crucial at this point so that students can learn from the experience.
- **Involve students in the assessment of their presentations.** When given the chance to assess each others' presentations they take them more seriously and will learn from the experience. Students merely watching each others' presentations tend to get bored and can switch off mentally. If they are evaluating each presentation using an agreed set of criteria, they tend to engage themselves more fully with the process, and in doing so learn more from the content of each presentation.
- **Ensure that the assessment criteria span presentation processes and the content of the presentations sensibly.** It can be worth reserving some marks for students' abilities to handle questions after their presentations.
- **Make up grids using the criteria which have been agreed.** Allocate each criterion a weighting, and get all of the group to fill in the grids for each presentation. The average peer-assessment mark is likely to be at least as good an estimate of the relative worth of each presentation as would be the view of a single tutor doing the assessment.
- **Be realistic about what can be achieved.** It is not possible to get twelve five-minute presentations into an hour, as presentations always tend to overrun. It is also difficult to get students to concentrate for more than an hour or two of others' presentations. Where classes are large, consider breaking the audience into groups, for example dividing a class of 100 into four groups, with students presenting concurrently in different rooms, or at different timetabled slots.
- **Think about the venue.** Students do not always give of their best in large, echoing tiered lecture theatres (nor do we!). A more intimate flat classroom is less threatening particularly for inexperienced presenters.
- **Consider assessing using videotapes.** This can allow the presenters themselves the opportunity to review their performances, and can allow you to assess presentations at a time most suitable to you. Viewing a selection of recorded presentations from earlier rounds can be useful for establishing assessment criteria with students. This sort of evidence of teaching and learning is also useful to show external examiners and quality reviewers.
- **Start small.** Mini-presentations of a few minutes can be almost as valuable as 20-minute presentations for learning the ropes, especially as introductions to the task of standing up and addressing the peer group.
- **Check what other presentations students may be doing.** Sometimes it can seem to students that everyone is including presentations in their courses. If students find themselves giving three or four within a month or two, it can be very demanding on their time, and repetitious regarding the processes.

11 Vivas – oral exams

Viva-voce exams have long been used to add to or consolidate the results of other forms of assessment. They normally take the form of interviews or oral examinations, where students are interrogated about selected parts of work they have had assessed in other ways. Such exams are often used to make decisions about the classification of degree candidates whose work straddles borderlines.

Advantages

- **Vivas are useful checks on the ownership of evidence.** It is relatively easy to use a viva to ensure that students are familiar with things that other forms of assessment seem to indicate they have learnt well.
- **Vivas seem useful when searching for particular things.** For example, vivas have long been used to help make decisions about borderline cases in degree classifications, particularly when the written work or exam performance has for some reason fallen below what may have been expected for particular candidates.
- **Candidates may be examined fairly.** With a well-constructed agenda for a viva, a series of candidates may be asked the same questions, and their responses compared and evaluated.
- **Vivas give useful practice for interviews for employment.** Sadly, for most vivas, what is at stake is more serious than a possible appointment, so it is worth considering using vivas more widely but less formally to allow students to develop the appropriate skills without too much depending on their performance.

Disadvantages

- **Some candidates never show themselves well in vivas.** Cultural and individual differences can result in some candidates underperforming when asked questions by experts and figures of authority.
- **The agenda may 'leak'.** When the same series of questions is being posed to a succession of students, it is quite difficult to ensure that candidates who have already been examined are not able to commune with friends whose turn is still to come.
- **The actual agenda covered by a viva is usually narrow.** Vivas are seldom good as measures of how well students have learnt and understood large parts of the syllabus.
- **Vivas cannot be anonymous.** Lecturers assessing viva performance can be influenced by what they already know about the students' work. However, it is possible to use lecturers who do not know the students at all, or to include such lecturers in a viva panel.

Using vivas

- **Remind yourself what the viva is for.** Purposes vary, but it is important to be clear about it at the outset. For example, the agenda could include one or more of the following: confirming that the candidates did indeed do the work represented in their dissertations, or probing whether a poor examination result was an uncharacteristic slip, or proving whether students' understanding of the subject reached acceptable levels.
- **Prepare your students for vivas.** Explain to them what a viva is, and what they will normally be expected to do. It helps to give them opportunities to practise. Much of this they can do on their own, but they will need you to start them off on the right lines, and to check now and then that their practice sessions are realistic.
- **Think about the room layout.** Sitting the candidate on a hard seat while you and your fellow assessors sit face-on behind a large table is guaranteed to make the candidate tremble. If possible, sit beside or close to the candidate. Where appropriate, provide students with a table on which to put any papers they may have with them.
- **Think about the waiting room.** If candidates are queuing together for long, they can make each other even more nervous. If you are asking the same questions of a series of students (in some situations you may be *required* to do this for fairness), the word can get around about what you are asking.
- **Prepare yourself for vivas.** Normally, if you are a principal player at a viva, you will have read the student's work in some detail. It helps if you come to the viva armed with a list of questions you may ask. You do not have to ask all of them, but it helps to have some ready. Normally, you may need to have a pre-viva discussion with other members of the examining panel, and you need to be seen to have done your homework.
- **Prepare the agenda in advance, and with colleagues.** It is dangerously easy (and unfair to students) for the agenda to develop during a series of interviews with different students. Prepare and use a checklist or pro forma to keep records. Memory is not sufficient, and can be unreliable, especially when different examiners conducting a viva have different agendas.
- **Do your best to put the candidate at ease.** Students find vivas very stressful, and it improves their confidence and fluency if they are greeted cheerily and made welcome at the start of a viva.
- **When vivas are a formality, indicate this.** When students have done well on the written side of their work, and it is fairly certain that they should pass, it helps to give a strong hint about this straight away. It puts students at ease, and makes for a more interesting and relaxed viva.
- **Ensure there are no surprises.** Share the agenda with each candidate, and clarify the processes to be used. You are likely to get more out of candidates this way.

- **Ask open questions which enable students to give full and articulate answers.** Try to avoid questions which lead to minimal or 'yes/no' replies.
- **Let students do most of the talking.** The role of an examiner in a viva is to provoke thought and prompt candidates into speaking fluently about the work or topics under discussion, and to spark off an intellectual dialogue. It is not to harangue, carp or demonstrate the examiner's intelligence, or to trick candidates.
- **Prepare to be able to debrief well.** Write your own notes during each viva. If you are dealing with a series of such events, it can become difficult to remember each feedback point that you want to give to each student. Vivas can be very useful learning experiences, but much of the experience can be lost if time is not set aside for a debrief. Such debriefing is particularly useful when students will encounter vivas again.
- **When debriefing, ask students for their opinions first.** This can spare them the embarrassment of having you telling them about failings they already know they have. You may also find useful food for thought when students tell you about aspects of the vivas that you were unaware of yourself.
- **Be sensitive.** Vivas can be traumatic for students, and they may have put much time and effort into preparing for them. Choose words carefully particularly when giving feedback on aspects which were unsuccessful.
- **Be specific.** Students will naturally want to have feedback on details of things they did particularly well. As far as you can, make sure you can find something positive to say even when overall performance was not good.
- **Consider recording practice vivas on video.** This is particularly worthwhile when one of your main aims is to prepare students for more important vivas to follow. Simply allowing students to borrow the recordings and look at them in the comfort of privacy can provide students with useful deep reflection on their performance. It is sometimes more comfortable to view the recordings in the atmosphere of a supportive student group.
- **Run a role-play afterwards.** Ask students to play both examiners and candidates, and bring to life some of the issues they encountered in their vivas. This can allow other students observing the role-play to think about aspects they did not experience themselves.
- **Plan for the next step.** Get students to discuss strategies for preparing for their next viva, and ask groups of students to make lists of 'dos and don'ts' to bear in mind next time.
- **Get students to produce a guidance booklet about preparing for vivas and taking part in them.** This may be useful for future students, but is equally valuable to the students making it as a way of getting them to consolidate their reflections on their own experience.

12   Student projects

In many courses, one of the most important kinds of work undertaken by students takes the form of individual projects, often relating theory to practice beyond the college environment. Such projects are usually an important element in the overall work of each student, and are individual in nature.

Advantages

- **Project work gives students the opportunity to develop their strategies for tackling research questions and scenarios.** Students' project work often counts significantly in their final-year degree performance, and research opportunities for the most successful students may depend primarily on the skills they demonstrated through project work.
- **Projects can be integrative.** They can help students to link theories to practice, and to bring together different topics (and even different disciplines) into a combined frame of reference.
- **Project work can help assessors to identify the best students.** Because project work necessarily involves a significant degree of student autonomy, it does not favour those students who just happen to be good at tackling traditional assessment formats.

Disadvantages

- **Project work takes a lot of marking.** Each project is different, and needs to be assessed carefully. It is not possible for assessors to 'learn the scheme, and steam ahead' when marking a pile of student projects.
- **Projects are necessarily different.** This means that some will be easier, some will be tough, and it becomes difficult to decide how to balance the assessment dividend between students who tackled something straightforward and did it well, as opposed to students who tried something really difficult and got bogged down in it.
- **Projects are relatively final.** They are usually one-off elements of assessment. When students fail to complete a project, or fail to get a difficult one started at all, it is rarely feasible to set them a replacement one.

Designing student projects

Setting, supporting and assessing such work can be a significant part of the work of a lecturer, and the following suggestions should help to make these tasks more manageable.

- **Choose the learning by doing to be relevant and worthwhile.** Student projects are often the most significant and extended parts of their courses, and it is important that the considerable amount of time they may spend on them is useful to them and relevant to the overall learning outcomes of the courses or modules with which the projects are associated.

- **Work out specific learning outcomes for the projects.** These will be of an individual nature for each project, as well as including general outcomes relating to the course area in which the project is located.
- **Formulate projects so that they address appropriately higher-level skills.** The aims of project work are often to bring together threads from different course areas or disciplines, and to allow students to demonstrate the integration of their learning.
- **Give students as much opportunity as possible to select their own projects.** When students have a strong sense of ownership of the topics of their projects, they put much more effort into their work, and are more likely to be successful.
- **Include scope for negotiation and adjustment of learning outcomes.** Project work is necessarily more like research than other parts of students' learning. Students need to be able to adjust the range of a project to follow through interesting or important aspects that they discover along the way. Remember that it is still important to set standards, and the scope for negotiation may sometimes be restricted to ways in which students will go about accumulating evidence to match set criteria.
- **Make the project briefings clear, and ensure that they will provide a solid foundation for later assessment.** Criteria should be clear and well-understood by students at the start of their work on projects.
- **Keep the scope of project work realistic.** Remember that students will usually have other kinds of work competing for their time and attention, and it is tragic when students succeed with project work, only to fail other parts of their courses to which they should have devoted more time alongside their projects.
- **Liaise with library and information services colleagues.** When a number of projects make demands on the availability of particular learning resources or information technology facilities, it is important to arrange this in advance with such colleagues, so that they can be ready to ensure that students are able to gain access to the resources they will need.
- **Ensure that a sensible range of factors will be assessed.** Assessment needs to relate to the whole of the project, and not be unduly skewed towards such skills as writing-up or oral presentation. These are likely to be assessed in any case in other parts of students' work.
- **Collect a library of past projects.** This can be of great help to students starting out on their own projects, and can give them a realistic idea of the scope of the work likely to be involved, as well as ideas on ways to present their work well.
- **Arrange staged deadlines for projects.** It is very useful for students to be able to receive feedback on plans for their project work, so that they can be steered

away from going off on tangents, or from spending too much time on particular aspects of a project.

- **Allow sufficient time for project work.** The outcomes of project work may well include that students develop time-management and task-management skills along the way, but they need time and support to do this. Arrange contact windows so that students with problems are not left too long without help.
- **Consider making projects portfolio-based.** Portfolios often represent the most flexible and realistic way of assessing project work, and allow appendices containing a variety of evidence to be presented along with the more important parts showing students' analysis, thinking, argument and conclusions.
- **Encourage students to give each other feedback on their project work.** This can be extended to elements of peer assessment, but it is more important simply to get students talking to each other about their work in progress. Such feedback can help students sort out many of the problems they encounter during project work, and can improve the overall standard of their work.
- **Think about the spaces and places which students will use to do their project work.** Some of the work may well occur off-campus, but it remains important that students have access to suitable places to write up and prepare their project work for assessment, as well as facilities and support to help them analyse the data and materials they accumulate.
- **Include a self-evaluation component in each project.** This allows students to reflect on their project work, and think deeper about what went well and where there may have been problems. It can be particularly useful to students to get feedback about the quality of their self-evaluation.

13   Poster displays and exhibitions

When students are asked to synthesize the outcomes of their learning and/or research into a self-explanatory poster (individually or in groups), which can be assessed on the spot, it can be an extremely valuable process. More and more conferences are providing poster-display opportunities as an effective way of disseminating findings and ideas. This kind of assessment can provide practice in developing the skills relevant to communicating by such visual means.

Advantages

- **Poster displays and exhibitions can be a positive step towards diversifying assessment.** Some students are much more at home producing something visual, or something tangible, than at meeting the requirements of traditional assessment formats such as exams, essays or reports.

- **Poster displays and exhibitions can provide opportunities for students to engage in peer assessment.** The act of participating in the assessment process deepens students' learning, and can add variety to their educational experience.
- **Such assessment formats can help students to develop a wide range of useful, transferable skills.** This can pave the way towards the effective communication of research findings, as well as developing communication skills in directions complementary to those involving the written (or printed) word.

Disadvantages

- **However valid the assessment may be, it can be more difficult to make the assessment of posters or exhibitions demonstrably reliable.** It is harder to formulate 'sharp' assessment criteria for diverse assessment artefacts, and a degree of subjectivity may necessarily creep into their assessment.
- **It is harder to bring the normal quality assurance procedures into assessment of this kind.** For example, it can be difficult to bring in external examiners, or to preserve the artefacts upon which assessment decisions have been made so that assessment can be revisited if necessary (for example for candidates who end up on degree classification borderlines).
- **It can take more effort to link assessment of this sort to stated intended learning outcomes.** This is not least because poster displays and exhibitions are likely to be addressing a range of learning outcomes simultaneously, some of which are subject-based, but others of which will address the development of key transferable skills.

Planning assessed poster displays and exhibitions

- **Use the assessment process as a showcase.** Students are often rather proud of their achievements, and it can be invaluable to invite others in to see what has been achieved. Think about inviting moderators, senior staff, students on parallel courses and employers. Gather their impressions, either using a short questionnaire, or verbally asking them a couple of relevant questions about their experiences of seeing the display.
- **Use posters as a way to help other students to learn.** For example, final-year students can produce posters showing the learning they gained during placements. This can be a useful opportunity for students preparing to find their own placements to adjust their approaches and base them on others' experiences.
- **Get students to peer assess each other's posters.** Having undertaken the task of making posters themselves, they will be well prepared to review critically the work of others. This also provides chances for them to learn from the research undertaken by the whole cohort rather than just from their own work.
- **Consider asking students to produce a one-page handout to supplement their posters.** This will test a further set of skills, and will provide all reviewers with an aide memoire for subsequent use.

- **Give sufficient time for the debrief.** Lots of learning takes place in the discussion during and after the display. The tendency is to put poster displays and exhibition sessions on during the last week of the term or semester, and this can give little time to unpack the ideas at the end.
- **Make careful practical arrangements.** Large numbers of posters take up a lot of display space, and to get the best effect they should be displayed on boards. Organizing this is possible in most universities, for example by borrowing publicity display boards, but it needs to be planned in advance. Allow sufficient time for students to mount their displays, and make available drawing pins, adhesive putty, tape, sticky pads, demountable display equipment and so on.
- **Stagger the assessment.** Where peers are assessing each others' posters, to avoid collusion, 'fixing' and outbursts of spite, it is valuable to arrange that half the display is in one room and the rest in another, or to run successive displays at different times. Number the posters and get one half of the group to assess the odd-numbered posters and the other half to assess the even-numbered ones, and average the data which is produced.
- **Consider getting groups to produce a poster between them.** This encourages collaborative working and can reduce the overall numbers of posters – useful when student numbers are large. You could then consider getting students within the group to peer assess (intra) their respective contributions to the group as well as to assess collaboratively the posters of the other groups (inter-peer-group assessment).
- **Link assessment of poster displays to open days.** Students coming to visit the institution when they are considering applying for courses may well get a good idea about what students actually do on the courses, from looking at posters on display.
- **Prepare a suitable assessment sheet.** Base this firmly on the assessment criteria for the exercise. Provide space for peers' comments. This paves the way towards plenty of opportunity for peer feedback.
- **Use assistance.** When working with large numbers of peer-assessed posters, you may need help in working out the average scores. Get the students to do the number work, either for themselves or for each other (and advise them that the numbers will be randomly checked to ensure fair play). Alternatively, press-gang colleagues, partners, administrators, or progeny to help with the task.
- **Provide a rehearsal opportunity.** Let the students have a practice run at a relatively early stage, using a mock-up or a draft on flipchart paper. Give them feedback on these drafts, and let them compare their ideas. This can help them to avoid the most obvious disasters later.
- **Let everyone know why they are using poster displays.** This method of assessment may be unfamiliar to students, and to your colleagues. It is therefore valuable if you can provide a clear justification of the educational merits of the method to all concerned.

- **Brief students really carefully about what is needed.** Ideally, let them see a whole range of posters from previous years (or some mock-ups, or photographs of previous displays) so that they have a good idea about the requirements, without having their originality and creativity suppressed.
- **Use the briefing to discuss criteria and weighting.** Students will need to know what level of effort they should put into different elements such as presentation, information content, structure and visual features. If students are not clear about this, you may well end up with brilliantly-presented posters with little relevance to the topic, or really dull, dense posters that try to compress the text of a long report onto a single A1 sheet.
- **Give students some practical guidelines.** Let them know how many A1 sheets they can have, where their work will be displayed, what size of font the text should be to be readable on a poster, what resources will be available to them in college, and how much help they can get from outsiders such as friends on other courses who take good photographs or who have the knack of writing in attractive script.
- **Attach a budget to the task.** In poster displays, money shows! If you were to give a totally free hand to students, the ones with best access to photocopiers, photographic resources, expensive papers, word processors and so on may well produce better-looking products than students who have little money to spend on their posters or displays (although it does not always turn out this way). Giving a notional budget can help to even out the playing field, as can requiring students to only use items from a given list, with materials perhaps limited to those provided in workshops in the college.
- **Keep records of poster displays and exhibitions.** Take photographs, or make a short video. It is not possible to retain complete displays and exhibitions, but a handy reminder can be very useful for use when planning the next similar event. Evidence of the displays can also be interesting to external examiners and quality reviewers.
- **Get someone (or a group) to provide a 'guide booklet' to the exhibition.** This helps the students undertaking this task to make relative appraisals of the different items or collections making up the exhibition as a whole.
- **Consider turning it into a celebration as well.** After the assessment has taken place, it can be pleasurable to provide some refreshments, and make the display or exhibition part of an end-of-term or end-of-course celebration.

14   Dissertations and theses

Students invest a great deal of time and energy in producing dissertations and theses, usually in their final year. Sometimes these arise from the results of their project work. We therefore owe it to them to mark them fairly and appropriately.

Advantages

- **Dissertations and theses are individual in nature.** There are reduced possibilities regarding plagiarism and cheating, and a greater confidence that we are assessing the work of individual students.
- **There is usually double or multiple marking.** Because dissertations and theses are important assessment artefacts, more care is taken to ensure that the assessment is as objective as possible.
- **There is usually further triangulation.** External examiners are often asked to oversee the assessment of at least a cross-section of dissertations or theses, and sometimes see all of them. The fact that such triangulation exists is a further pressure towards making the assessment reliable and valid in the first instance.

Disadvantages

- **Assessment takes a long time.** Even more so than with student projects, dissertations or theses are so individual that it is not possible for assessors to 'get into their stride' and forge ahead marking large numbers of these in a given period of time.
- **Assessment can involve subjectivity.** For example, it is less possible to achieve 'anonymous' marking with large-scale artefacts such as these, as the first assessor at least is likely to have been supervising or advising the candidate along the route towards assessment.
- **Assessment can be over-dominated by matters of style and structure.** While both of these are important and deserve to contribute toward assessment of dissertations or theses, there is abundant evidence that a well-structured, fluent piece of work where the actual content is quite modest, attracts higher ratings than a less well-structured, somewhat 'jerky' piece of work where the content has a higher quality.

Tips on assessing dissertations and theses

- **Make sure that the assessment criteria are explicit, clear, and understood by the students.** This may seem obvious. However, theses and dissertations are normally very different in the topics and themes they address, and the assessment criteria need to accommodate such differences. Students will naturally compare marks and feedback comments. The availability of clear criteria helps them see that their work has been assessed fairly.

- **Get students to assess a few past dissertations.** You cannot expect them to do this at the same level as may be appropriate for 'real' assessment, but you can (for example) issue students with a one-sided pro forma questionnaire to complete as they study examples of dissertations. Include questions about the power of the introduction, the quality and consistency of referencing, and the coherence of the conclusions.
- **Offer guidance and support to students throughout the process.** Dissertations usually take students quite some time to complete. Students appreciate and need some help along the route. It is worth holding tutorials both individually and with groups. This takes good planning, and dates need to be set well in advance, and published on a notice board or handout to students.
- **Ensure that student support mechanisms are available.** With large class sizes, we cannot afford to spend many hours of staff time with individual students. However, much valuable support can be drawn from the students themselves, if we facilitate ways of them helping each other. Consider introducing supplemental instruction processes, or setting up friendly yet critical student syndicates. Running a half-day workshop with students counselling each other can be valuable.
- **Beware of the possibility of bias.** Sometimes dissertations involve students writing on topics of a sensitive cultural or political nature. We need to be aware of any prejudices of our own, and to compensate for any bias these could cause in our assessment. Whenever possible, dissertations should be second-marked (at least!).
- **Provide students with equal opportunity regarding selecting their dissertation themes.** Research for some dissertations will involve students in visiting outside agencies, finding materials for experiments, building models and so on. With resource limitations becoming more severe, students may be forced to avoid certain topics altogether. Try to suggest topics where financial implications are manageable to students.
- **Check whether dissertations always have to be bound.** This may depend on which year of the course they are set in. It may be worth reserving binding for final-year dissertations, to help save students money.
- **Help students to monitor their own progress.** It helps to map the assessment criteria in a way that helps students to keep track of their own progress and achievements. Computer programs are now available which help students work out how they are getting on, and prompt them to the next steps they should be considering at each stage.
- **When assessing dissertations, collect a list of questions to select from at a forthcoming viva.** Even if there is not going to be a viva, such lists of questions can be a useful addition to the feedback you return to students.
- **Use post-its while assessing dissertations and theses.** These can be placed towards the edges of pages, so that notes and questions written on the post-its can be found easily again. They help you avoid having to write directly on the pages of the dissertation or thesis (especially when your questions are found to be addressed two pages later!).

15   Work-based learning

Increasing use is being made of assessment based on students' performance in the workplace, whether on placements, as part of work-based learning programmes, or during practice elements of courses. Often a variety of assessors are used, sometimes giving rise to concerns about how consistent assessment practice between the workplace and the institution can be assured. Traditional means of assessment are often unsuitable in contexts where what is important is not easily measured by written accounts. Many courses include a placement period, and the increasing use of accreditation of prior experiential learning in credit accumulation systems means that we need to look at ways of assessing material produced by students in work contexts, rather than just things students write up when back at college after their placements.

Advantages

- **Work-based learning can balance the assessment picture.** Future employers are likely to be at least as interested in students' work-related competencies as in academic performance, and assessing work-based learning can give useful information about students' competencies beyond the curriculum.
- **Assessing placement learning helps students to take placements more seriously.** As with anything else, if they are not assessed, some students will not really get down to learning from their placements.
- **Assessing placement learning helps to make your other assessments closer to practice.** Although it is difficult to assess placement learning reliably, the validity of the related learning may outweigh this difficulty, and help you to tune in more successfully to real-world problems, situation and practices in the rest of your assessment practice.
- **Assessing placement learning can bring you closer to employers who can help you.** It is sometimes possible to involve external people such as employers in some in-college forms of assessment, for example student presentations, interview technique practising, and so on. The contacts you make with employers during placement supervision and assessment can help you to identify those who have much to offer you.

Disadvantages

- **Reliability of assessment is difficult to achieve.** Placements tend to be highly individual, and students' opportunities to provide evidence which lends itself well to assessment can vary greatly from one placement to another.
- **Some students will have much better placements than others.** Some students will have the opportunity to demonstrate their flair and potential, while others will be constrained into relatively routine work practices.

Assessing work-based learning

The following suggestions may help you to strike an appropriate balance between validity and reliability if your assessment agenda includes assessing work-based learning, whether associated with work placements, or arising from a need to accredit prior experiential learning.

- **Explore how best you can involve employers, professional supervisors and colleagues.** They will need careful briefing, and negotiation may also be required to achieve their full cooperation, as they (like you) are often very busy people. Ways of involving them include asking them to produce testimonials, statements of competence, checklists, grids and pro formas, or simply to sign off students' own statements of competence or achievement.
- **Be clear about the purpose of the assessment.** Is the assessment being done to satisfy a funding body, or because it is required by the university, or because the employers wish it to be done? Or is the assessment primarily to aid students' learning? Or is the assessment primarily designed to help students develop skills and experience which will aid their future careers? Clarifying the purposes can help you decide the most appropriate forms of assessment.
- **Get the balance right.** Work out carefully what proportion of students' overall assessment will be derived from their placements. Decide whether the related assessment should be on a pass–fail basis, or whether it should be attempted to classify it for degrees.
- **Expect placements to be very different.** If a group of students are spread through a number of companies or organizations, some will have a very good experience of placement, and others through no fault of their own can have an unsatisfactory experience. It is important that factors outside students' control are not allowed to prejudice assessment.
- **Consider carefully whether a mentor is well placed to assess.** There can sometimes be complex confusions of role if the person who is the professional supporter or friend of the student whose performance is being assessed is also the person who has to make critical evaluations for assessment purposes.
- **Decide carefully whether to tutor assess during workplace visits.** Visiting students on placement certainly gives tutors opportunities to gather data that may be relevant to assessment, but if assessment is on the agenda the whole nature of such visits changes. One way of separating the assessment ethos from the workplace environment is to handle at least some face-to-face meetings with the student off site rather than at the workplace.
- **Consider including the assessment of a work log.** Some professions prescribe the exact form such a log or work diary should take; in other work contexts it is possible for the course team or the students themselves to devise their own formats. It is often helpful if such logs include lists of learning outcomes, skills, or

competencies that students are expected to achieve and demonstrate, with opportunities to check off these and add comments as appropriate. It can be even better to encourage students to express as learning outcomes *unanticipated* learning that they discover happening to them during a placement. Some of these outcomes may be more important than the intended ones.

● **Ask students to produce a reflective journal.** This can be a much more personal kind of a document, and might include hopes, fears and feelings as well as more mundane accounts of actions and achievements. Assessing reflective journals can raise tricky issues of confidentiality and disclosure, but ways round such issues can be found, particularly if students are asked to submit for assessment edited extracts from their reflective journals.

● **Consider using a portfolio.** A portfolio to demonstrate achievement at work can include suitably anonymized real products from the workplace (with the permission of the employer) as well as testimonials from clients, patients, support staff and others.

● **Help to ensure that assessment does not blind students to their learning on placement.** Consider asking students who have completed work placements to write up their experiences in the form of a journal article, perhaps for an in-house magazine or journal. A collection of these can help to disseminate their experiences. Joint articles written with employers are even more valuable, and help make links with employers better.

Feedback and assessment

Quality of feedback

If 'assessment is the engine that drives learning' (John Cowan), then the ways in which we give feedback are important in gearing and lubricating the engine so that maximum effect is achieved from the effort put in by all concerned. This section of the chapter explores a variety of ways in which feedback can be given to students, and includes many suggestions for optimizing the usefulness of such feedback.

How can we best give feedback to students? We can select from a wide range of processes, but we also need to address as many as possible of a range of qualities and attributes in our strategy for providing feedback. For example, feedback needs to be:

■ **Timely** – the sooner the better. There has been plenty of research into how long after the learning event it takes for the effects of feedback to be significantly eroded. Ideally feedback should be received within a day or two, and even better almost straight away, as is possible (for example) in some computer-aided learning situations, and equally in some face-to-face contexts. When marked work is returned to students weeks (or even months) after submission, feedback is often totally ignored because it bears little relevance to students' current needs. Many institutions nowadays specify in their Student Charters that work should be returned within two to three weeks, enabling students to derive greater benefits from feedback. When feedback is received very quickly, it is much more effective, as students can still remember exactly what they were thinking as they addressed each task.

- **Intimate and individual.** Feedback needs to fit each student's achievement, individual nature and personality. Global ways of compiling and distributing feedback can reduce the extent of ownership which students take over the feedback they receive, even when the quality and amount of feedback is increased. Each student is still a person.

- **Empowering.** If feedback is intended to strengthen and consolidate learning, we need to make sure it does not dampen learning down. This is easier to ensure when feedback is positive, of course, but we need to look carefully at how best we can make critical feedback equally empowering to learners. We must not forget that often feedback is given and received in a system where power is loaded towards the provider of the feedback rather than the recipient – for example where we are driving assessment systems.

- **Oriented to opening doors, not closing them.** In this respect, we have to be particularly careful with the words we use when giving feedback to students. Clearly, words with such 'final language' implications as 'weak' or 'poor' cause irretrievable breakdowns in the communication between assessor and student. To a lesser extent, even positive words such as 'excellent' can cause problems when feedback on the next piece of work is only 'very good' – why wasn't it excellent again? In all such cases it is better to praise exactly what *was* very good or excellent in a little more detail, rather than take the short cut of just using the adjectives themselves.

- **Manageable.** There are two sides to this. From our point of view, designing and delivering feedback to students could easily consume all the time and energy we have – it is an endless task. But also from students' points of view, getting too much feedback can result in them not being able to sort out the important feedback from the routine feedback, reducing their opportunity to benefit from the feedback they need most.

The suggestions overleaf unpack how you can set about trying to ensure that the feedback you provide for your students addresses the factors listed above. Furthermore, some of these suggestions are intended to help you to maintain high-quality feedback to your students without consuming inordinate amounts of your precious time and energy.

1 **Try to do more than put ticks.** Tempting as it is to put ticks beside things that are correct or good, ticks do not give much real feedback. It takes a little longer to add short phrases such as 'good point', 'I agree with this', 'yes, this is it', 'spot on', and so on, but such feedback comments do much more to motivate students than just ticks. Think about how students will feel when they get marked work back. Students can be in states of heightened emotion at such points. If their scripts are covered with comments in red ink (even when it is all praise) it is rather intimidating for them at first.

2 **Avoid putting crosses if possible.** Students often have negative feelings about crosses on their work, carried forward from schooldays. Short phrases such as 'no', 'not quite', 'but this wouldn't work', and so on can be much better ways of alerting students to things that are wrong.

3 **Try to make your writing legible.** If there is not going to be room to make a detailed comment directly on the script, put code numbers or asterisks, and write your feedback on a separate sheet. A useful compromise is to put feedback comments on post-its stuck to appropriate parts of a script, but it is worth still using a code, asterisk or some such device so that if students remove the post-its as they read through their work, they can still work out exactly which points your comments apply to.

4 **Try giving some feedback before you start assessing.** For example, when a class hands in a piece of work, you can issue at once handouts of model answers and discussions of the main things that may have caused problems. Students can read such information while their own efforts are still fresh in their minds, and can derive a great deal of feedback straight away. You can then concentrate, while assessing, on giving them *additional* feedback individually, without going into detail on things that you have already addressed in the general discussion comments you have already given them.

5 **Give feedback to groups of students sometimes.** This helps students become aware that they are not alone in making mistakes, and allows them to learn from the successes and failures of others.

6 **Let students argue.** When giving one-to-one feedback, it is often useful to allow students the opportunity to interrogate you and challenge your comments (orally or in writing) so that any issues which are unclear can be resolved.

7 **Feedback should be realistic.** When making suggestions for improvement of student work, consider carefully whether they can be achieved. It may not have been possible (for example) for students to gain access to certain resources or books in the time available.

8 **Feedback should not be linked to wealth.** Check that you are not giving feedback on the amount of money that was spent on the work you mark, for example when some students can submit work produced by expensive desktop publishing systems, while other students have no access to such facilities.

9 **Feedback should be honest.** When there are serious problems of which students need to be made aware, feedback comments should not skirt round these or avoid them. It may be best to arrange for individual face-to-face feedback sessions with some students, so you can give any bad news in ways in which you can monitor how they are taking it, and provide appropriate comfort at the same time.

10 **Feedback can be given before scores or grades.** Consider whether sometimes it may be worth returning students' work to them with feedback comments but no grades (but having written down your marks in your own records). Then invite students to try to work out what their scores or grade should be, and to report to you in a week's time what they think. This causes students to read all your feedback comments earnestly in their bid to work out how they have done. Most students will make good guesses regarding their grades, and it is worth finding out which students are way out too.

11 **Think about audio tapes for giving feedback.** In some subjects, it is quite hard to write explanatory comments on students' work. For example, in mathematical problems, it can be quicker and easier to 'talk' individual students through how a problem should be solved, referring to asterisks or code-numbers marked on their work. Such feedback has the advantages of tone of voice for emphasis and explanation. Another advantage is that students can play it again, until they have fully understood all of your feedback.

12 **Consider giving feedback by e-mail.** Some students feel most relaxed when working at a computer terminal on their own. With e-mail, students can receive your feedback when they are ready to think about it. They can read it again later, and even file it. Using e-mail, you can give students feedback asynchronously as you work through their scripts, rather than having to wait till you return the whole set to a class.

Feedback and competence development

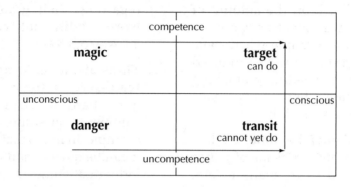

Figure 2.1   Linking feedback to competence development

In Chapter 1, I included a model tracking the development of conscious competence. Feedback is important in all four 'states' represented in the diagram in Figure
2.1.

Feedback addressing conscious competence

Giving students feedback on things they can already do well, and *know* they are
already competent at doing, is trickier than may seem obvious. When students *know*
that they have done something well, any feedback which smacks of 'faint praise' can
be quite damning. However, if we wax too lyrical in our praise, it can be seen as
condescending. We need to pit our wits towards helping students to take ownership
of their successes in this scenario, for example:

- I'm sure you already realize you've done a really good job with this; or
- Do stop for a moment and think about how well you've done this, and how
  useful it will be for you to continue to hone these skills. Don't lose them!

Feedback addressing conscious uncompetence

We are more practised at giving this sort of feedback. Much of the feedback we
routinely give students is directed towards helping them to become better at things
they already know they cannot yet do. We can help by giving them suggestions about
what to do first in their attempts to move things upwards out of the 'transit' box on
the diagram. We can help them prioritize *which* things are worth trying to move, and
which are not important enough to bother with.

Feedback addressing unconscious uncompetencies

This is by far the most importance area for feedback. One of the main points of having assessed coursework is to use this sort of feedback to help students find out much more about what they did not yet know that they could not yet do. In other words, we use feedback to help students to move things out of their danger box and into their transit box, on the way towards the target box.

It could be said that the art of teaching lies in helping students to explore their danger box, and to identify important elements hiding there, bringing them out into the open, then moving them towards conscious competence.

The fact that this is an everyday part of helping students to learn does not mean that it is an easy part. For a start, we are talking about giving feedback addressing *unconscious* uncompetencies. Therefore, the first hurdle is gently alerting students to things that they did not know were there. There is an element of surprise. Some of the surprises will be unpleasant ones – where (for example) students had thought that they were consciously competent in the aspect concerned. It is the 'bad news' box. The good news is that the things identified will not be bad news any more, once moved.

Feedback addressing unconscious competence

This is another surprise box, but this time it is a 'good news' box. For example, part-time mature students bring to their educational experience a wide range of unconscious competencies. These are things that they are good at, but do not know how useful and important the things themselves could turn out to be. For example, they are often really skilled at time-management and task-management. Their life experience has often allowed them to develop skills at handling a number of different agendas at once, and prioritizing between competing demands.

Moving these unconscious competencies towards the conscious level almost always results in an increase of confidence and self-esteem. If you have just been helped to see that you are actually very good at something that you had not ever suspected was among your strengths, would you not feel good about it?

Reducing your load: short cuts to good feedback

Keep records carefully

Keeping good records of assessment takes time, but can save time in the long run. The following suggestions may help you organize your record-keeping:

- **Be meticulous.** However tired you are at the end of a marking session, record all the marks immediately (or indeed continuously as you go along). Then put the marks in a different place from the scripts. Then should any disasters befall you (briefcase stolen, house burnt down and so on) there is the chance that you will still have the marks even if you do not have the scripts any longer (or vice versa).
- **Be systematic.** Use class lists, when available, as the basis of your records. Otherwise make your own class lists as you go along. File all records of assessment in places where you can find them again. It is possible to spend as much time looking for missing marksheets as it took to do the original assessment.
- **Use technology to produce assessment records.** Keep marks on a grid on a computer, or use a spreadsheet, and save by date as a new file every time you add to it, so you are always confident that you are working with the most recent version. Keep paper copies of each list as an insurance against disaster. Keep backup copies of disks or sheets: simply photocopying a handwritten list of marks is a valuable precaution.
- **Use technology to save you from number-crunching.** The use of computer spreadsheet programs can allow the machine to do all of the subtotalling, averaging and data handling for you. If you are afraid to set up a system for yourself, a computer-loving colleague or a member of the information systems support staff will be delighted to start you off.
- **Use other people.** Some universities employ administrative staff to issue and collect in work for assessment, and to make up assessment lists and input the data into computers. Partners, friends and even young children can help you check your addition of marks, and help you record the data.

Reduce your burden

Straightforward ways to lighten your assessment and feedback load are suggested below:

- **Reduce the number of your assignments.** Are all of them strictly necessary, and is it possible to combine some of them, and completely delete others?

- **Use shorter assignments.** Often we ask for 2,000, 3,000 or 5,000-word assignments or reports, when a fraction of the length can be just as acceptable. Some essays or long reports could be replaced by shorter reviews, articles, memorandum-reports or summaries. Projects can be assessed by poster displays instead of reports, and exam papers can include some sections of multiple-choice questions, particularly where these could be marked by optical mark scanners, or using computer managed assessment directly.
- **Use assignment return sheets.** These can be pro formas which contain the assessment criteria for an assignment, with spaces for ticks/crosses, grades, marks and brief comments. They enable rapid feedback on routine assessment matters, providing more time for individual comment to students when necessary on deeper aspects of their work.
- **Consider using statement banks.** These are a means whereby your frequently-repeated comments can be written once each then printed or e-mailed to students, or put onto transparencies or slides for discussion in a subsequent lecture.
- **Involve students in self or peer assessment.** Start small, and explain what you are doing and why. Involving students in some of their assessment can provide them with very positive learning experiences.
- **Mark some exercises in class time using self or peer marking.** This is sometimes useful when students have prepared work expecting tutor assessment, to the standard that they wish to be seen by you.
- **Do not count all assessments.** For example, give students the option that their best five out of eight assignments will count as their coursework mark. Students satisfied with their *first* five need not undertake the other three at all then (which is three less for you to mark!).

When you still find yourself overloaded

No one wants to have to cope with huge piles of coursework scripts or exam papers. However, not all factors may be within your control, and you may still end up overloaded. The following wrinkles may be somewhat soothing at such times:

- **Put the great unmarked pile *under* your desk.** It is very discouraging to be reminded continually of the magnitude of the overall task. Put only a handful of scripts or assignments in sight – about as many as you might expect to deal with in about an hour.
- **Set yourself progressive targets.** Plan to accomplish a bit more at each stage than you need to. Build in safety margins. This allows you some insurance against unforeseen disasters (and children), and can allow you to gradually earn some time off as a bonus.

- **Make an even better marking scheme.** Often, it only becomes possible to make a really good marking scheme after you have found out the ways in which candidates are actually answering the questions. Put the marking scheme where you can see it easily. It can be useful to paste it up with Blu-Tack above your desk or table, so you do not have to rummage through your papers looking for it every time you need it.
- **Mark in different places.** Mark at work, at home, and anywhere else that is not public. This means of course carrying scripts around as well as your marking scheme (or a copy of it). It does, however, avoid one place becoming so associated with doom and depression that you develop place-avoidance strategies for it.
- **Mark one question at a time through all the scripts, at first.** This allows you to become quickly skilled at marking that question, without the agenda of all the rest of the questions on your mind. It also helps ensure reliability and objectivity of marking. When you have completely mastered your marking scheme for all questions, start marking whole scripts.

Involving students in their own assessment

Nothing affects students more than assessment, yet they often claim that they are in the dark as to what goes on in the minds of their assessors and examiners. Involving students in peer and self-assessment can let them in to the assessment culture they must survive. Increasingly peer assessment is being used to involve students more closely in their learning and its evaluation, and to help enable students to really understand what is required of them. It is not a 'quick fix' solution to reduce staff marking time, as it is intensive in its use of lecturer time at the briefing and development stages. It can have enormous benefits in terms of learning gain. The following suggestions may help you get started with student peer assessment.

Reasons to consider using student peer assessment

Introducing student peer assessment can seem a daunting and hazardous prospect, if you are surrounded by an assessment culture where lecturers undertake all of the assessing. There are, however, several good reasons why the prospect should not be seen as so formidable, and some of these are proposed below:

- **Students are doing it already.** Students are continuously peer assessing, in fact. One of the most significant sources of answers to students' pervading question, 'How am I doing?' is the feedback they get about their own learning achievements and performances by comparing them with those of others. It is true that feedback from tutors is regarded as more authoritative, but there is less such feedback available from tutors than from fellow learners. Setting up and facilitating peer assessment therefore legitimizes and makes respectable something in which most students are already engaged.

- **Students find out more about our assessment cultures.** One of the biggest dangers with assessment is that students often do not really know how their assessment works. They often approach both exams and tutor-marked coursework like black holes that they might be sucked into! Getting involved in peer assessment makes the assessment culture much more transparent, and students gain a better idea of exactly what will be expected of them in their efforts to demonstrate their achievement of the intended learning outcomes.

- **We cannot do as much assessing as we used to do.** With more students, heavier teaching loads and shorter timescales (sometimes caused by moves to modularization and semesterization), the amount of assessment that lecturers can cope with is limited. While it is to be hoped that our assessment will still be valid, fair and reliable, it remains the case that the amount of feedback to students that lecturers can give is less per capita. Peer assessment, when facilitated well, can be a vehicle for getting much more feedback to students.

- **Students learn more deeply when they have a sense of ownership of the agenda.** When peer assessment is employed using assessment criteria that are devised by the students themselves, the sense of ownership of the criteria helps them to apply their criteria much more objectively than when they are applying tutors' criteria to each other's work.

- **The act of assessing is one of the deepest learning experiences.** Applying criteria to someone else's work is one of the most productive ways of developing and deepening understanding of the subject matter involved in the process. Measuring and judging are far more rigorous processes than simply reading, listening and watching.

- **Peer assessment allows students to learn from each other's successes.** Students involved in peer assessment cannot fail to take notice of instances where the work they are assessing exceeds their own efforts. When this learning from each other is legitimized and encouraged, students can benefit a great deal from the work of the most able in the group.

- **Peer assessment allows students to learn from each other's weaknesses.** Students peer assessing are likely to discover all sorts of mistakes that they did not make themselves. This can be really useful for them, as their awareness of what not to do increases, and they become much less likely to fall into traps that might otherwise have caused them problems in their future work.

Getting students to formulate their peer-assessment criteria

As mentioned already, peer assessment works at its best when students own the assessment criteria. Furthermore, it is important that the criteria are clearly understood by all the students, and their understanding is shared. The best way of developing a set of good criteria is to involve the students from the outset in the process. It is crucial not to put words in students' mouths during this process, otherwise the assessment agenda can revert to academic terminology which students do not understand. The following processes can be used to generate a set of peer-assessment criteria from scratch. I have used this process with groups of nearly 200 students, as well as with more intimate groups of 20 upwards.

It really does not matter what the task that students are going to peer assess involves. The process below will be described in terms of students peer assessing a presentation, but the process could be identical for generating student-owned assessment criteria for an essay, a report, a poster display, an interview, an annotated bibliography, a student-devised exam paper and countless other assessment possibilities.

It is possible to go through all the processes listed below, with a group of over 100 students, in less than an hour. The more often you do this with students, the faster and better you will become at it (and at taking short-cuts where appropriate, or tailoring the steps to your own subject, and to the particular students, and so on).

In practice, you are very unlikely to need to build in all 18 of the steps outlined in the list below in any given instance of negotiating criteria with a group of students. Usually, at least some of the processes below may be skipped, but it is worth thinking through the implications of all of the stages before making your own decision about which are most relevant to the particular conditions under which you are planning to facilitate peer assessment:

- **Brainstorming.** Ask all students to jot down individually a few key words in response to, 'What makes a really *good* ten-minute presentation? Jot down some of the things you would look for in an excellent example of one.'
- **Sharing.** Get students to work in groups. Even in a large lecture theatre, they can work in groups of four or five with their near neighbours. Alternatively, if students are free to move around the room where the exercise is happening, they can be put into random groups (alphabetical, or by birthday month, or allowed to form self-selecting groups). Ask the groups to share and discuss for a few minutes *all* of their ideas for a good presentation.
- **Prioritizing.** Ask the groups to make a shortlist of (say) 'The most important *five* features of a good ten-minute presentation'. Ask each group to appoint a scribe to note down the shortlist.
- **Editing.** Get the groups to look carefully at the wording of each item on their shortlists. For example, tell them that when they report back an item from their list, if you cannot tell exactly what it means, you will ask them to tell you, 'What

it *really* means is...'. Maybe mention that some of the more academic words such as 'coherence', 'structure' and 'delivery' may need some translation into everyday words (maybe along the lines of 'hangs well together, one point following on logically to the next...' , 'good interest-catching opening, logical order for the middle, and firm solid conclusion', and 'clearly-spoken, well-illustrated, backed up by facts or figures...'). However, do not put too many words of any kind into students' minds; let them think of their own words.

- **Re-prioritizing.** Remind the groups about the shortlisting process, and to get their five features into order of priority. This may have changed during the editing process, and meanings became clearer.

- **Turning features into checklist questions.** Suggest that the groups now edit each of their features into a question format. For example, 'Was there a good finish?', or 'How well was the material researched?'. The point of this is to pave the way for a checklist of criteria that will be more straightforward as a basis for making judgements.

- **Collecting the most important questions in the room.** Now start collecting 'top' feature-questions. Ask each group in turn for the thing that came top of its list. Write these up, one at a time, on a flipchart or overhead transparency, so that the whole class can see the emerging list of criteria. Where one group's highest-rating point is very similar to one that has already been given, either put a tick beside the original one (to acknowledge that the same point has been rated as important by more than one group), or (better) adjust the wording slightly so that the flipcharted criterion reflects *both* of the sources equally. Continue this process until each of the groups has reported its top criterion.

- **Fleshing out the agenda.** Now go back round the groups (in reverse order) asking for the second most important thing on each list. At this stage, the overlaps begin to occur thick and fast, but there will still emerge new and different checklist questions based on further features identified by the groups. Use ticks (maybe in a different colour from the overlaps of top-rated questions) to make the degree of concurrence visible to the whole group as the picture continues to unfold. With a large class, you may need to use more than one flipchart-sheet (or overhead transparency), but it is important to try to keep all of the agenda that is unfolding visible to the whole class. This means posting up filled flipcharts where everyone can see them, or alternating the transparencies so that students remember what has already come up.

- **Any other business?** If the degree of overlap has increased significantly, and after gaining all the second-round contributions, the flow of new ideas has slowed down, it is worth asking the whole group for 'Any fairly-important things that still aren't represented on your list?' Usually, there will be a further two or three significant contributions at this stage.

- **Numbering the agenda.** When all of the criteria questions have been noted down, *number them*. Simply write numbers beside each criterion, in the order that they were given. During this stage, if you notice that two criteria are more or less the same, it can be worth asking the class whether you can clump them together.

- **Weighting individually.** Next, ask students to work individually again. Ask them to weight each criterion, using an agreed total number of marks. Choosing the total number needs care. If there are 10 criteria, 100 marks would be too tempting, since there is the possibility of some students just giving each criterion 10 marks, and avoiding the real business of making prioritizing decisions again. Thirteen criteria and 60 marks works better, for example. Ask every student to ensure that the total marks number adds up to the agreed figure. Allow students to ignore any criteria that they individually do not think are important: 'If you think it is irrelevant, just score it zero.'

- **Recording everyone's weighting publicly.** The next stage is to record everyone's marks on the flipcharts or transparencies. This means starting with criterion number 1, and writing beneath it *everyone's* marks-rating. It is worth establishing a reporting-back order round the room first, so that every student knows who to follow (and encouraging students to nudge anyone who has lost concentration and is failing to give you a score). 'Can you shout them out as fast as I can write them up?' usually keeps everyone (including you) working at speed.

- **Optional separating.** It can be worth starting with two flipcharts from the outset. For example, you may wish to record separately the criteria relating to *content* and those relating to *structure*. This may pave the way for peer-assessment grids which help to separate such dimensions.

- **Discussing divergent views.** Then go through all the remaining criteria in the same way. Do not worry that sometimes consecutive scores for the same criterion will be quite divergent. When this happens, it will be a rich agenda for discussion later, and if you are writing the scores up in the same order each time, it is not too hard to pinpoint the particular individual who gave an unusually high or low rating to any criterion. You can, for example, ask the student who rated criterion 8 highest to argue briefly with the student who rated it lowest, and see what the causes of the divergence may be.

- **Averaging.** Next, average out all the scores. If there are students with calculators in the group, the average rating may be forthcoming from the group without any prompting. Otherwise, it is usually possible to do some averaging and rounding up or down to the nearest whole number just intuitively by looking at the numbers. Ask the whole group 'Does criterion 7 get a 5 or a 6 please? Hands up those who make it a 5' and so on.

- **Shedding weak criteria.** Look back at the whole range of criteria and ratings. At this point, there will usually be one or more criteria that can safely be dropped from the agenda. They may have seemed like a good idea at the time to some of the students, but the visible ratings tell their own story.

- **Confirming ownership.** 'Are you all happy to proceed with the averaged-out version of the ratings, and with these criteria?' is the question to ask next. Mostly, there will be no dissent. Just occasionally, a student with a different view of the ratings may wish to speak out against the consensus. It is worth then offering that any individuals who feel strongly about the ratings can choose to be peer assessed by their own idiosyncratic rating scales, but that these must now be shared with the whole group for approval. Students rarely wish to do this, particularly if the feeling of ownership of the set of weighted criteria is strong in the group as a whole.
- **Administrating.** Turn the criteria questions into a grid, with the criteria down the left-hand side, and the weighting numbers in a column alongside them, with spaces for students to write in their peer-assessment ratings. If students are going to be asked to peer assess several instances of the task involved (for example, maybe 10 short presentations) the grids could be marked up so that students use the same grid for the successive presentations (see Figure 2.2). Alternatively, if the peer-assessment grids are going to be used for a small number of assessments (for example, where all students mark three essays or reports, and each of theirs is to be marked by three students), it is worth having

Peer assessment: grid for multiple examples									
Your name:	Date:	Session:							
Example being assessed:	Mark out of:	A	B	C	D	E	F	G	H
Criterion 1	6								
Criterion 2	8								
Criterion 3	4								
Criterion 4	8								
Criterion 5	5								
Criterion 6	5								
Criterion 7	2								
Criterion 8	4								
Total	40								

Figure 2.2 Example of a grid where students peer assess A to H (for example) presentations

separate sheets, with a column for individual feedback comments relating to the score awarded for each of the criteria (see Figure 2.3).

The list of processes above may appear daunting, but in fact it is quite a lot easier to do in practice than it is to write out a description of it! Also, some of the steps are in fact very quick to do. Furthermore, as the culture of peer assessment becomes better known to students, they themselves become better at generating and weighting criteria, and more skilled at applying them well.

Setting up self-assessment tutor dialogues

Think of the following scenario. A piece of coursework is to be handed in and tutor assessed. This could be just about anything, ranging from a practical report to a fieldwork report, a dissertation, and even an essay or set of answers based on a problems sheet.

Peer assessment with feedback: grid for a single example			
Your name:	Date:	Session:	
Example being assessed:	Mark:	Score	Feedback comments
Criterion 1	6		
Criterion 2	8		
Criterion 3	4		
Criterion 4	8		
Criterion 5	5		
Criterion 6	5		
Criterion 7	2		
Criterion 8	4		
Total	40		

Figure 2.3   Pro forma for individual peer assessments of (for example) essays or reports, with feedback

Imagine that students are briefed to self-assess their efforts at the point of submitting the work for tutor assessment, and are supplied with a pro forma for this self-assessment, of no more than two pages' length. Suppose that the pro forma consists of a dozen or so short, structured questions, asking students to make particular reflective comments upon the work they are handing in, and that the principal purposes behind these questions are to:

- get students to reflect on what they have done;
- give tutors assessing their work additional information about 'where each student is' in relation to the tasks they have just attempted;
- form a productive agenda to help tutors to focus their feedback most usefully;
- save tutors time by helping them to avoid telling students things about their submitted work, which they know all too clearly already;
- give students a sense of ownership of the most important elements of feedback which they are going to receive on the work they have submitted.

Some ideas for self-assessment agendas

Each of the suggestions below could take the form of a relatively small box on the pro forma, requiring students to give their own reply to the question, but allowing space for tutors to add a sentence of two in response to each student's reply. Sometimes, of course, tutors would wish to (or need to) enclose additional response information on separate sheets – often pre-prepared handout materials dealing with anticipated problem areas or frequently-made errors.

A reminder: the menu of questions below is exactly that – a menu – from which individual assessors will need to select carefully only a few questions, those which are most relevant to the nature of the assessed task. Also, for every separate task, it is vitally important that the self-assessment questionnaires are patently task-specific, and that students *do not* see the same (or similar) questionnaires more than once. (We all know how 'surface' students' responses become to repetitively-used course evaluation questionnaires, and how limited is the value of the feedback we receive from such instruments.)

For each of the questions I include below, I have added a sentence or two about *why* or *when* it may prove useful to assessors and students. Some parts of the menu below are much more 'obvious' than others, and I believe that those most likely to set up deep tutor–student dialogue are among the less common ones:

- What do you honestly consider will be a fair score or grade for the work you are handing in?
  - Most students are surprisingly good at estimating the worth of their work. Only those students who are more than 5 per cent out (or one grade point)

need any detailed feedback on any differences between the actual scores and their own estimates. This saves tutors' time.

■ What do you think was the thing you did best in this assignment?
- The fact is that assessors know soon enough what students actually did best, but that is not the same as knowing what they *think* they have done well. Where both are the same thing there is no need for any response from assessors, but on the occasions when students did something else much better (or did the original thing quite poorly) feedback is vital, and very useful to students.

■ What did you find the hardest part of this assignment?
- Assessors know soon enough what students do least well, but that is not always the thing they found hardest. When a student cites something that was completely mastered – in other words, the assignment gives no clue that this was a struggle – it is quite essential that the student is congratulated on the achievement involved. For example, a few words such as 'You say you found this hard, but you've completely cracked it – well done!' go a long way.

■ If you had the chance to do this assignment again from scratch, how (if at all) might you decide to go about it differently?
- This question can save assessors hours. Students usually know what is wrong with the approach they have engaged in. Let them tell you about this. This saves you having to go on at length telling them about it. Moreover, when students themselves have diagnosed the weaknesses in their approach, the ownership of the potential changes to approach lie with them, rather than our having to take control of this.

■ How difficult (or easy) did you find this assignment?
- Do not use number scales. Provide words or phrases which students can underline or ring. Use student language, such as 'dead easy', 'tough in parts', 'straightforward', 'a real pain', 'took longer than it was worth', 'hard but helped me learn' and so on.

■ What was the most important thing that you learnt about the subject through doing this assignment?
- Answers to this question give us a lot of information about the extent to which the assignment is delivering learning payoff to students.

■ What was the most important thing that you learnt about *yourself* while doing this assignment?
- Such a question gives us information about how well (or badly) the assignment may be contributing to students' development of key transferable skills, including self-organization.

■ What do you think are the most important things I am looking for in this assignment?
- This question can be sobering for assessors – it can show us how students perceive our activities, and it can often show us a lot about how we are found

to be assessing. Students can benefit from feedback on their responses, when their perceptions of the purposes of an assignment have gone adrift.

■ How has doing this assignment changed your opinions?
- Not all assignments have anything to do with developing students' views, attitudes or opinions, but some do this, and it is important that we acknowledge this when such issues are intentional. Such a question is better than simply asking, 'Has your opinion changed?', where the expectation is clearly for a 'Yes' response.

■ What is the worst paragraph, and why?
- This question is particularly useful as a feedback dialogue starter when assign-ments are substantial, such as long reports or dissertations. Students quite often know exactly where they were trying to firm up an idea, but struggling to express it. Their help in bringing to our attention the exact positions of such instances can save us hours in finding them, and can ensure that we have the opportunity to respond helpfully and relevantly to students' needs.

Conclusions

None of the forms of assessment discussed in this chapter is without its merits or its limitations in the context of assessing various facets of the skills, knowledge and performances of students. The challenges caused by greater numbers of students and increased assessment workloads provide an opportunity to make a radical review of the ways we assess our students. The requirement placed upon us to match assessment criteria to intended learning outcomes give us further opportunity to adjust our assessment so that we are attempting to measure that which is important, rather than merely that which is relatively straightforward to measure.

In particular, we must ensure that our attempts to meet these challenges do not lead to a retreat from those forms of assessment which are less cost-effective, but which help students to get due credit for a sensible range of the knowledge and skills they demonstrate. Probably the best way to do our students justice is to use as wide a mixture of the assessment methods outlined above as possible, allowing students a range of processes through which to demonstrate their respective strengths and weaknesses. Moreover, the 15 assessment methods discussed in some detail in this chapter are only a cross-section of those which could be used. Ideally, for each area of students' learning, we should be asking, 'What is the most appropriate way to measure this fairly, validly and reliably?'

Finally, we need to ensure that learning is not simply assessment-driven. It can be argued that presently we have far too much assessment, but that neither the quality nor the diversity of this assessment is right. Students are highly intelligent people; if we confront them with a game where learning is linked to a rigid and monotonous diet of assessment, they will learn according to the rules of that game. To improve their learning, we need to improve our game.

3: Refreshing your lecturing

Intended outcomes of this chapter

When you've looked through this chapter, and applied the most appropriate ideas it contains to your teaching, you should be better able to:

- gain confidence in preparing and delivering lectures;
- develop your work with large groups of students so that their learning is more productive in your sessions;
- think consciously about how your students learn in lectures, and about ways you can address the principal factors underpinning successful learning in your lectures;
- make good use of audio–visual aids when giving lectures;
- use presentation managers well in lectures;
- use handout materials to help to structure students' learning, both during and after lectures;
- choose from a variety of ways to get feedback on your lectures from your students;
- prepare your large-group teaching so that it will be seen to be successful when your teaching is observed or reviewed;
- make use of, or adapt to your own purposes, a self-assessment pro forma, and a peer-assessment version, to help you to evaluate your own performance in lectures, and to gather evidence of your own professional performance.

Those who may need their lecturing refreshing

I have developed this chapter with five groups of colleagues in mind:

- those who are new to large-group teaching, and who would appreciate a little help on how best to get started on such work;
- those for whom student class sizes have expanded recently, and who may wish for some ideas on how to work well with larger groups;
- experienced colleagues who simply would like to explore whether there are fresh approaches they may wish to try out in their large-group work with students;
- old hands at lecturing, who may be thinking of introducing computer-based presentation managers to replace overheads or slides;

- colleagues who already make extensive use of handout materials, who may be concerned that students 'switch off' when they know that they will get most of the important information in their handouts.

This chapter is based around workshops on large-group teaching which I run with lecturers, and on some of the exercises I ask them to try during such workshops.

The importance of the act of lecturing

Giving lectures is the most public side of the work of most higher education lecturers. Attending lectures is part of the life of most higher education students. Although some parts of this chapter are specifically about lecturing, most of the suggestions apply to the processes of working with large groups of students. Suggestions in this chapter include ways to help large-group sessions deliver increased learning payoff to students. In effect, I explore many of the ways in which the principles of active, interactive learning can be brought into the lecture room or large-group classroom.

Later in the chapter, attention is turned to some of the technologies used by most lecturers, starting with overhead projectors, and leading into suggestions for using computer-managed presentation systems well.

The chapter concludes with some suggestions about ways to make the most of the benefits of observing others at work in the lecture room, and to learn from feedback when your own work is observed. Familiarity with teaching observation pays dividends when subject review or other forms of external scrutiny come your way.

The history of the lecture stems from times when there were very few books, and the most efficient way of communicating information was to read it out to people, who could take notes of their own, and store it. Although it was indeed possible to communicate *information* in this way, it was soon recognized that this did not amount to communicating *knowledge.* Despite the fact that this situation is long gone, most educational systems continue to place considerable value on the lecture situation, not least because it is something that is visible and accountable, and because many lecturers enjoy lecturing! Nowadays quite a lot of doubt hangs over the effectiveness of lectures as a means of helping students to learn, but this is mainly because some lecturers continue to regard lectures as occasions when they perform, and believe this is all that is necessary for their students to learn. Now that all kinds of information-technology-based curriculum delivery approaches are available, the central role of lectures is even more in doubt. Nevertheless, in this chapter I will explore how large-group sessions can in fact be made very productive in terms of students' learning, by making optimum use of occasions when students are together.

When you are appointed as a 'lecturer', it may seem reasonable to suppose that this is the most important part of your job. This belief is increased when the main specification of your job turns out to be a timetable, with lecture slots as the principal fixed teaching duties each week. Most people new to lecturing approach their first encounters with the process with some trepidation – some with sheer terror. Indeed, if measurements were taken of pulse-rate, palm sweat and blood pressure during the first few minutes on stage as a lecturer, the results would give every indication of quite a lot of stress.

Given how important lecturing is taken to be, you may be surprised that in Chapter 2 in this book I addressed assessment even before teaching. My justification is simple enough: students can survive bad lectures, but they may be damaged by bad assessment. Whatever else we do, we need to link assessment well to what students are intended to learn; *how* they learn it, *when* they learn it and *where* they learn it are of much less importance. It is also fair to say that despite the fears that new lecturers have about lecturing, the fears they have about wielding a red pen in assessment mode for the first time are often even more substantial.

'But all their eyes are on me!'

If you are naturally at home on the stage in a theatre, stage fright will not worry you – you may even enjoy it. However, for perhaps 19 out of 20 of us, we are not particularly comfortable being the focus of attention of so many eyes. Fortunately, there are many ways to divert students from watching us, and at the same time help them to think about the topics of our lectures. These diversion tactics include:

- using overheads or PowerPoint slides – and even dimming the lights so the slides are more easily seen – and we are less visible;
- giving out handouts, so that every now and then all the eyes will be looking at printed sheets rather than at us;
- giving students things to do during lectures: for example, decisions to make about which of three options – on-screen or in their handouts – would be preferable;
- getting students to discuss an idea with their immediate neighbours for a minute or two, then sounding out the conclusions they have reached.

But it is not enough just to look after our own comfort levels in lectures; we need to be thinking of what is happening in the minds of each and every member of our audience. Some of the diversion tactics listed above do indeed have direct links to helping students to learn.

Reasons to have lectures

There has been quite a lot written about how ineffective the traditional lecture can be in terms of learning payoff to students. However, we are stuck with slots with large groups on our timetables, so it is worth thinking about how we can make best use of such time. Long ago, the beginning of the culture of giving lectures was probably owing to the fact that only the 'lecturer' had the books. When books had to be copied by hand, they were rare and valuable. Now, students can have relatively easy access to all the original books and papers, not to mention a vast amount of further material available on the Internet and computer-based learning materials and databases. So why does the practice of giving lectures continue? There are good reasons and bad ones. Let us look at the worst ones first.

Some bad reasons

- simply to respond to some students' expectations that they are going to be taught all they need to know;
- to fill up students' timetables, so that a 'course' or 'programme of study' is seen to exist;
- to fill up your own timetable so that you are seen to be gainfully employed;
- to keep students 'under control';
- because 'that's the way it's always been done here';
- because 'that's what happened to me when I was a student'.

Some good reasons

Even nowadays when students can have their own access to source material, books, handouts and a range of electronic learning resources, there are still several things that can best be achieved in large-group sessions with classes. Some reasons for continuing to use large-group sessions with students include the following:

- to give students a shared learning experience and provide a focus, where everyone gets together regularly;
- to whet students' appetites, so that they go away and really want to get down to studying;
- to give students the chance to make sense of things they already know;
- to clarify intended learning outcomes, and define the standards of students' performance which will be linked to these outcomes;
- to give students the opportunity of learning by doing, where they can get feedback from an 'authority' and from each other;
- to add the power of tone of voice, emphasis, facial expression and body language to printed words, helping learners to see what's important, and what is not;
- to provide material for later discussion, exploration and elaboration;
- to challenge students' preconceptions, assumptions and beliefs;

- to change or develop students' attitudes and perspectives;
- to create occasions when some at least of the students present can 'first see the light' on tricky concepts and ideas, and consolidate this by sharing the experience of 'the light dawning' with fellow-students who've not yet seen the light;
- to give large groups of students a common 'briefing' for major assessment-related tasks which they are to undertake as they study the subject further.

Most of the above reasons for continuing to give lectures are more concerned with the broad experience of studying than with the activities which students engage in during a particular lecture. However, it is indeed possible to follow up our exploration of learning processes from Chapter 1 to set out to *cause* students to learn things *during* a lecture. This can still be achieved, even with very large student groups, by concentrating on what the students themselves actually do during such lectures, and ensuring that the processes relate to effective learning. Let us look next at some ways of achieving this.

Some things students do in lectures

I have asked many hundreds of lecturers what they believe their students do during lectures, and many thousands of students what they *really* do. As you may expect, many of the things students do during lectures are far from connected to the content of the lectures. Some of the most common things students do in lectures are listed below.

- Copying down things from the blackboard or screen.
- Copying down verbatim things said by the lecturer.
- Summarizing things discussed by the lecturer.
- Gazing out of the windows (if there are any).
- Looking at other students.
- Worrying because they cannot understand what is being talked about.
- Watching the clock – waiting for lunchtime, for example.
- Doodling, yawning, fidgeting, shuffling, daydreaming – even sleeping.
- Reading things that have nothing to do with the lecture.
- Listening to the match on a personal radio.
- Thinking about coursework soon to be submitted for *other* subjects.
- Actually *doing* coursework due to be handed in for other subjects.
- Worrying about accommodation problems, cash flow problems, relationships.
- Feeling generally unwell – hangover, tiredness, 'flu.

(Please continue this list if you wish!)

Only one of the things mentioned so far is a useful learning experience in its own right: 'summarizing'. This involves processing the content of the lecture, making decisions about the relative importance of different things, and generally 'digesting' the material.

Most of the remainder of the things in the list above are neither productive in terms of learning payoff, nor linked to achieving the intended learning outcomes. In particular, *copying* things down (whether from the screen, or from what has been said) is far from being as useful as people think it is. Most students will admit having been to lectures where they had copied all sorts of things down (even transcribed verbatim dictated episodes), but without actually thinking about the material at all at the time. They confirm that if they were to be quizzed about the notes they had just copied out, their answer would have to be along the lines 'Sorry, I haven't actually *read* it yet – ask me again later!'

In other words, the fact that a large group of students may look very busy writing during a lecture is in itself no indication that any deep learning is occurring then and there. It is true that students will often get down to learning what they have copied *later*, but that does not alter the fact that during the lecture itself they were in effect wasting their time and energy on processes with no direct learning payoff. It would have been better if they had been issued with the material they copied down, for example in the form of a handout. However, there are problems with straight handouts, in particular the danger that students believe that they have already captured the content of the lecture, and think that they may safely switch off mentally altogether.

Some productive lecture processes

A number of further activities that students can engage in during lectures can be productive in terms of learning. As we saw in Chapter 1, five overlapping processes which underpin successful learning are:

- wanting to learn – motivation, interest, enthusiasm;
- needing to learn – seeing the reason for putting in some hard work;
- learning by doing – practising, trial-and-error, learning from mistakes;
- getting feedback on how the learning is going – other people's reactions, comments, seeing tangible evidence for one's achievements using what has been learnt;
- making sense of what has been learnt – 'digesting' it, getting one's head round it.

Figure 3.1   Processes underpinning successful learning

Below I have tried to link some of these productive student actions to these five central processes.

> - becoming excited about the subject, and enthused (wanting);
> - wishing to find out more about things discussed (wanting);
> - seeing *why* something is important (needing);
> - solving problems (learning by doing);
> - trying out theoretical principles in practice-based examples (learning by doing);
> - making decisions (learning by doing, also digesting);
> - explaining things to fellow students sitting nearby (doing, digesting, feedback);
> - asking questions (seeking feedback);
> - working out questions to find out the answers to later (preparing to seek feedback);
> - prioritizing issues and information (digesting);
> - summarizing (digesting);
> - making notes in a way so that important things 'stand out from the page' (digesting, learning by doing);
> - answering questions (learning by doing, getting feedback).

As you read the discussion below, think further how you can construct your lectures in ways that directly address these active processes (and help to avoid the occurrence of some of the unproductive processes mentioned earlier).

Using handouts to enhance students' learning

The use of handouts in large-group lectures has increased dramatically over the last few years. This is not least due to the advent of better, faster, cheaper photocopying and reprographic technologies. It is also linked with students' expectations. Furthermore, handout materials provide evidence for quality review purposes, illustrating not only the content of teaching programmes, but also the processes adopted to address student learning in lectures.

There are many advantages accompanying the use of handout materials. Not least is the fact that in a few pages of handout materials, far more information can be made available to students than they would ever have been able to write down for themselves during the lecture.

However, the dangers accompanying the use of handouts are becoming ever more apparent. For example, students may feel little real ownership of a 'straight' handout (as opposed to an 'interactive' one, which is more akin to a learning resource). Straight handouts are still 'other people's words' to students. The principal danger is that students can be tempted to switch off mentally, if they believe that they will be receiving (or have already got in their hands) everything important that is being covered in a lecture.

Many advocates of the use of handout materials agree that it is what students *do* with the handouts that really matters. Handouts should be learning tools, not just compendia of information. Ownership of knowledge is much more than simply possessing the information.

The following pages contain an extensive checklist against which you can interrogate your own usage of handout materials. I do not suggest that each handout should achieve all of the factors included in the checklist below, but that across your range of handouts you may find it useful to address most of them in one way or another, as seems most appropriate to you in the context of your own discipline.

Using handouts: some practical suggestions

The following suggestions summarize some of the ways in which you can ensure that your use of handout materials helps your students to learn effectively during (and after) your lectures. Furthermore, they may help you to take steps to demonstrate the quality of your thinking about how your students learn, through the design of your handouts as artefacts evidencing your approach to teaching:

- Make handouts look attractive. Gone are the days when a plain handwritten or typed summary of a lecture was enough. The quality of the message is now inextricably associated with the quality of the medium; scrappy handouts tend not to be valued.

- Use the start of a handout to remind students what its purposes are. It can be useful to state on each handout the intended learning outcomes of the particular element of work involved.
- Use plenty of headings. There is little more off-putting than a solid page of unbroken text. Where possible, make headings stand out, by using bold print, or large-size print. When a glance at a handout gives information about the structure of its contents, it has already started to help people learn.
- Use white space. For students to develop a sense of ownership of handouts, they need to have room to write their own notes on them. Space between paragraphs, space at the top and bottom of pages, or a wide margin on one side are all ways of giving them this possibility of ownership.
- Make handouts interactive. In other words, include tasks and activities for students to do, either in the group session where the handout was issued, or as later follow-up activities.
- Include 'committed space' for students to do things in handouts. Structured tasks are best, such as, 'Think of six reasons why the economy is in recession and list them below'. The fact that space has been provided for students' answers helps persuade them (often subconsciously) to have a try at the tasks rather than simply skip them.
- Use tasks as chances for students to learn by doing, and to learn by getting things wrong. Multiple-choice questions are useful for this. The handout can serve as a useful reminder of 'wrong' options chosen, as well as a pleasant reminder of 'correct' choices.
- Use handouts to get students making notes, not just taking notes. Use handouts to avoid the wasteful process of students simply writing down things you say, or transcribing things they see on the screen or board. Copying things down is a low-level learning activity. Having such information already in handout form allows you to spend face-to-face time getting your students probing into the meaning of the information, interpreting it, questioning it, extrapolating from it, analysing it and so on.
- Work out what you intend students to add to the handout during your session. For example, leave spaces for individual 'brainstorms' (such as 'List five symptoms of anaemia'), and for the products of buzz-group discussions (such as putting some factors in order of importance). The aim should be that the handout students take away at the end of the session is much more valuable than the blank one they were given at the start.
- Include annotated bibliographies in handout materials. A few words about what to look for in each particular source can make a big difference to the ways in which students follow up references.
- Where possible, store your handout materials on disk. Go for small print runs. It is then easy to make considerable adjustments and additions to handouts each successive time you use them. Avoid the waste associated with piles of handouts which you have subsequently replaced with updated, improved versions.

Table 3.1 Interrogating your handouts

Key questions	Links to effective learning, further questions	Your notes and action points
Setting the scene		
What are the intended learning outcomes?	Can students see what they need to be able to achieve?	
How much will students want to achieve these outcomes?	Motivation – wanting to learn.	
Is it clear which of the learning outcomes is the most important one?	Can students see priorities to address in their learning?	
Does the handout show how students' achievement of the learning outcomes could be measured in due course?	Motivation – needing to learn.	
Does the handout make links between the present agenda, and topics already covered, and/or to be covered in future?	Digesting – gaining a sense of the place of the particular session in the overall picture.	
Is the handout designed on a realistic scale, so that it can be used fully in the timescale available in the session?	If it is accompanying a one-hour lecture, can it all be covered in 45 minutes or so?	
Learning by doing – interactivity		
Are instructions for tasks clear and helpful?	Can students see exactly what they are intended to be doing?	
Does the handout include some past assessed tasks, for students to practise upon?	Is it encouraging learning by practice?	
Feedback to students		
Does the handout give opportunities for students to gain feedback about their own performance and learning?	For example, where students have undertaken tasks around the content of the handout, are the debriefings clear and useful?	
Can the handout be used to get students to work together in small groups during the session?	Does this allow useful peer feedback to be exchanged?	
Does the handout include answers or responses giving students feedback on the tasks they attempted using the handout?		

Table 3.1 *contd*

Key questions	Links to effective learning, further questions	Your notes and action points
Depth, tone, style		
Is the handout fun? Is the handout a tool for learning, rather than just an information source?	Will students want to learn from it?	
Is the depth of the content appropriate for the purpose of the session?	Helping students to distinguish between information and expected knowledge.	
Does the handout challenge students' thinking, rather than just inform them?	Does it help them to make sense of the topic, rather than just know it?	
Is all the information in the handout essential and relevant?	Will it be regarded by students as an important learning resource?	
How clearly are important concepts and rules expressed, if applicable?	Saving students from routine copying of important material.	
Is the language level pitched appropriately for the students concerned?	Making sure that the learning agenda is not obscured by language sophistication or simplicity.	
Is the style thought-provoking rather than just information-providing?	Will students be caused to think for themselves?	
Layout, appearance		
Is there dedicated space for students to make notes, write their own thoughts, write their own questions?	Is it encouraging participative learning rather than passive receiving?	
Is the layout clear and attractive?	Will students want to use it again and again?	
Is the design simple?		
Is the handout sufficiently concise?	Can students see the wood from the trees?	
Are there headers and page numbers to help students to navigate the handout again later?	Will they be able to use the handout again weeks later, and still remember the context in which it was first used?	
Does the handout contain pictures, drawings, graphs, diagrams and so on to add visual impact to the words?	Does it help by triangulating learning using different approaches?	

Table 3.1 *contd*

Key questions	Links to effective learning, further questions	Your notes and action points
Follow-up after the session		
Does the handout contain tasks for students to try after the session?	Making sense of what has been learnt – gaining understanding.	
Will the handout make a useful revision aid for students?		
Does the handout cite appropriate reference material for students to follow up after the session?		
Are the briefings to external resources active and focused rather than general?	For example, not just 'read Chapter 3 of…' but ' Use pp.45–48 of Chapter 3 to decide why…' and so on.	
Authenticity, quality, topicality and so on		
Has the handout been frequently changed, edited, updated?	Or is it just being used yet one more time as it stands?	
How old is the handout? Could it be regarded as dated?		
Is the content topical and up to date?	Will students find it sufficiently relevant?	
Does the handout look professional?	Is the message being well supported by the medium?	
Will it be possible to use the handout again?	Economy of scale, workload, and so on.	
What changes will be made after this use, and before the next use?		
Student attendance		
Would having a copy of the handout be a sufficient substitute for attending the session?	If 'yes', perhaps the session is not really putting the handout to real use.	
Feedback to the lecturer		
Does the handout include a tear-off short questionnaire to give the lecturer feedback on the particular session?	If 'yes, is the questionnaire sufficiently different from other ones to avoid 'death by questionnaire'?	

Linking learning to teaching in lectures

To summarize our thinking on how we can use large group sessions with students to maximize the learning payoff they derive from them, I would like you to think once again about the practical model of learning introduced in Chapter 1, and the five underpinning processes: wanting, needing, doing, feedback, and digesting. Next, let us take each of these in turn, and remind ourselves of some of the ways in which they can be embraced within the lecture situation. Your own subject-specific ideas are by far the most important aspect of your own agenda for turning your lectures into interactive learning experiences. Nevertheless, I will explore below some further general factors, which I hope will add to your own ideas.

Lectures and wanting to learn

Lectures can be a very effective way of creating the want to learn. Lectures can be occasions where the want is rekindled or amplified. Even if this was the *only* result of a particular lecture, it would be a useful one. Some ways we can attempt to develop students' want to learn include:

- radiating infectious enthusiasm for the subject;
- posing interesting questions which excite students' curiosity;
- helping students to see how much they can already do, increasing their confidence;
- illustrating to students that complex problems can often be solved one step at a time;
- clarifying targets, performance standards and intended learning outcomes, so that students can see exactly what they are aiming for;
- helping students to identify the difference between what they *need to know*, and those things that are simply *nice to know*;
- relating materials being taught to course objectives, and exam questions (establishing the *need to know* dimension).

Lectures and needing to learn

While, as hinted at above, wanting to learn is a much happier driving force for the learning process than needing to learn, the latter is much better than nothing. We can use the shared, large-group situation to help our students to see exactly what is entailed in the expected learning outcomes associated with each topic or theme. Some of the approaches with which we can help students to take ownership of their particular learning needs include:

- explaining what students may be required to do to demonstrate their learning of the topics covered by the lecture;
- helping students to see the purpose of learning and become competent in particular aspects of the material covered;
- allowing students to see that some parts of the subject content are expected to be hard, but that it will be worthwhile for students to spend some energy on these parts.

Lectures and learning by doing

I have already suggested that simply writing down what is heard or seen during a lecture is not a particularly useful kind of 'doing'. However, there are many other activities, which can be used even with hundreds of students sitting tightly in rows, which all connect to 'learning by doing'. Here are some possibilities:

- students making decisions – for example, picking the best option from several alternatives shown on the screen or in their handouts, and working out why other options are less good or even incorrect;
- students solving problems – using information given to them on the screen or board, or in their handouts;
- students working out what the important issues or questions are, using information given by the lecturer, or from their own experience;
- students engaging in mini-brainstorms for a few minutes with their immediate neighbours, for example, working out what they think may be the main issues which need to be addressed in a scenario or case-study;
- students placing given factors in order of importance, prior to a class discussion which shows them whether their prioritizing was effective.

Lectures and learning through feedback

The old-fashioned sort of lecture where students were seen and not heard offered little opportunity for learning through feedback. However, the potential which can be derived from feedback in modern large-group learning environments is high, by facilitating student actions including:

- students comparing notes with each other regarding decisions they made individually when given options to choose;
- students working together in small clusters of two or three, to make decisions, or solve problems, or prioritize the importance of issues, or formulate questions, and so on;

- students finding out where they stand, for example in 'show of hands' episodes where the positions or views of all the members of even the largest group can be surveyed in seconds;
- students explaining things to each other, or arguing with each other;
- students receiving feedback from the lecturer, on decisions they have reached or options they have selected;
- students doing self-assessment exercises built into interactive handout materials (at their own pace and in their own way), then turning to the back of their handouts to find feedback responses designed to let them see how well they had tackled the questions.

Lectures and digesting: making sense of what is being learnt

Sadly, many students are only too willing to connect lectures to *indigestion* – especially 12.00–13.00 pm lectures – when they are hungry not for concepts but for food! However, the digesting stage of the learning process can be embraced by lectures, in ways including:

- giving students the chance to explain things to each other: the act of putting an idea into words is often the fastest way to get a real grip on the idea, especially when coupled with feedback;
- helping students to see the big picture, in other words to make sense of what they have already learnt, and to see how it links to the things they will study next;
- helping students to find out how successful their learning has been so far – and where the black spots are;
- giving students tasks where they apply what they have learnt from previous lectures in the series to new data or scenarios;
- helping students to find out where they stand, for example, letting them see how their views and beliefs compare with those of the rest of the group by show-of-hands episodes in a lecture.

Beginnings, middles and endings

It has been said that a good lecture should involve three stages:

1 Tell them what you are going to tell them.
2 Tell them it.
3 Remind them what you have told them.

Linked to the student-centred model of learning we have been looking at, however, it might be wiser to rephrase this along the following lines:

1 Alert students to what they are going to be doing. (Create the want or the perceived need – explain the intended learning outcomes of the session.)
2 Help students get down to learning by doing – practising, experiencing, and learning by trial and error and receiving quick feedback on their learning in progress.
3 Help students to make sense of what they have been doing, and the feedback they have derived (such as by reminding them of the intended learning outcomes that they should now have at least started to achieve).

I have already explored stage 2 of the above processes, but it is perhaps worth saying a little more about beginnings and endings.

Beginnings

Some ways of getting a lecture off to a productive start include:

- Expressing the intended learning outcomes for the lecture, for example using words such as:
  - 'By the end of this lecture you'll be able to do the following four things.'
  - 'In this lecture, we'll explore three ways of analysing social policy.'
  - 'When you've worked through the examples we'll discuss in this lecture, you'll be able to use the Second Law of Thermodynamics to solve problems.'
  - 'After this lecture, you should be able to begin to formulate your own project outline.'
- Giving a checklist of points that will be covered in the lecture.
- Posing a list of questions that the lecture will address.
- Providing the exam question on last year's paper to which the material you are about to cover relates.

In other words, it is productive to use the first two or three minutes of a lecture to set the agenda for that particular lecture – and also to link the agenda to things that have already been covered, and things to come later on.

Human nature being what it is, however, there are good reasons for not just reciting the agenda or intended learning outcomes – it is better if they can be seen in print in a handout, and/or on the screen or board. The reasons for putting the outcomes in print as well as speech include:

- Some students may arrive late, and miss the agenda, or disturb others' reception of the agenda.
- If the outcomes are visible in a handout, they continue to serve as an agenda right through the session, rather than being subsumed or forgotten as time goes on.

■ If questions and issues are planted in students' minds, as the answers and solutions evolve during the session, students are more receptive. It is useful to have students searching (even subconsciously) for the knowledge constituting the answers to questions.

Endings

It is so easy for time to run out, so that we feel our only option is to stop the lecture in mid-flow. Saving the last five or even ten minutes for a deliberate ending phase for a lecture pays dividends. For a start, any observer (or appraiser) will then recognize the signs of a structured approach to using lecture situations. Even when time does run out, it is more important to have a good ending than to get through all of the agenda that has been presented. In other words, cut short some of the middle, and leave room for the ending. This is in fact quite easy to do, when the middle has been centred round student-centred activities that I explored under the 'learning by doing' and 'learning through feedback' headings earlier – simply miss out an activity, or cut one a little.

Some ways of coming to a robust conclusion include:

■ Go back to the agenda of intended learning outcomes, and briefly summarize how each has been addressed (this helps students with the digesting stage of their learning).
■ Pick out any unfinished business from the agenda, to be included in a future lecture, or to be diverted to tutorial sessions for in-depth exploration. (Note that this allows you to turn occasions when time runs out on you into what seems like a deliberate strategy.)
■ Formulate a new agenda for the next lecture, to whet students' appetites for what is to come next, and to give them the opportunity to do some preparation for the next lecture.
■ Set a task for all students to complete before the next lecture, or for them to bring along to forthcoming tutorial sessions.
■ Present in advance the intended learning outcomes for the next lecture, giving students the opportunity to add focus to their preparatory work or reading.

In some ways, regularly ending by giving students something to do is a useful ploy: it helps to reduce the fidgeting that so often occurs when a lecture is obviously about to wind up – closing of books, rustling of papers, shifting of chairs and so on. When students need to listen carefully so that they know exactly what a task is, such fidgeting is almost completely avoided.

Ways of holding students' attention till the very end include:

■ At the end of each lecture, put up an overhead slide with the task briefing for students to note down, for example for their preparation for future tutorials on the topic.

■ Give out slips of paper with printed task briefings already on them. (Students are unlikely to begin slipping out from the lecture if they know an important, further handout – however small – is still to be issued at the end.)

Any of these techniques is better than simply having an 'Any questions?' episode right at the end of a lecture. An open-ended offer to take questions can lead to the majority of students with no particular questions feeling that for them the lecture is over, and the group gradually dissolving into shuffling and movement.

Planning 60 minutes for learning: an example for discussion

Timetables are usually developed around one-hour slots (even though concentration spans are measured in seconds and minutes, rather than hours). Suppose you have a lecture scheduled from 10.00–11.00 am. Students will often have to be in some other lecture or tutorial in the next slot, starting at 11.00 – and many may have already been at something else scheduled from 09.00–10.00. The possibility of giving a 60-minute lecture (or even of *facilitating* a 60-minute learning experience) is remote! If your lecture goes on past 11.00, there may be hundreds of students (and a frustrated colleague) milling around outside the lecture room waiting to get in. Therefore, it is clear that there are advantages in 'reasonable punctuality' – in both starting and finishing. Here are some suggestions. Let me say at once, however, that I am not suggesting an inflexible regime for conducting large-group sessions, merely a frame of reference to apply and customize as the occasion demands.

10.00 (or earlier, if the room is empty) Arrive on the dot if not earlier – punctuality and professionalism are closely connected in many people's minds. Get your handouts ready, and get the overhead containing your agenda (or list of questions to be considered during the lecture, or objectives for the lecture) ready. Check the projector if you are going to use it, clean the board if necessary and so on.

If you are using video or slides, computer-delivered projection (for example PowerPoint) or giving a practical demonstration, it is worth booking the room from **09.00** (or even earlier) if possible, and doing all this without time pressure. If you cannot book the room from 09.00, and have a lot of setting up to do, you can often arrange to do it before 09.00, and arrange with whoever is using the room from 09.00–10.00 that your preparations will be guarded.

10.01 Maybe (if *you* are quite ready to start) chat with some of the students who arrive first. Make them feel good about being punctual. Start circulating handouts.

10.05 If more than half of the class is there, make a definite start. For example, do the 'beginnings' bits. Reveal the agenda of intended learning outcomes relating to the next 40-odd minutes, and discuss it. Remind the class of the important things they should have remembered from last time. Or tell an anecdote or joke. Ignore as best you can stragglers who arrive late. Let the punctual students make latecomers feel resented.

10.10 Enter the 'middle' phase – preferably with a student-centred activity rather than a direct input from you. You can give your input *in response* to the results of the student centred activity soon enough. Continue activities, buzz-group discussions, open discussions, and short inputs from you, with no single thing taking more than 10–15 minutes, until about 10.40.

10.40 Take 'control' again, for example by asking for general questions – or if none are forthcoming, asking questions yourself and putting one or two students 'on the spot' (but not unkindly).

10.45 Do the 'winding up' bits. Go briefly through the intended outcomes again, perhaps this time elaborating on how these are linked to forthcoming assessment criteria; set a task, and so on. Aim to finish at around 10.50.

10.50 Finish! This is best done 'visually', for example by replacing your papers in your case or bag, switching off the projector, cleaning the board and so on. However, there are still five more minutes available, if there are pressing questions from the class, and if you want to deal with them at this stage. However, surprising as it may seem, few students are seriously disappointed when a lecture finishes a few minutes early!

10.55 If you have not managed to do so already, *definitely finish* and **walk out**! Especially with large groups, it can easily take five minutes for one group of students to leave and another to take their places. This may mean choosing phrases on your way such as 'Sorry, but I really must go now'; 'I'll take this up next week'; 'We'll look further into this on Thursday at the tutorials'; 'Anyone who wants some further help on this, please come along to my room this afternoon after four.'

If you still wish to talk to a few students until 11.00, do it *outside* the room, so that the next class can (if punctual) walk straight in before 11.00.

A way of helping students to be punctual in appointments to see you individually is to advertise an 'open hour' when you will be pleased to see them in your room, and to post a 'make your own appointment' sheet (maybe in five-minute intervals) on your door. This gives you the further advantage that you will often be armed with the names of students intending to call to see you – a luxury when dealing with large groups of students where it can otherwise be quite impossible to link names to faces.

Practical pointers on preparing and giving lectures

These tips are designed to optimize the learning potential of lectures, in particular with reference to teaching and learning processes, and to remind you of ways in which large-group sessions can pay real dividends to students. Later sets of tips in this chapter will look more specifically at using visual aids, handout materials, and computer-managed presentation packages.

1 **Make the most of opportunities when you have the whole group together.** There are useful benefits of whole-group shared experiences, especially for setting the scene in a new subject, and talking students through known problem areas. Use these as sessions to develop whole-group cohesion, as well as to give briefings, provide introductions, introduce keynote speakers, and hold practical demonstrations.

2 **Make sure that lectures are not just 'transmit–receive' occasions.** Little is learnt by students just writing down what the lecturer says, or copying down information from screens or boards. There are more efficient ways of providing students with the information they need for their learning, including the use of handout materials, textbooks and other learning resource materials.

3 **Be punctual, even if some of your students are late.** Chat to the nearest students while people are settling in. Ask them, 'How's the course going for you so far?' for example. Ask them, 'What's your favourite topic so far?' or, 'What are the trickiest bits so far?'

4 **When you are ready to start, capture students' attention.** It is often easier to do this by dimming the lights and showing your first overhead, than by trying to quieten down the pre-lecture chatter by talking loudly. Do your best to ignore latecomers. Respect the courtesy of punctuality of those already present, and talk to them.

5 **Make good use of your specific intended learning outcomes for each lecture.** Find out how many students think they can already achieve some of these – and adjust your approach accordingly. Explaining the outcomes at the start of the session, or including

them in handout materials given out to students, can help them to know exactly what they should be getting out of the lecture, serving as an agenda against which they can track their individual progress during the minutes which follow.

6 **Help students to place the lecture in context.** Refer back to previous material (ideally with a short summary of the previous lecture at the beginning) and give them fore-warning of how this will relate to material they will cover later.

7 **Use handout material to spare students from copying down lots of information.** It is better to spend time discussing and elaborating on information that students can already read for themselves.

8 **Face the class when using an overhead projector, or computer-aided presentations on-screen in the lecture room.** Practise in a lecture room using your trans-parencies or slides as an agenda, and talking to each point listed on them. By placing a pen on a transparency you can draw attention to the particular point on which you are elaborating, maintaining vital eye contact with your students.

9 **Work out some questions which the session will address.** Showing these questions as an overhead at the beginning of the session is a way of helping students to see the nature and scope of the specific learning outcomes they should be able to address progressively as the session proceeds.

10 **Give your students some practice at note-making (rather than just note-taking).** Students learn very little from just copying out bits of what they see or hear, and may need quite a lot of help towards summarizing, prioritizing, and making their notes their own individual learning tools.

11 **Get students learning by doing.** Just about all students get bored listening for a full hour, so break the session up with small tasks such as problems for students to work out themselves, applying what you have told them, reading extracts from their handout material, or discussing a question or issue with the students nearest to them. Even in a crowded, tiered lecture theatre, students can be given things to do independently for a few minutes at a time, followed by a suitable debriefing, so that they can compare views and find out whether they were on the right track.

12 **Variety is the spice of lectures.** Make sure that you build into large-group lectures a variety of activities for students, which might include writing, listening, looking, making notes, copying diagrams, under-taking small discussion tasks, asking questions, answering questions, giving feedback to you, solving problems, doing calculations, putting things in order of impor-tance and so on.

13 **Ask the students how you are doing.** From time to time ask, 'How many of you can hear me clearly enough?', 'Am I going too fast?', 'Is this making

sense to you?' Listen to the answers and try to respond accordingly.

14 **Use lectures to start students learning from each other.** Getting students to work in small groups in a lecture environment can allow them to discuss and debate the relative merits of different options in multiple-choice tasks, or put things in order of importance, or brainstorm possible solutions to problems. After they have engaged with each other on such tasks, the lecturer can draw conclusions from some of the groups, and give expert-witness feedback when needed.

15 **Use lectures to help students make sense of things they have already learnt.** It is valuable to make full use of the times when all students are together to give them things to do, to allow them to check out whether they can still do the things they covered in previous sessions.

16 **Use lectures to help shape students' attitudes.** The elements of tone of voice, facial expression, body language and so on can be used by lecturers to bring greater clarity and direction to the attitude-forming shared experiences which help students set their own scene for a topic or theme in a subject.

17 **Genuinely solicit students' questions.** Do not just ask, 'Any questions?' as you are picking up your papers at the end of a class. Treat students' questions with courtesy even if they seem very basic to you. Repeat the question so all students can hear, and then answer in a way that does not make the questioner feel stupid.

18 **Do not waffle when stuck.** Do not try to bluff your way out of it when you do not know the answers to some of the questions students may ask. Tell the questioners that you will find out the answers to their questions before your next lecture with them – they will respect you more for this than for trying to invent an answer.

19 **Use some lecture time to draw feedback from students.** Large group sessions can be used to provide a useful barometer of how their learning is going. Students can be asked to write on slips of paper (or post-its) questions that they would like you to address at a future session.

20 **Use whole-class time to explain carefully the briefings for assessment tasks.** It is essential that all students have a full, shared knowledge of exactly what is expected of them in such tasks, so that no one is disadvantaged by any differentials in their understanding of the performance criteria or assessment schemes associated with the tasks.

21 **Show students how the assessor's mind works.** This can be done by devising class sessions around the analysis of how past examples of students' work were assessed, as well as by going through in detail the way in which assessment criteria were applied to work that the class members themselves have done.

22 **Record yourself on video every now and then.** Review the video to help you see your own strengths and weaknesses, and look for ways to improve your performance. Your keenest critic is likely to be yourself, so do not try to resolve every little habit or mannerism at once; just tackle the ones that you think are most important, little by little. It may also be useful for a group of colleagues together to look at each other's videos, and offer each other constructive comments. This is excellent practice for inspection or other quality assessment procedures.

23 **Use all opportunities to observe other people's lectures.** You can do this not only in your own department, but also at external conferences and seminars. Watching other people helps you to learn both from what others do well, that you might wish to emulate, and from awful sessions where you resolve never to do anything similar in your own classes.

24 **Put energy and effort into making your lectures interesting and stimulating.** A well-paced lecture which has visual impact and in which ideas are clearly communicated can be a motivating shared experience for students. Become comfortable using overhead projectors and audio–visual equipment in imaginative ways.

25 **Watch the body language of your audience.** You will soon learn to recognize the symptoms of 'eyes glazing over' when students are becoming passive recipients rather than active participants. That may signal the time for one of your prepared anecdotes, or better, for a task for students to tackle.

26 **Do not tolerate poor behaviour.** You do not have to put up with students talking, eating or fooling around in your lectures. Ask them firmly but courteously to desist, and as a last resort, ask them to leave. If they do not do so, you should leave yourself for a short period to give them a cooling-down period.

27 **Do not feel you have got to keep going for the full hour.** Sometimes you will have said all you need to say, and still have ten or fifteen minutes in hand. Do not feel you have to waffle on. It may come as a surprise to you, but your students may be quite pleased to finish early occasionally!

28 **Do not feel that you have to get through all your material.** Even very experienced lecturers, when preparing a new lecture, often over-estimate what they can cover in an hour. It is better to cover part of your material well, than to try to rush through all of it. You can adjust future sessions to balance out the content.

29 **Use large-group sessions to identify and answer students' questions.** This can be much more effective, and fairer, than just attempting to answer their questions individually and privately. When one student asks a question in a large-group session,

there are often many other students who only then realize that they too need to hear the answer.

30 **Help the shy or retiring students to have equal opportunity to contribute.** Asking students in large groups to write questions, or ideas, on post-its helps to ensure that the contributions you receive are not just from those students who are not afraid to ask in public. It can be comforting for students to preserve their anonymity in asking questions, as they are often afraid that their questions may be regarded as silly or trivial.

31 **Come to a timely conclusion.** A large-group session must not just fizzle out, but should come to a definite and robust ending. It is also important not to overrun. It is better to come to a good stopping place a few minutes early, than to end up rushing through something important right at the end of the session.

Using the tools of the trade in lecture rooms

Decades ago, the only equipment to be found in most lecture rooms was a lectern, and perhaps a blackboard. Nowadays, some lecture theatres abound with technology. The simplest technologies still include blackboards (or whiteboards), but most lecture theatres are equipped at least with an overhead projector. In this section of the chapter, I present selected tips on using each of a range of technological tools, all with two main aims in mind:

- to help you to keep your cool when using visual aids;
- to help you to design your use of such aids, keeping your students' learning from them in mind.

These tips are dos and don'ts based on views gathered from countless colleagues and students. Some of them are likely to seem too obvious to deserve stating, but I hope that in each of the lists which follows you will find at least some suggestions which will trigger you to experiment with how you use technology in your lectures.

Working with overhead projectors

The overhead projector is one of the most common ways of displaying visual information to students, particularly in large-group situations. Two major advantages of overhead projection are that you can face your audience as you speak, and you do not need to darken the room. The following guidelines (overleaf) may help your students to get the most from your use of the overhead projector:

1 **Know your machine.** Most machines have a focus control, but this is located differently on different types of projector. Most machines also have a red–blue adjustment lever (or fringe control). It is well worth your time to take steps to become familiar with the particular machine you are going to work with. Do not be afraid to move it to get it into good focus, across the whole of the screen area. When you can, adjust the height and positioning of the projector to avoid 'keystoning' (the top of the image being a different width from the bottom).

2 **Ensure that your transparencies will fit any projector.** Many projectors have a plate of approximately A4 size (and can usually be arranged for vertical or lateral display). Some projectors have square screens, wider but less deep vertically than A4 size.

3 **Get the machine position right.** The aim is to ensure that all your students can see the screen without anything obstructing their vision (particularly *you!*). Put on a slide, and sit in various seats in the room (before the students are there) so that you know that the screen is clearly visible, and that the average overhead will be easily seen.

4 **Be ready for problems.** If the bulb should suddenly go, is there a 'switchable' spare? If there is, check in any case that this works. Alternatively, have a spare projector (which you know works) sitting inconspicuously in a corner of the room.

5 **When all else fails…** Have one or two exercises up your sleeve which do not depend at all on the availability of an overhead projector. Plan these so that while your students are engaged on them you give yourself the time to arrange a new projector.

6 **'The medium is the message.'** Good-quality overheads can add credibility to your messages. It is worth using desktop publishing programmes to make your principal overhead transparencies look professional and believable. With inkjet and laser colour printers, it is nowadays relatively easy to produce coloured transparencies with graphics.

7 **Be careful with coloured print or writing.** Some colours, especially red, are harder than you might imagine to see from the back of a large room. Throw away any orange or yellow ones from your set of overhead pens – unless you are using them for colouring in blocks on diagrams or flowcharts, for example.

8 **Do not use typewritten overheads.** To be clearly visible, most fonts need to be at sizes 18, 24 or larger – considerably bigger and bolder than typical typewritten materials. Make sure that each transparency you prepare will be visible from the back of the largest room you are likely to use, even by someone without perfect eyesight.

9 **Keep the number of words down.** A good overhead transparency only needs to contain the main ideas, not the details. You can add the details as you discuss the main points on the

transparencies. Your own 'crib' notes can then be written onto a paper copy of each transparency.

10 **Use landscape rather than portrait orientation.** This helps you to make the best use of the top half of the screen, which is usually more easily visible to most of your audience.

11 **Watch students' eyes.** As soon as you notice students having to move their head positions to see something on one of your transparencies, it is worth trying to move that part up so that they can see it without moving their gaze.

12 **Get your transparencies into the right order before your lecture.** There is nothing worse than watching a lecturer sifting and sorting to try find the right overhead. It is sometimes worth arranging them into two sets: ones you will *definitely* use, and ones you *might* wish to use if time permits, or if anticipated questions arise.

13 **Use the top half of the screen.** By sliding your transparencies up, you can normally make the most important pieces of information appear towards the top of the screen – more easily visible by students at your sessions.

14 **Try not to read out your overheads.** Your students can read much faster than you can speak. People do not like having things read out to them that they can read for themselves.

15 **Give people time to take notes if they wish.** Sometimes, you may have copies of your transparencies in handout materials you issue to students. Otherwise, expect that at least some students will want to jot down the main points they see on the screen, and make sure that they have done this before you move on to another transparency.

16 **Minimize passive transcribing by students.** Copying down words from transparencies is not the most productive of learning activities. Where possible, issue handout materials which already contain the wording from your principal overhead transparencies.

17 **Do not point at the screen itself.** This would mean losing eye contact with your students. Use a pen or pencil to rest on the transparency, indicating the part you are talking about.

18 **Be prepared to add things to your transparencies during discussions.** This ability to edit slides 'live' is an advantage of overhead projectors over computer-based presentation managers, and can help your students to feel that their comments are important and valued. With transparencies produced from ink-jet printers, however, do not write on your original; put a blank sheet of acetate over it.

19 **Do not over-use 'progressive reveal' techniques** (showing transparencies a bit at a time by gradually moving a masking sheet of paper). Some students feel manipulated if they are continually 'controlled' in this way. It can be better to build up a complex overhead using multiple overlays.

20 **Make your own masking sheet.** Tape a pen or short ruler to what will be the top edge, or stick a piece of adhesive putty there. The extra weight will help to ensure that the sheet does not slip off your transparencies prematurely revealing your last line or two (which may be punch lines!).

21 **Remember to switch the projector off.** Most overhead projectors make at least some noise. When you are not actually showing something, it is important that both visually and auditorily you are not distracting your students.

Computer-aided presentations

The package most commonly used for computer-aided presentations in lectures is Microsoft PowerPoint. Most educational institutions run training sessions to help lecturers gain skills in using this sort of medium, but there is no substitute for simply getting on with your experimenting, and learning by trial and error. However, this can be helped by thinking about a range of dos and don'ts to help you not make all the mistakes which other people have already made. The suggestions that follow relate to the PowerPoint program, but apply to most other presentation management software too.

First of all, however, have you thought through your *reasons* for using computer-aided slides in your lectures? Here are some reasons people give. You can decide which are closest to your own:

- **Because you want to make a good impression on your audience.** Some people may think if you are just using old-fashioned ways of giving presentations in your teaching that your message itself may be outdated. However, the quality of your use of the medium is actually more important than simply choosing an up-to-date medium.

- **Because you want to be able to edit your presentation easily and frequently.** Computer-generated presentations are very easy (and very inexpensive) to edit, even to restructure completely. It is much easier to adjust a computer-delivered presentation after every experience of giving it, than it would be to prepare a new set of overhead transparencies each time.

- **Because you want your handout material to relate directly to your presentation.** In PowerPoint presentations, for example, you can print off handout pages containing multiple slides. You can also annotate individual slides to make handouts with additional notes and background information. The strongest advantage of printing out your slides as handout materials is that your students then do not need to do menial tasks such as simply copying your slides into their own notes, but can do more active things such as writing their own notes onto their print-outs of your slides.

■ **Because you want to show things that cannot be shown using traditional methods.** For example, if you want to show your students pictures, moving images or graphics which would be difficult or impossible to do using overhead transparencies, you can be fairly sure that you are justified in making your presentations computer-aided.

■ **Because you want to be able to have *all* of your teaching presentations available.** A single floppy disk can carry hundreds of slides of presentation material. If your teaching repertoire is wide and varied, it might be impossible to carry it all around with you on overheads or handouts. Carrying a few disks is much more feasible, and you can customize a new presentation from your repertoire quite easily once you have had some practice at editing, and print off those handouts you need locally.

■ **Because you want your students to be able to have another look at your presentation later.** You can give students your computer-managed presentation on disk, to work through at a machine in the resources centre, or at home. You can e-mail the presentation to students at a distance, or place it in a virtual library or conference area on your computer network.

Some *don'ts* for presentation managers

Any presentation medium can be used well or badly. The following suggestions should help you to avoid some of the most common pitfalls:

1 **Don't just use computer-aided presentations because everyone else seems to be using them.** This may be a reason for making at least some of your presentation computer-aided, but it is worth thinking hard about whether computers provide the best medium for the exact purposes of each element of your presentations. It is better to mix and match, rather than to switch blindly to a different way of supporting your presentations.

2 **Don't just use computer-aided presentations because the equipment happens to be there.** Some institutions lay on computer-delivered presentation systems as a matter of routine. It is still possible to use overhead projectors, marker boards and flipcharts too! Sometimes, these may be pushed out of sight to make room for the computer and projector, but they are usually not far away.

3 **Don't cause 'death by bullet point'.** Even though computer-aided presentation packages can introduce bullet points to slides in a variety of ways (fly from left, dissolve, and so on), bullet points can quickly become tiresome to an audience. It is worth having a good reason for building any slide step by step.

4 **Don't underestimate the problems that can arise.** You may not be able

to get the room dark enough for students to see your presentation properly. There may be compatibility problems between the software version you have used to create your presentation, and the version on the computer through which you wish to show it. The image size on your laptop may not be compatible with that required by the data projector. The resolution of the projection equipment may not be sufficient to show fine details of images that you carefully placed into your presentation.

5 **Don't overdo the special effects.** Doing the whole presentation in a single format becomes boring for your audience, but programming a random sequence of slide builds tends to be irritating for you as presenter, as you do not know what build sequence will be produced when you move to your next slide. Similarly, don't go overboard on the snazzy changes from one slide to the next.

6 **Don't use it just like an overhead projector substitute.** Simply transferring the contents of your overhead transparencies into a computer-delivered presentation does not make full use of the medium. Try to do *other* things with computer-aided presentations, for example making good use of the possibilities of moving images, graphics and so on.

7 **Don't forget that it is not that bright.** Most computer-aided presentation packages rely on projection equipment that is not nearly as bright as a good overhead projector. This means that you may need to take particular care with room lighting, daylight from windows, and (worst of all) direct sunlight. If you use a liquid crystal display tablet, it is not a good idea to place it on top of an ordinary overhead projector; you need a high powered one (1,000 W or more) for reasonable visibility.

8 **Don't forget to check the focus before you start.** Some projection systems are fine for video projection, but turn out to be too fuzzy for computer-managed presentation projection. Modern systems have easy ways of adjusting the focus, but older systems may need to be set up in considerable detail before an acceptable image quality is produced, or may just not be capable of producing clear still images. Looking for any length of time at fuzzy images can give some members of your audience headaches, as their eyes try in vain to compensate for the fuzziness.

9 **Don't forget the conditions appropriate for human sleep.** Turning down the lights, sitting comfortably in the same place for more than a few minutes, and listening to the sound of your voice may be just the right conditions for your audience to drop off, particularly if the images are unclear.

10 **Don't forget that sunlight moves.** If you are setting up a teaching room first thing in the morning, you may need to plan ahead for where any sunlight may be later in the day.

11 **Don't put too much on any slide.** There still seem to be few computer-aided presentations where *all* of the slides are perfectly readable from the back of the room. It is better to have twice as many slides, rather than to cram lots of information onto each slide. It usually takes two or more slides to project the same amount of information as would have fitted onto one overhead transparency.

12 **Don't put important text in the lower half of slides.** Unless all members of your audience have an uninterrupted view of the screen, people sitting at the back may have to peer around their nearer neighbours to read any text at the bottom of the screen. Unlike overhead projection, you cannot simply move a transparency up the platen to make the final points visible to people at the back.

13 **Don't use portrait layout.** You will usually have the choice between landscape and portrait, so use land-scape to make the most of the top part of the screen. You may already have found that the same applies to overhead transparencies.

14 **Don't import tables or text files.** The fact that you *can* import such files into a computer managed pres-entation package leads many into temptation. These are very often the slides which cannot be read from the back (or even from the front). It is normally better to give students such information as handouts, rather than to try to show them it on screen.

15 **Don't use the wrong colours.** Colours that look good on a computer screen do not always show up so well when they are projected. If most of your presentations will be in rooms with natural daylight, it is usually best to stick to dark colours for text, and light (or even white) back-grounds. If you know you are going to be working in a lecture theatre where you have full control of the lighting, you can then be more adven-turous, and use light lettering against dark backgrounds (not forgetting that you may be lulling your audience to sleep when you turn down the lights).

16 **Don't use the same slide format for all of your slides.** Computer-managed presentation packages may allow you to switch your whole pres-entation into different pre-prepared styles, but the result can be that your slides all look too similar to have an optimum learning payoff for your viewers. Vary the layout, colours and backgrounds, so that each new slide makes its own impact.

17 **Don't leave a slide on when you have moved on to talk about some-thing else.** It is better to switch the projection off, rather than to leave up information that people have already thought about. If you are within reach of the computer keyboard, pressing 'B' on some systems causes the display to go black, and pressing 'B' again brings the display back. This is far simpler and safer than switching the projector to standby, and risking having to wait for it to warm up again when you want to

project your next slide. An alternative is to insert a 'black' slide, where you wish to stop your audience from looking at the screen. Don't, however, forget where you've placed these, and panic about where your display has gone!

18 **Don't talk to the screen.** With overhead projectors, it is easy to develop good habits, including looking at the transparency rather than at the screen, and avoiding turning your back on your audience. With projected images, you may have no alternative but to watch the screen, but you need to make sure that you talk to your audience. If you can arrange things so that you can look at a computer screen rather than the projection screen, the problem can be partly solved.

19 **Don't go backwards for too long.** If you need to return to a slide you showed much earlier, it is better to switch the display off, and find the slide you want without your audience seeing every step. The same applies to returning to your original place in your presentation.

20 **Don't forget to rehearse your presentation.** With overhead transparencies you always know what is coming next; with presentation managers it is all too possible to forget. If *you* look surprised when your next slide appears, it does not do much for your credibility with your audience.

21 **Don't underestimate the potential of remote controls surprising you.** Many systems allow you to change slides with a remote control connected to your computer, or to the projection equipment. Pressing the wrong button on this can switch the system to something quite different (for example video input), and can mean that you can find yourself unable to get back to your presentation without losing your cool. It is best to find out in advance which buttons *not* to press, and possibly to place some adhesive tape over them to reduce the possibility of pressing them.

22 **Don't forget to check your spelling.** PowerPoint, for example, can do this for you, but you have to instruct the software appropriately. Be careful not to let the software replace words automatically, or you will get some strange slides if you are using unfamiliar words.

23 **Don't fail to get feedback on your presentation before you run it.** It is really useful to get someone else to watch your slides, and to ask about anything that is not clear, or point out anything that could irritate an audience. It is also useful to check your timing, and the overall length of your presentation in practice.

24 **Don't miss out on seeing your presentation on paper.** Consider printing out your slides, for example six per page. This helps you to get an overview of your presentation, and can sometimes alert you to where to insert an additional slide or two. It is also useful to have such pages in front of you as you present, so that

you can easily remind yourself of what's on the next slide.

25 **Don't neglect to adjust and improve your slides.** It is so easy to alter a set of slides that there is no real excuse for not editing your presentation frequently so that it is always finely tuned to the particular audience and context. The most beneficial additions are often new slides inserted to address frequently-asked questions in advance.

26 **Don't stop watching other people's technique.** This is one of the fastest ways of improving your own presentations. Look for things that work well for other people, and find out how the effects were achieved, then emulate them. More importantly, look for things that do not work, and make sure that you avoid them.

27 **Don't forget your overheads.** It is still useful to have at least some of your computer slides on traditional acetate. Computers can go down. More likely, you can still press the wrong button on a remote control, and switch your projector onto video or off altogether. At such times, it can seem life-saving to be able to go to overhead projector, at least temporarily.

Using video recordings in your large-group teaching

Video recordings play valuable roles in helping to show students things that they would not be in a position to explore on their own. You may already use video extracts in your teaching. Well-equipped lecture theatres usually include the means to project video sequences onto the main screen, whether from videotape or DVD (digital video disk), or indeed from within computer-based presentation managers.

Most people who have incorporated video sequences into their large-group lectures can tell horror stories of how the technology let them down, or how they lost their place on the videotape, and so on. However, the main danger is linked to the fact that the act of watching material on a lecture-theatre screen (or even a television screen) is *not* one of the most powerful ways through which students actually learn, unless the video extracts are carefully planned into their learning programme. The following suggestions may help you to help your students to make the most of any video extracts you weave into your large-group teaching sessions:

1 **Decide what the intended learning outcomes directly associated with the video extracts will be.** It is important that any video extracts are not just seen as an optional extra by your students. The best way to prevent this from happening is to tell students exactly what they are intended to gain from each extract of video material.

2 **Decide why video is the best medium for your purposes.** Ask yourself, 'What is this video extract doing that could not be done just in print, or on slides?' Video extracts can be invaluable for showing all

sorts of things that students could not experience directly, as well as for conveying the subtleties that go with body language, facial expression, tone of voice, and interpersonal interactions, skills and techniques.

3 **Decide *how* the video material is planned to help your students to learn**. Is it primarily intended to whet their appetites and stimulate their motivation? Is it designed to help them to make sense of some important ideas or concepts which are hard to learn without seeing things? Is it designed to give them useful briefings about things they themselves are intended to do after watching the material?

4 **Consider whether your students will need further access to the video.** If they are intended to watch the video sequence a number of times, you may be able to arrange that the materials can be viewed on demand in a resources centre. If so, make sure that there are mechanisms enabling students to book a time-slot when they can see the video material.

5 **Decide what your students will take away after watching the video.** One of the dangers with video extracts is the 'now you see it, then it's gone' situation. If the video is serving important purposes for your students, they will need to have something more permanent to remind them of what they learnt from it.

6 **Work out what (if anything) will be assessed.** If the video is just 'icing on the cake' and there is nothing arising from the video material that will

directly be involved in any form of assessment, tell your students that this is the case. When things they derive from using the video elements *are* involved in their assessment, explain this to them, to help them give the video materials appropriate attention.

7 **Use short extracts one at a time.** People are conditioned to watch quite long episodes of television, but to do so in a relatively passive way. Make sure that your students approach video extracts in a different way than that which they normally use for watching television. It is better to split up a 30-minute video into half a dozen or so separate episodes if there are several different things you wish your students to get out of the material.

8 **Set the agenda for your students before each episode of video.** Ensure that your students are set up with questions in their minds, to which the video extracts will provide answers.

9 **Consider giving your students things to do while they view the video extracts.** You could brief them to note down particular observations, or to make particular decisions, or to extract and record specific facts or figures as they watch the video extracts.

10 **Consider asking your students to do things after they have watched each extract.** This can help them to consolidate what they have gained from watching the extracts. It can also prompt them to have a further look at any extract where they may

have slipped into passive viewing mode and missed important points.

11 **Do not underestimate the importance of printed support materials.** To make the most of video elements, students need something in another medium to remind them about what they should be getting out of the video, and where it fits into the overall picture of their learning. Video recordings often work best when supported by a printed workbook, into which students write their observations and their interpretations of what they see. Their learning from such workbooks can be reviewed by looking again at them, even without looking again at the recording.

Peer observation of lecturing

The final part of this chapter is about making the most of what you can learn about lecturing by being observed by colleagues, and (even more sometimes) by observing them at work. Many institutions build teaching observation into quality assurance procedures as a matter of routine. In some, however, a stranger in the classroom or lecture theatre is less common.

It is useful to couple peer observation of your lectures with self-evaluation of the same lectures. The real benefits come when you combine both for a particular lecture. Afterwards both you and your observer write down your observations and reflections, then sit down together to compare notes, and discuss some of the finer details which may have applied to the particular lecture.

The suggestions which follow are intended to help you to see the benefits of taking part in a peer-observation system. In particular, they aim to help you to get the most out of seeing others teach, and getting feedback from colleagues on your own teaching. Since the most significant arena of observation is likely to be in the context of one or other variety of inspection (such as subject review visits in universities in the UK), many of the suggestions below relate to using teaching observation as preparation for such events.

1 **Value feedback from your colleagues.** It is useful to get used to taking critical feedback from someone you know, as preparation to taking it well from someone you do not know. It is useful to actively encourage staff from other parts of the institution, who already have some experience regarding quality visits, to make this experience available to you.

2 **Do not allow practising to go wrong.** Sometimes it is harder to take critical feedback from someone you know than from someone vested with authority from outside. The criticism may be just as valid, however. Make sure that everyone involved in mock visits feels that the visitors are allowed to role-play rather than make enemies.

3 **Accept observation as normal.** This means that when the practice is really needed, prior to a real visit, for example, it is much easier to find the time for it to happen. It also means that many of the potential problems will have already been recognized and dealt with.

4 **Make use of opportunities to be observed, in staff development programmes.** The sooner you become accustomed to the experience of other people watching your teaching performance, the greater becomes your confidence at handling such situations.

5 **Make appropriate use of existing checklists.** Your institution may well have specific checklists relating to key features of lectures or classroom work, on aspects such as 'planning and preparation', 'use of resources', 'involving students', 'responding to individual needs' and so on.

6 **Lead in new colleagues gently.** Avoid the situation of the performances of new staff being observed against a framework of detailed criteria intended for practised and experienced teachers.

7 **Make sure that not too much emphasis is placed on presentation skills.** Include room for the quality of handouts, overheads, media elements, and class exercises to be covered in the observation criteria. This can help spread the load, so that colleagues are not overly anxious about their presentation skills.

8 **Remind yourself that in real teaching you are not being observed every second.** While it is possible that some students will notice slips you may make, you are unlikely to have the undivided attention of the whole class at any such time (or any other time!).

9 **Beware of the possibility of getting into a rut.** When anyone has been teaching a particular topic for a considerable time, it is natural to tend to go on autopilot, and be less aware of what is actually happening during teaching sessions. Teaching observation can act as a powerful aid to refreshing your approach.

10 **Take advantage of team-teaching opportunities.** When you are regularly in the position of observing parts of your colleagues' teaching, and vice versa, a considerable amount of automatic staff development occurs as you learn from each other's triumphs and disasters.

11 **It does not take long.** Suppose an observer gives you (say) three tips at the end of an hour; this can be very good value compared to just reading a book on teaching practices, where you may not happen to read the things you may most need to find out.

12 **Involve students.** Give students practice in giving feedback to visitors, by getting them to give you the same sorts of feedback as they may be asked for by visitors. Explain why you welcome their comments, and then tell them what you will intend to do differently as a result of their feedback.

13 **Make case studies out of existing feedback.** Use published feedback to other institutions as a means of developing the skills of interpreting

feedback comments, and role-playing responses to such feedback, and the decision making that would have been appropriate on the basis of such feedback. All this paves the way to being better able to deal with the real feedback your institution will derive from quality visits.

14 **When you have observed someone else teach, always give positive feedback first.** Help to put the colleague you are observing at ease by giving the good news first (and indeed making sure there is always some good news). We are all much more likely to take on board the 'could do betters' if we have received the positive statements first.

15 **Try to give three positives for every one 'could do better'.** Even when there is much to comment adversely on, it is important to give sufficient good news. If people are given too much adverse comment, they may lose track of which are the most important parts of the agenda that they need to address.

16 **When you have been observed, treat it as free consultancy.** 'Isn't it wonderful to have a colleague or friend who finds time to engage in an educational conversation with me?' is a much better approach than 'I haven't time for all this practising, let us just hope it goes all right on the day.'

17 **Take the attitude that all feedback is potentially useful.** Feedback is an important part of everyday learning, and it is constructive to regard quality visits not so much in terms of the verdicts which may be reached, but in terms of the availability of valuable feedback which they may bring.

18 **Be prepared to receive positive feedback.** In many cultures, there is a sense of embarrassment when receiving praise. This leads people to shrug it off, and to fail to really take on board the value of finding out more about what is regarded as successful. It is worth practising *receiving* positive feedback, and verbally acknowledging it, and thanking the people who deliver it.

19 **Get practising for receiving negative feedback.** Regard criticism as useful feedback. Avoid the temptations to become hostile, or to justify your position, or to make excuses for things that were found to be lacking. When critical feedback is felt to have been openly received and taken note of, the people giving such feedback are much more satisfied that their job has been done effectively, than when they are not at all sure that the feedback has been listened to and heeded.

20 **Practise eliciting feedback.** Gain skills in drawing out feedback, and getting the people giving it to clarify it and expand on it when necessary. 'What do you consider the *best* thing about the way we are handling so and so?' and 'What is the first thing about this that you would suggest we try to change?' are the sort of questions that help in this process.

21 **Share feedback on your teaching with your students.** They like to feel involved. Ask them what they think of feedback you have received. Ask them what actions they might suggest that you consider. Explain why you might be doing something different; this could lead to more feedback.

4: Making small-group teaching work

Intended outcomes of this chapter

When you have thought through the suggestions included in this chapter (and tried out the most relevant ones) you should be better able to:

- confront some of the behaviours (student ones and tutor ones) which can reduce the success of small-group work;
- decide the optimum size of student groups for particular collaborative tasks you set;
- choose the best way to establish the group membership for your purposes;
- select from a range of processes such as rounds, buzz-groups, syndicates, snowballing, fishbowls, crossovers, brainstorming and pair-dialogues, to help your students to learn productively and actively in small-group environments.

Why small-group learning is so important

My aim in this chapter is to help colleagues increase the interest and diversity of the processes used in small-group work with students. A common theme running throughout this chapter is the need to help students to participate fully in small-group situations, so that the learning payoff they derive from such occasions is maximized.

Small-group learning may be more important than we think. When most people think about teaching in universities and colleges, the image that frequently comes to mind is of a large lecture theatre full of students listening intently (or not) to a lecturer in full spate of erudition. Actually, a large proportion of the most meaningful learning in higher education happens when students are working in small groups, in seminars, tutorials, practicals and laboratories. Moreover, even more learning can be happening in small-group situations beyond timetabled sessions, where students interact spontaneously with each other, and learn from each other. With increasing pressure on us all to deliver the curriculum in ever more efficient and effective ways, the methods by which we manage small-group teaching, and harness the potential learning payoff, come under close scrutiny. This chapter is intended to help you to explore how we can do this to best effect.

Group learning is about getting people to work well together, in carefully set-up learning environments. The human species has evolved on the basis of group learning. Learning from other people is the most instinctive and natural of all the learning contexts we experience, and starts from birth. Although learning can only be done by the learner, and cannot be done 'to' the learner, the roles of other people in accelerating and modifying that learning are vitally important. Other people can enhance the quality of our learning, and can also damage it. But *which* other people?

We hear much of collaborative learning, as if it is the most natural activity in the world. But it often seems like the least natural, particularly amongst strangers. Sociological research tells us repeatedly that it is human nature *not* to be involved with people we do not know. We might make a mistake, or look stupid, or be attacked. We will, however, get involved with people we do know. We will help them with their problems and even defend them. One key to working and learning with other people is, therefore, the ability to lower barriers and become friends with people who had been strangers, while acknowledging differences and respecting different viewpoints.

Furthermore, much is now said about transferable skills, or key skills, particularly including oral communication skills, problem-solving skills, self-organization skills and reflection. Many of these skills can only be learnt from, and with, other people, and cannot be developed solely by reading and studying what others have written about them. It is now increasingly accepted that the most important outcomes of education and training are about developing people, and not just what people know or understand. Employers and managers plead for employees who are able to work well with others, and organize themselves. Working in small groups can allow students to embrace a range of interactive and collaborative skills which are often hard to develop in individual study situations, and impossible to develop in large-group environments such as lectures. The small-group skills are precisely those required in employment and research, where graduates need to be able to:

- work in teams;
- listen to others' ideas sympathetically and critically;
- think creatively and originally;
- build on others' existing work;
- collaborate on projects;
- manage time and processes effectively;
- see projects through to a conclusion;
- cope with the normal difficulties of interactions between human beings.

The last of these may be the most important of all. Learning in groups allows students to develop cohesion with their peers, when classes are becoming so large as to preclude feelings of whole-group identity, particularly under modular schemes where large cohorts of students come together from disparate directions to study together on a unit.

Group learning has never been as important as it now is. Yet we are still in a world where most teachers, educators and trainers are groomed in instruction rather than facilitation. Despite the increased status of group learning, there is nothing fundamentally new in people learning together.

Some lecturers find working with small groups more anxiety-provoking than lecturing, because of the necessity to work with students as individuals rather than in the anonymity of large groups. Sometimes there are worries about student behaviour, that they might become too challenging, disruptive or unfocused. Otherwise, there are often anxieties about organizational issues, such as how to run a number of parallel seminars, based on a single lecture, with several tutors and research assistants working with different groups. This chapter addresses some of the reasons for persevering nevertheless, and offers some practical suggestions on overcoming a wide range of difficulties.

Deciding on group size

A number of choices exist about the selection of group size and group membership, depending on the context of the group work and the nature of the learning outcomes which are intended to be achieved by students working in groups. If assessed work is to be an outcome of group work, it is worth thinking in advance how appropriate credit for the overall product can best be coupled with credit for individual contributions to the product, particularly where there is the possibility of the contributions being unequal. There are no rights or wrongs to the following suggestions about ways of establishing student groups: basically it is best to make informed decisions (or inspirational leaps) based on the context and the occasion. It is useful to consider group size first.

The choice of group size will often depend on the size of the whole class, as well as on the sizes of, shapes of and facilities available in the rooms in which small-group work is carried out. Sometimes, episodes in small-group format can be conducted even in a large, full lecture theatre, with groups being formed between students sitting close enough to participate together. However, the most important occasions where group size is likely to be crucial involve subdividing the students present at seminars, tutorials and practical classes.

Pairs. In some regards a pair is not really a group. It is usually relatively easy to group students in twos, either by choosing the pairs yourself, random methods or friendship pairs. Advantages include a low probability of passenger behaviour, and the relative ease for a pair to arrange meeting schedules. Pairs are good for small-scale tasks, where both students know each other well. Pairs can also be useful where a stronger student can help a weaker one. Problems can occur when pairs fall out, or either student is absent, or lazy or domineering. It is normally unwise to use the same pairs for long-term tasks, but useful to ring the changes of constitution of pairs over different tasks.

Couples. In any class of students, there are likely to be some established couples. When they work together on collaborative work, the chances are that they will put a lot more into group work than ordinary pairs, not least because they are likely to spend more time and energy on the tasks involved. The risks include the possibility of the couple becoming destabilized, which can make further collaborative work much more difficult for them.

Threes can work well, as communication between three people is still easy and work can often be shared out in manageable ways. Trios represent a very popular group size. The likelihood of passenger behaviours is quite low, and trios will often work well together, sharing out tasks appropriately. It is easier for trios to arrange meetings schedules than for larger groups. The most likely problem is for two of the students to work together better than with the third, who can gradually (or suddenly) become, or feel, marginalized. Threes can be difficult if two gang up on one, and the group is still fairly vulnerable if one member is often absent, or when present, does not take an equal responsibility.

Fours. This is still quite small as a group size. Passenger behaviour is possible, but less likely than in larger groups. When subdividing group tasks, it can be useful to split into pairs for some activities, and single individuals for others. There are three different ways in which a quartet can subdivide into pairs, adding variety to successive task distribution possibilities. Fours can be very effective, and can be a good critical mass for sharing out large projects, with opportunities for both delegation and collaboration. Students with different abilities and qualities can play to their own strengths within a foursome, giving each member a chance to contribute something and feel valued. Fours do have a tendency, however, to split into two pairs, and tensions can arise. With four members (or any other even number) there is no possibility of a 'casting vote' if the group is evenly split between two courses of action.

Fives have many of the advantages of fours, and are a favoured group size for many tasks, not least because of the 'casting vote' opportunity when making decisions. There are sufficient people to provide a range of perspectives, but the group is not of unmanageable proportions. In a group this size, however, a determined slacker may still be able to hide, unless suitable precautions are taken. The possibility of passenger behaviour begins to increase significantly, and it becomes more important for the group to have a leader for each stage of its work. However, because of the odd number, there is usually the possibility of a casting vote when making decisions, rather than the group being equally divided over a choice of action. There are many ways that a group of five can subdivide into twos and threes, allowing variety in the division of tasks among its members.

Sixes. The possibility of passenger behaviour is yet more significant, and group leadership is more necessary. The group can, however, subdivide into threes or twos, in many different ways. It is now much more difficult to ensure equivalence of tasks for group members.

Seven to ten or so. Such numbers are still workable as groups, but the larger the number, the greater the possibility of idlers loafing and shy violets being over-shadowed by the more vociferous and pushy members of the group. It can be argued that groups of this size are only really viable if a really substantial task is to be undertaken and if considerable support and advice is given on project and team management. Such groups can still be useful for discussion and debate, before splitting into smaller groups for action. Passengers may be able to avoid making real contributions to the work of the group, and can find themselves outcasts because of this. When it is necessary to set up working groups which are larger than six, the role of the leader needs to change considerably. A skilled facilitator is needed to get a large group collaborating well. It can be advanta-geous for the facilitator to become somewhat neutral, and to concentrate on achieving consensus and agreement rather than attempting to set the direction of the group.

Ways of forming groups

Strict rules on how to form groups cannot be provided, as such decisions depend so strongly on context and purpose. The following discussion points out some of the advantages and disadvantages of different ways of constituting student-group membership. There are many different ways in which you can create groups of students from a larger class. All have their own advantages and disadvantages, and it is probably best to use a mixture of methods so that students experience a healthy level of variety of group composition, and maximize the benefits of learning from and with each other.

Groups with some historical or social basis

Friendship groups. If you let students select themselves into their own groups, often strategic high-flyers will quickly locate each other, then the middle-ability ones will realize what is happening and form groups among themselves, then the last ones left will tend to be the less able, and they will clump together through lack of any alternative. Allowing students to arrange themselves into groups has the advantage that most groups feel a sense of ownership regarding their composition. However, there are often some students 'left over' in the process, and they can feel alienated through not having been chosen by their peers. Friendship groups may also differ quite widely in ability level, as high-fliers select to work with like-minded students. This method is effective if you want to be sure that marks will be distributed, but is not such a useful method of group selection if you want peers to support each other.

Geographical groups. Simply putting students into groups according to clusters as they are already sitting (or standing) in the larger group is one of the easiest and quickest ways of dividing a class into groups. This is likely to include some friendship groups in any case, but minimizes the embarrassment of some students who might not have been selected in a friendship group. The ability distribution may, however, be skewed, as it is not unusual for the students nearest the tutor to be rather higher in motivation than those in the most remote corner of the room!

Alphabetical (family name) groups. This is one of several random ways of allocating group membership. It is easy to achieve if you already have an alphabetical class list. However, it can happen that students often find themselves in the same group, if several tutors use the same process of group selection. Also, when working with multicultural large classes, several students from the same culture may have the same family name, and some groups may end up dominated by one culture, which may not be what you intend to occur.

Other alphabetical groups. For example, you can form groups on the basis of the last letter of students' first names. This is likely to make a refreshing change from family-name alphabetical arrangements. Students also get off to a good start in seeing each others' first names at the outset.

Random groups

Many tutors find this to be the easiest and fairest way of selecting groups of students to work together. Using lottery systems or random-number generators, students are allocated to the groups in which they are to work. Problems can arise using this method from difficulties with group dynamics, particularly if the students have been given no preparation on how to be a good team member. However, in industrial and commercial contexts, graduates are often required to work in allocated teams, so this may be regarded as good preparation for real life.

The following ways of randomizing group composition can add variety to student group work.

Number groups. When students are given a number (for example, on a class list), you can easily arrange for different combinations of groups for successive tasks, by selecting a variety of number permutations (including using a random-number generator if you have one on your computer). Groups of four could be 1–4, 5–8 and so on for task 1, then 1, 3, 5, 7; 2, 4, 6, 8 and so on for the next task, then 1, 5, 9, 13 and so on.

Class-list rotating syndicates. Where a succession of small-group tasks is to be used, say with group size being four, it can be worth making a printed list (or overhead transparency) of the whole class, and starting off by forming groups by writing AAAA, BBBB, CCCC, DDDD etc down the list. Next time round, write ABCD, ABCD, ABCD and so on, so that everyone is in an entirely new group. Such rotation can minimize the problems that can be caused by the occasional difficult or uncooperative student, whose influence is then spread around, rather than lumbering the same group each time. It is worth, however, avoiding the grouping being too much influenced by any alphabetical factors; all too often students find themselves in alphabetically-determined situations, and it is useful to break free of this unwitting constraint in deciding group membership.

Astrological groups. When selecting group membership from a large class, it makes a change to organize the selection on the basis of calendar month of birthdate. Similarly, 'star signs' could be used – but not all students know when (for example) Gemini starts and finishes in the year. This method often leads to groups of somewhat different sizes, however, and you may have to engineer some transfers if equal group size is needed. Participants from some religions may also find the method bizarre or inappropriate.

Crossovers. When you wish systematically to share the thinking of one group with another, you can ask one person from each group to move to another group. For example, you can ask the person with the earliest birthday in the year to move to the next group clockwise round the room, carrying forward the product or notes from the previous group and introducing the thinking behind that to the next group. The next exchange could be the person with the latest birthday, and so on. When doing this, you need to make sure that not too many students end up stuck in the same physical position for too long.

Coded name labels. Give out self-adhesive labels for students to write their names, but with a series of codes already on the labels. A three-digit code of a Greek letter, normal letter, and a number can lead to the possibility of all students finding themselves in three completely different groups for successive tasks. Six of each letters and numbers allows an overall group of 36 students to split into different sixes three times, for example, with each student working cumulatively with 15 other students.

Further ways of forming groups

Performance-related groups. Sometimes you may wish to set out to balance the ability range in each group, for example by including one high-flier and one low-flier in each group. The groups could then be constituted on the basis of the last marked assignment or test. Alternatively, it can be worth occasionally setting a task where all high-fliers and all low-fliers are put into the same group, with most of the groups randomly middle-fliers, but this (though appreciated by the high-fliers) can be divisive to overall morale.

Skills-based groups. For some group tasks (especially fairly extended ones), it can be worthwhile to try to arrange that each group has at least one member with identified skills and competencies (for example, doing a Web search, using a word-processing package, leading a presentation). A short questionnaire can be issued to the whole class, asking students to self-rate themselves on a series of skills, and groups can be constituted on the basis of these.

Hybrid groups. This is a compromise solution. You may sometimes wish to organize learners by ability or in learning teams, and may at the same time wish to help them avoid feeling that they are isolated from everyone they already know. You can permit students to select one other person they would like to work with, and then juggle pairs to ensure some balance of ability. This can work really well, but can be fraught with difficulty, for example, when pair choice is not coincident! It can also make for difficulties if you try to pair up two self-selecting high-flyers with two of the less able students: resentment and conflict can ensue. In order to avoid this problem, you can sometimes pair middle-ability pairs, which make up the bulk, with more able and less able pairs, using your best judgement on factors such as friendship and cooperative ability. You need to recognize, however, that when group work is assessed, the likely mark achieved by each group can be affected by your choices and may not be seen as fair, even though it works well in adding value to most students' learning experience.

Learning teams. If your aim is to build upon students' prior experience and ability, it is possible to select group members with specific criteria in mind. You might suggest that groups form themselves (or are formed by the tutor) into teams which include, for example, one with proven competence in numeracy, one with excellent communication skills, an IT specialist, someone fluent in a language other than English, someone with experience in the world of work and so on. This provides the opportunity for team members to take account of each other's divergent abilities and to value them. There may be problems with task allocation, however. Do you allocate the task of doing the drawings to the former draughtsperson or to the group member who is inexperienced in this kind of work? Do you give the IT tasks to the technophile or the technophobe? The team's marks will be better if the former choice is made, but there may be more learning gain if the novice undertakes the task with guidance from the specialist. Will the team work to its strengths, and achieve the intended outcomes well, or should it be encouraged to work to its weaknesses and maximize the learning payoff resulting from the tasks? If group work is assessed, it is no surprise that teams will do the former. Forming learning teams also relies on the students and tutors having a good knowledge of prior abilities and competence, and may take some considerable organization.

Small-group process techniques

The most significant single enemy of small-group work with students is their non-participation. There is a wide range of small-group processes from which we can select a variety of ways to help students to learn actively. A balanced programme of different kinds of activities can then be devised which will promote learning to the satisfaction not only of external quality assessors but also of the students themselves, who are likely to benefit from being stretched. Effective small-group techniques help students derive increased learning payoff from the time students spend working together, by:

- enhancing their motivation to learn, by raising interest levels, and helping them see the relevance of the topics they are working with;
- giving them learning-by-doing opportunities, and allowing them to practise relevant activities, and to learn by trial and error in a safe and supportive environment;
- allowing students to gain a considerable amount of feedback from each other, and from the facilitator of the small-group session;
- helping students make sense of things that they are learning together, particularly by explaining things to each other, and making decisions together.

This chapter continues with some suggestions regarding how you may use each of eight different ways of helping students to be participative in group situations. Some lend themselves to large-group situations, and can be ways of helping interactive learning to occur in packed lecture theatres as well as in smaller-group settings.

---

1   Rounds

Where groups are not too large, say around 20 or fewer, go around everyone in the group and ask them to respond (for example) to a given sentence-starter, or to give a sentence or two about what they want to find out about the topic to be explored. People often use rounds as icebreakers or equally as part of the winding-up of a session, when it can be productive to ask students for (for example) 'one thing you learnt, one thing you liked, and one thing you did not like'.

Try not to make the round too daunting for students. It helps to provide some guidance on what is expected of them (for example, 'I want everyone to give their name and then identify one aspect of the course programme they know nothing about but are looking forward to learning about', or 'Let's go round and find out which single aspect of today's session has been most useful for each person'). In big rounds, students can be quite nervous, so make it clear that it is acceptable to say 'pass', and if people at the beginning have made the point the student had planned to make, that concurrence with ideas expressed already is sufficient. Alternatively, ask everyone to write down the point they intend to give, for example on a post-it, and as the round continues stick all the post-its on a chart or wall, so that they are all seen to be equally important. Those students who are reticent orally are often less nervous when they have already jotted down the point they wish to contribute.

A drawback with rounds is that it can be boring if the group is large, and the answers are repetitive. Contributions late in the round tend not to be valued as they add nothing new, and the contributors can feel their ideas are rejected.

2   Buzz groups

Give pairs, threes, fours or larger subdivisions of the whole class, small timed tasks which involve them talking to each other, creating a hubbub of noise as they work. Their outcomes can then be shared with the whole group through feedback, on a flipchart sheet poster, on an overhead projector transparency or otherwise as appropriate. This technique can also work well in large-group lecture situations, though it is not usually appropriate to do more than collect the feedback from selected groups on such occasions, otherwise reporting-back becomes too tedious, repetitive and time consuming. The noise level in a large lecture theatre full of students 'buzzing' can be quite alarming for lecturers used only to the sound of one or two voices at a time, but when it is remembered that a lot of learning by explaining and learning through feedback is occurring in such a noisy room, the use of the time spent is certain to be accompanied by significant learning payoff.

Buzz groups often work best when they are buzzing about several different things at once. For example, in a large-group lecture, provide several buzz-group tasks, and get different groups of students addressing selected tasks. Report-back from buzz groups is then not tedious or repetitive, and the interest level of the large group can be maintained.

3   Syndicates

This is a term often used to describe activities undertaken by groups of students working to a brief, usually issued by the tutor, but under their own direction. Syndicate activities can take place within the room where a larger group is working, or student groups can be briefed to go off and undertake a task on their own. For example, students in syndicates can be asked to undertake literature searches, debate an issue, explore a piece of text, prepare an argument, design an artefact, prioritize a list of options, prepare an action plan, or many other tasks. To achieve productively, they will need an explicit brief, appropriate resources and a clear description of the intended outcomes.

Specialist accommodation is not always necessary; syndicates can work in groups spread out in a large room or, where facilities permit, go away and use social areas of the campus or designated areas of the learning resource centre. On crowded campuses, however, do not just assume that students will be able to find somewhere suitable to work. If the task is substantial, the tutor may wish to move from group to group, or may be available on a 'help desk' at a central location, or available by e-mail online at specified times.

It is important to have clear (sometimes quite rigid) deadlines for syndicate report-back, as it can be very tedious when punctual syndicates have to await tardier colleagues before a plenary sharing session can begin. Outcomes from syndicate work may be delivered in the form of assessed work from the group, or produced at a plenary meeting of the whole class as report-backs, poster displays, and so on.

4   Snowballing

This is also known as pyramiding. Start by giving students an individual task of a fairly simple nature such as listing features, noting questions or identifying problems. Then ask them to work in pairs on a slightly more complex task, such as prioritizing issues or suggesting strategies. Thirdly, ask them to come together in larger groups, fours or sixes for example, and undertake a task involving perhaps synthesis, assimilation or evaluation. Ask them, for example, to draw up guidelines, or to produce an action plan, or to assess the impact of a particular course of action. They can then feed back to the whole group if required.

It can be useful to issue sheets of overhead transparency, and brief the groups to report back using these to present summaries of their outcomes. If several groups are involved in feedback on the same final task, it can become somewhat repetitive, and it is often useful to give separate contributory elements of the overall task to different groups, so that interest levels are maintained during the final report-back stage.

5   Fishbowls

Fishbowling ad hoc: ask for a small group of up to half a dozen or so volunteers to sit in the middle of a larger circle comprising the rest of the group. Give the inner circle a task to undertake that involves discussion, problem solving or decision making, with the group around the outside acting as observers. Usually it is worth having an agreed substitution process, to allow someone from the outer circle to take the place of someone in the inner group, but only when both agree on the exchange. Make the task you give the inner circle sufficiently simple in the first instance to give them the confidence to get started. The levels of the tasks can be enhanced once students have had practice and become more confident.

Fishbowling post hoc: where several groups have undertaken a task (or some complementary tasks) in parallel, form the inner circle using one member from each group (a volunteer or a conscript) and start the inner circle processing the findings of the groups. Arrange that substitution can occur when necessary or when useful, for example to allow another group member from the outer circle to come in when the representative already in the inner circle is stuck. This method can be a useful method for managing students who are over-dominating a group, because it gives them permission to be the centre of attention for a period of time. After a suitable interval, you can ask others from the outer circle to replace them, thus giving the less vocal ones an opportunity for undisturbed air time. Fishbowls can also be useful ways of getting representatives from buzz groups to feed back to the whole group. Some students will find it difficult to be the focus of all eyes and ears, so it is as well not to coerce anyone to take centre stage (although gentle prompting can be valuable). A 'tag wrestling' version can be used, with those in the outer circle who want to join in gently tapping the shoulders of people in the middle whom they want to replace, and taking over their chairs and opportunities of talking. Fishbowls can work well with quite large groups too.

6   Complete changeover groups

Often we want to mix students up in a systematic way so they work in small groups of different compositions, and give and receive feedback from many more people than are involved in the group size they are working in at any given time. One way of predetermining a wide variation in group membership is to use sticky labels or post-its (or just small pieces of paper) to make a name-badge for each student which also bears a unique code as follows.

Imagine that you have, for example, 25 students, and that the table below is your sheet of sticky labels, and that you write on them codes of one Greek letter, one normal letter, and one number, as in Figure 4.1.

αA1	βA2	γA3	δA4	εA5
αB2	βB3	γB4	δB5	εB1
αC3	βC4	γC5	δC1	εC2
αD4	βD5	γD1	δD2	εD3
αE5	βE1	γE2	δE3	εE4

Figure 4.1   Codes for 25 students

Give these labels out randomly (and ask students to write their names on them, especially when it will be useful for them to become more familiar with each other's names). Then you can use three entirely different group configurations, each with five groups of five, as follows:

- grouping by Greek letters;
- grouping by normal letters;
- grouping by numbers.

So in this example, by the third group each student would have worked with 12 different students from the whole group of 25, and would have encountered entirely different students in each successive group.

Where the group tasks are successive stages of a larger whole, there is no need for whole-group feedback on the first two tasks, because each individual can act as rapporteur on the outcomes of their previous task in the last configuration. This means that everyone is a rapporteur, and each group can benefit from everything which happened in all the groups without the repetition of plenary report-back. As with snowballing or pyramids, you can make the task at each stage slightly more difficult, and ask for a product from the final configuration if desired.

Crossovers are useful in making sure everyone in the group is active, and also help to mix students up outside their normal friendship, ethnic or gender groups. It takes a little forethought to get the numbers and letters right for the cohort you are working with. It can be useful to have some templates of the different number–letter combinations, so that you can cut up a sheet of paper or card and give students their individual numbers. (This helps avoid the possibility of duplicating numbers when writing them out by hand in the actual session.) You can, however, do crossovers on the spur of the moment using post-its and quick calculations.

7 Brainstorming

This can be a valuable way of stimulating creative free thinking, and is particularly useful when looking for a solution to a problem or in generating diverse ideas. Start with a question like 'How can we... ?' or 'What do we know about... ?' and encourage the group to call out ideas as fast as you can write them up. (Perhaps use two scribes on separate boards if the brainstorm flows well.) Make it clear that this is supposed to be an exploratory process, so set ground rules along the following lines:

- A large quantity of ideas is desirable, so everyone should be encouraged to input at whatever level they feel comfortable.
- Quick snappy responses are more valuable at this stage than long, complex, drawn-out sentences.
- Ideas should be noted without comment, either positive or negative; no one should say, 'That wouldn't work because...' or, 'That's the best idea we've heard yet' while the brainstorm is in progress, as this might make people feel foolish about their contributions or unduly narrow the focus of further contributions.
- Participants should 'piggy-back' on each other's ideas if they set off a train of thought.
- 'Logic circuits' should be disengaged, allowing for a freewheeling approach.

It can be useful to generate these rules with the group at the start of the brainstorm, and write them up on a flipchart or overhead transparency so that everyone remains aware of them.

Alternatives to these ground rules include gathering contributions from everyone in turn, and allowing people to say 'pass' if they have nothing to add at the time. This helps to prevent the products of the brainstorm being unduly influenced by those members of the group who are most vocal or who have most ideas, though it can be argued that this is not brainstorming in the truest sense. The mass of ideas thus generated can then be used as a basis for selection of an action plan, a programme of development, or a further problem-solving task.

One of the most effective ways of following up a brainstorm is to get everyone involved in some sort of prioritization of the products. For example, everyone can be invited to vote for their own top three of the things written up on the flipcharts, maybe giving three points to what they consider to be the most important point, two for the next most important point and so on. The numbers can then be added up, and a global view of the prioritization can be seen. It can be useful to get students to vote privately first, so that voting does not become influenced by the initial trends that may be seen as votes begin to point towards favourite items.

Brainstorming is often the basis of a technique for gathering feedback, known as 'nominal group technique', where groups of participants generate then prioritize ideas before reporting them back.

---

8   Pair dialogues: 'Five (or three) minutes each way'

This can be a useful way of getting students to make sense of their own thinking on a topic or an issue, by explaining and articulating their views uninterrupted for a few minutes. Ask students in pairs to take it in turn alternately to speak and to listen, talking without being interrupted for a few minutes on a given topic. They might find this quite difficult at first, but it is an excellent way of getting students to articulate their ideas, and also means that the quieter students are given opportunities to speak and be heard in a non-threatening situation.

The art of listening without interrupting (other than with brief prompts to get the speaker back on target if he or she wanders off the topic) is a useful one which many students will need to foster too. The products of such pair work can then feed into other activities.

Leading and following

Student group work, particularly when there is not the presence of a tutor, can depend a great deal on the skills which the group leader brings to bear on the group. However, no amount of leadership can work on its own, without a substantial investment in 'followership' by those who do not happen to be leading at the time. The following discussion highlights some of the important attributes needed to make the most of both leadership and followership.

Leadership

Much has been written about the qualities and attributes associated with effective leadership. It all, however, boils down to what leaders actually *do*. The following list of 'good leader behaviours' (not presented in any significant order here) can be used as a starting point for groups working out who will lead and how.

A good leader:

- does not confuse leadership with control, and invites participation from all group members;
- earns the respect of other group members;
- notices when someone feels an outsider, and tactfully draws them in;
- shows no favouritism to individual group members, and treats them as having equal potential;
- gets to know the strengths and weaknesses of group members, and apportions workload accordingly;
- keeps an eye on group dynamics, and defuses conflict before it gets out of hand;
- is always there, particularly at the start of group meetings;
- knows when to keep quiet, and let others take the initiative;
- makes space for lateral thinking, and off-the-wall ideas which may seem weird at first, but may enrich later thinking.
- allows group members to have ownership of their own best ideas;
- has the tact to guide choices without leaving those whose ideas were rejected feeling let down;
- finds something of value to commend even in the least able group member, and is unstinting in praise for those who contribute a great deal;
- is sensitive to issues of gender, race and age, and makes sure that no-one feels disadvantaged or excluded because of such factors;
- does not leap automatically to what seems the most obvious solution, but allows diverse views to be expressed and considered;
- has an active brief to ensure equivalence of contribution for group members, to that everyone feels they are being treated fairly;
- undertakes effective project planning, with built-in milestones and check points, to ensure that the group's task is achieved;
- keeps referring back to the task brief, to ensure that work is productive and on target;
- set SMART goals for the group, which are specific, measurable, achievable, realistic and time-specific;
- has an ever watchful eye for the evidence that will show the group will have achieved its intended objectives;
- manages group resources (including any project budget) carefully to ensure that targets are achieved;

- has contingency plans for when things go wrong;
- admits to mistakes, and shares responsibility when these cause the group's work to go off target;
- does not automatically blame others when things go wrong (unless it is genuinely caused by the destructive or lazy behaviour of others);
- knows how to delegate effectively, without making group members feel that they have been dumped on;
- puts as much energy into making sure that group process works, as in contributing towards generating the ultimate product;
- knows when to seek outside help, and when the group can continue autonomously;
- is methodical about ensuring that good records are kept of group meetings and delegated activities;
- ensures at the end of each group session that other participants are clear about when and where the next session will take place;
- clarifies for the group members exactly what each individual is expected to do prior to the next meeting;
- makes sure that when the group process ends there is a sense of closure, with a final 'washing-up' meeting and, if appropriate, some kind of celebration.

Followership

There will always need to be more followers than leaders. We all know the problems that occur when too many people try to lead a group. The suggestions below may help you to ensure that your leaders have skilled followers. They may also help to optimize the learning that can be achieved through well thought-out following:

1 **Brief groups about the importance of followership.** It can be important to legitimize followership as a vital factor to underpin the success of group work.

2 **Explain that followership should not be regarded as weakness.** When leadership is rotating between group members, they should regard their work when *not* leading as every bit as important as when they are directing the actions of the group.

3 **Accept that followership requires well-developed skills and attributes.** For example, patience may be needed. When it takes a little time for the purpose or wisdom of a leadership decision to become apparent, it is sometimes harder to wait for this to happen than to jump in and try to steer the group, or argue with the decision.

4 **More followers than leaders are needed.** It is virtually impossible to

have a successful group where all members are adopting leading stances at the same time. Though the credit for successful group work is often attributed to the leader, it is often the followers who actually own the success. It is more than good sense to acknowledge this right from the start of any group-work situation.

5 **Followership is a valuable, transferable key skill.** In all walks of life, people need to be followers at least for some of the time. It can be useful to employ group-work situations to help people develop skills which will make them good followers in other contexts of their lives and careers.

6 **Good followership is not the same as being 'easily led'.** Being 'easily led' usually is taken to imply that people are led into doing things against their better judgement. Good followership is closer to being easily led when the direction of the task in hand coincides quite closely to individuals' own judgement.

7 **Followership should not be blind obedience.** Encourage group members to think about how they are following, why they are following, for how long they are going to be content with following, and what they are learning through following.

8 **Suggest that group members experiment with a 'followership log'.** This could be private notes to themselves of their experiences of being led, but it is more important to make notes on their feelings as followers than to write down criticisms of the actions of the leaders. Whether the logs are treated as private or shared notes can be decided later by everyone involved in a group.

9 **Legitimize followership notes as authentic evidence of the operation of a group.** Such notes can tell their own stories regarding the relative contributions of members of the group, the group processes that worked well and those which worked badly. When it is known that followership records will count towards the evidence of achievement of a group, leadership itself is often done more sensitively and effectively.

10 **Followership is vital training for leadership.** People who have been active, reflective followers can bring their experience of followership to bear on their future leadership activities. Having consciously reflected on the experience of following informs leadership approaches, and makes their own leadership easier for others to follow.

11 **Good followership is partly about refraining from nit-picking.** When people have too strong a desire to promote their individuality, it often manifests itself in the form of expending energy in trying to achieve unimportant minor adjustments to the main processes going on in group work. Good followership involves adopting restraint about minor quibbles, and saving interventions for those occasions where it is important not to follow without question.

Things that can go wrong in small groups

Small-group teaching can provide excellent opportunities for participants to get to know each other, come to grips with their subject and learn actively, yet small-group-format classes are often seen by students as of questionable value compared to lectures and one-to-one sessions. Talking to students, they often express confusion about the tasks involved and uncertainty about their role, as well as lack of confidence about participating. They criticize tutors for inconsistency of approach and treatment, for disorganization and lack of structure and for hogging the sessions with their own views and opinions.

When things go wrong, sometimes it is the fault of the group members themselves. Sometimes the blame can be directed at the facilitator. In this section, I look in turn at some of the most common 'damaging behaviours', and offer for each a few suggestions which can alleviate the problems which can result from them.

Group member behaviours which damage group work

The following section looks at a range of learner behaviours which can damage or even destroy group work. These are based on the experience of many facilitators. For each of these behaviours, some tactics are offered below as to how facilitators can reduce the effects on group work.

Group members being late

Sometimes lateness is unavoidable, but even then it is seen as time-wasting for the group members who have managed to be punctual. Here are some approaches from which facilitators can select, to reduce the problem:

- **Lead the group towards including an appropriate ground rule on punctuality.** If the group members feel a sense of ownership of such a ground rule, they are more likely to honour it.
- **Point out that punctuality is related to courtesy.** Remind group members that when one of them is late, it is an act of discourtesy to all the other people who have been kept waiting, including the group facilitator if present.
- **Lead by example – do not be late yourself!** If the facilitator is late, it is not surprising that group members can fall into bad habits. Your own actions are seen as a reflection of how you value group learning.
- **Make the beginning of group sessions well worth being there for.** If group members realize that they are Wlikely to miss something quite important in the early minutes of a group session, they are likely to try harder to be punctual.

- **Give out something useful at the start of the session.** For example, issue a handout setting the scene for the session, or return marked assignments straightaway as the session starts.
- **Avoid queuing.** If the place where a group meeting is due to be held is frequently still occupied at the starting time for the group session, it can be worth rescheduling the group for five or ten minutes later, so that a prompt, punctual start can be made then, without those who arrive early having to hang around.

Group members not turning up at all

This is one of the most common complaints made by facilitators. Learner non-attendance can have a serious effect on group work, and a variety of approaches (and incentives) can be used to address the problem, including those listed below:

- **Ensure that it really is worth turning up.** If group members are not getting a lot out of group sessions, they naturally value them less, and this can lead to them being lower priority than they could have been.
- **Keep records of attendance.** Simply making notes of who is there and who is not gives the message that you are really expecting learners to turn up and join in. If keeping records is not enough, see below.
- **Assess attendance.** For example, state that 10 per cent of the coursework element of a programme of study will be based solely on attendance. This is one way of making quite dramatic improvements in attendance at small-group sessions. However, the downside of this way of inducing learners to attend is that some group members may be there in body but not in spirit, and can undermine the success of the group work.
- **Issue something during each session.** Learners do not like to miss handouts, task briefings or the return of assessed work. It is important to make missed paperwork available to learners who could not have avoided missing a session, but do not be too ready to do so for those who have no real reason for absence.
- **Cover some syllabus elements only in small-group sessions.** When learners know that these elements will be assessed alongside those covered in lectures and so on, their willingness to attend the small-group sessions increases.
- **Do not cancel small-group sessions.** Learners are quick to pick up the message that something that has been cancelled could not have been too important in the first place. This attitude then spreads to other people's small-group sessions.

Group members not preparing

Group members can get far more out of small-group sessions if they have done at least some preparation for them. However, many teachers and facilitators complain that learners still arrive without having thought in advance about what the session will be covering. It is difficult to cause *every* group member to come prepared, and over-zealous attempts to do this are likely to cause unprepared learners to decide not to come at all. The following suggestions may help you to strike a workable balance between getting well-prepared learners, and frightening them off:

- **Help learners to structure their preparation.** For example, issuing an interactive handout for them to complete and bring to the forthcoming session is better than just asking them to 'Read Chapter 3 of Smith and Jones'. You could ask them to 'Research your own answers to the following seven questions using Chapter 3' instead, and leave spaces beneath each question for them to make notes as they read.
- **Do not fail to build on their preparations.** If group members go to the trouble of preparing for a session, and then nothing is done with the work they have done, they are discouraged from preparing for the next session.
- **Try starting each session with a quick quiz.** Ask everyone one or two short, specific questions, and perhaps ask respondents themselves to nominate the recipient of your next question. This is a way of building on the preparation work that learners have done, and making sure that everyone is included, rather than just those who are most forthcoming when you ask questions.
- **Consider asking students to hand in their preparations sometimes.** This does not necessarily mean that you have to assess them, but you could sift through them while group members are busy with an activity, to gather a quick impression of who is taking preparation seriously. The fact that you do this occasionally will lead to learners to not wish to be found lacking should it happen again, and lead to better levels of preparation.
- **Get students to peer assess their preparations sometimes.** This has the advantage that they can find out how their own learning is going, compared to other learners. It also helps them learn from feedback from each other, and the act of giving a fellow learner feedback is just as useful as receiving feedback.

Group members not doing their jobs

A lot of time can be wasted when group members go off on tangents to their intended tasks, or procrastinate about starting the next stage of their work. Work-avoidance is human nature at least for some of the time for some people. The following approaches may help you to keep your group members on task:

- **Have clear task briefings in the first place.** It is usually better to have these in print, and for every learner to have a copy. Oral briefings are quickly forgotten, and are much more likely to lead to deviation from the intended tasks.
- **Make the first part of a group task relatively short and straightforward.** This can cause a group to gain momentum more quickly, and can help to ensure that later, more complex tasks are started without undue procrastination.

■ **Specify the learning outcomes clearly.** When learners know what they should be getting out of a particular activity, their engagement is enhanced.
■ **Set structured tasks, with staged deadlines.** Most effort is expended as the deadline approaches, especially if learners will be *seen* to have slipped if their task is not completed by a deadline. Act as timekeeper if you are facilitating group work: gentle reminders such as 'Six minutes to go, please' can cause a lot of work to be done.

Group members being disruptive

Group work is often damaged by one or more participants whose behaviour slows down or diverts the work of others. Disruption is more of a problem in small-group contexts than in formal lectures, for example, as it takes less courage to be disruptive in informal settings. Sometimes there is no easy solution for disruptive behaviour, but the following suggestions may help you to solve some such occurrences:

■ **Check that it really is disruption.** If you are a passing spectator to different groups, you may happen to arrive at one particular group just at the moment when one of its members is expressing a strong feeling, or arguing a point relatively forcefully. This may be fine with the other members of the group, and it gives the wrong message if the facilitator assumes the worst.
■ **Find out why a person is being disruptive.** Sometimes there are identifiable reasons for such behaviour, for example when a group as a whole has become dysfunctional, or when the task briefing is being interpreted in different ways by group members.
■ **Watch for the same group member being disruptive repeatedly.** It is then usually worth talking to the person concerned, to find out why this may be happening. If this does not improve the situation, it may be necessary to reconstitute the membership of groups for successive tasks, so that the disruptive element is fairly distributed across a wider range of learners, rather than a particular group becoming disadvantaged by recurring disruption.

A group member dominating

Such members can be among the most serious enemies of effective group learning. They need to be handled with considerable sensitivity, as their 'taking over' the work of a group may be well-intentioned:

■ **Get the group to reflect on how it is functioning.** For example, once in a while, give them a relatively small task to do as a group, even an exercise which is primarily for light relief. Then when they have completed it, ask them to *think* through their answers to questions such as the following:
    – How well do you think you did that as a group?

- Did someone take the lead, and if so, how did this come about?
- Who said most?
- Whose ideas are most strongly present in the solution to the task?
- Did you always agree with the ideas being adopted by the group?
- Was there anything you *thought* but did not actually say?

This can cause the group to reflect on any elements of domination which may have occurred, and can reduce the tendency for domination in future group activities.

- **Lead a discussion on the benefits and drawbacks of assertiveness.** Then ask group members to put into practice what they have learnt about assertiveness. This can lead to learners watching out for each other's assertive behaviours, and reduce the chance of a particular group member dominating for too long.
- **Confront the dominator privately.** For example, have a quiet word in a break, or before the next group session. Explain that while you are pleased that the dominant group member has a lot to contribute, you would like other learners to have more opportunity to think for themselves.
- **Intervene in the work of the group.** Sometimes it is helpful to argue politely with a person who seems to be dominating, to alert other group members to the fact that they could be being led off-target by this person. Be careful, however, not to put down the dominator too much. There is little worse for group dynamics than a sullen ex-dominator.

Group facilitator behaviours which can damage group work

There are many ways in which group learning facilitators can damage group work. Sometimes facilitators know about the things they do which undermine the success of group work, but more often they simply are not aware that things could be improved. When facilitators know they have a bad habit, it would be tempting to simply advise 'Stop doing it', but often this could lead to the reply, 'Yes, but how?' The following list of facilitator faults is rather longer than the learners' damaging behaviours already discussed, but it can be argued that facilitators are able to address their own short-comings even more directly than they can help learners to address theirs. As before, each situation is annotated with some suggested tactics for eliminating or reducing the various kinds of damage which can occur.

Facilitator ignoring non-participants

It is tempting to ignore non-participants, hoping either that they will find their own way towards active participation, or that other group members will coax them out of inactivity. Alternatively, facilitators sometimes take the understandable view that 'If they do not join in, they will not get as much out of the group work, and that's really up to them to decide.' However, there are indeed some straightforward steps from which facilitators may select, to make positive interventions to address the problem of non-participation as and when they see it:

- **Remind the whole group of the benefits of equal participation.** This is less embarrassing to the non-participants themselves, and can be sufficient to spur them into a greater degree of involvement.
- **Clarify the group-learning briefing.** Place greater emphasis on the processes to be engaged in by the group, and less on the product that the group as a whole is to deliver.
- **Consider making the assessment of contribution to the work of the group more explicit.** When non-participants know that participation counts, they are more likely to join in.
- **Confront a non-participant directly.** This is best done tactfully, of course. The simple fact that it was noticed that participation was not adequate is often enough to ensure that the situation does not arise again.
- **Try to find out if there is a good reason for non-participation.** There often is. Sometimes, for example, a non-participant may find it difficult to work with one or more particular people in a group situation, because of pre-existing disagreements between them. It may then be necessary to consider reconstituting the groups, or see whether a little 'group therapy' will sort out the problem.
- **Explore whether non-participation could be a cry for help.** The act of *not* joining in to the work of a group can be a manifestation of something that is going badly for non-participants, possibly in an entirely different area of their learning or their lives in general.
- **Check, with care, whether the problem is with the work rather than the group.** Non-participation can sometimes arise because of the nature of the task, rather than being anything to do with the composition or behaviour of the group. For example, if the group-learning task involves something to do with researching the consumption of alcoholic beverages, it is not impossible that someone whose religion forbids alcohol should resort to non-participation.
- **Check whether non-participation could be a reaction against the facilitator.** If someone does not like the way in which *you* are organizing some group learning, their reaction could be not to join in.

Facilitator allowing domineers

Domination has already been discussed under the bad habits that group members can engage in, and several tactics have already been suggested there. However, if you *allow* domination, it can be seen as your fault too. The following tactics may include remedies for situations where you notice group learning being undermined by domineers:

- **Have a quiet word with the domineer.** This is often enough to solve the problem. Having been seen to be too domineering is usually enough to make a domineer stop and think.
- **Get the whole group to do a process review.** For example, give them a relatively straightforward collaborative task to do, then ask them all to review who contributed most, why this happened, whether this was fair, and whether this is what they want to happen with the next (more important) group-learning task.
- **Watch out for why people dominate.** Sometimes, it is because they are more confident, and it is important not to damage this confidence. It can be better to acknowledge group members' confidence and experience, and gently suggest to them that they need to help others to develop the same, by being able to participate fully in the actions of the group.

Facilitator not having prepared adequately

We have already explored some of the tactics that can be used to solve the problem of lack of preparation by group members. This time, the issue is lack of preparation by the facilitator. The short answer is, of course, 'prepare'. However, the results of this preparation need to be visible to group members. The following approaches can help to ensure that group members can see that you are taking group work as seriously as you want them to do:

- **Make it obvious that you have prepared specially for the group session.** There are many ways of allowing your preparations to be visible, including:
  - coming armed with a handout relating to the particular occasion, rather than just any old handout;
  - having researched something that has just happened, ready to present to the group as material for them to work on;
  - arriving punctually or early, to avoid the impression you were delayed by getting your own act together ready for the session;
  - making sure that you have indeed done anything you promised to do at the last meeting of the group.
- **Keep records of group sessions, and have them with you.** You would not arrive to give a lecture or presentation without having your notes and resources with you, and doing the same for group sessions gives the message that you take such sessions just as seriously as larger-scale parts of your work.

Facilitator being too didactic or controlling

This is one of the most significant of the facilitator behaviours which can damage group learning, and experienced facilitators can be the most vulnerable. The quality of group learning is greatly enhanced when learners themselves have considerable control of the pace and direction of their own learning. The following suggestions (overleaf) may alert you to any danger you could be in:

- **Do not try to hurry group learning too much.** It is particularly tempting, when *you* know very well how to get the group to where it needs to be, to intervene and point out all the short-cuts, tips and wrinkles. It is much better, however, for group learners to find their own way to their goals, even when it takes somewhat longer to get there.

- **Hide your knowledge and wisdom sometimes.** In other words, allow group members to discover things for themselves, so that they have a strong sense of ownership of the result of their actions. As mentioned previously, this may be slower, but leads to better learning. Do not, however, make it show that you are withholding help or advice. When you feel that you may be giving this impression, it is worth declaring your rationale, and explaining that it will be much better for your group learners to think it out for themselves before you bring your own experience to their aid.

- **Allow group members to learn from mistakes.** Tempting as it is to try to stop learners from going along every blind alley, the learning payoff from some blind alleys can be high. Help them *back* from the brick wall at the end of the blind alley, rather than trying to stop them finding out for themselves that there is a brick wall there.

- **Plan processes rather than outcomes.** It is well worth spending time organizing the *ways* in which group learners can work towards their goals, rather than mapping out in too much detail the things they are likely to experience on the way. The achievement of the group-learning outcomes will be much more enduring when the group has ownership of the learning journey towards them.

- **Ask your learners.** Many of the things that can go wrong in teaching or training could have been avoided if feedback had been sought on the way. The best way of getting feedback is to ask for it, not to wait for it. To get feedback on important things (such as whether or not you are being too didactic or controlling) there is no faster way than asking for exactly that.

- **Learn from selected colleagues.** Feedback from other group-learning facilitators is always useful. However, it is worth going out of your way to seek feedback from colleagues who have a particular gift for making group learning productive, and being duly selective in the tactics you add to your own collection.

Facilitator showing lack of cultural sensitivity

This is a serious group-damaging behaviour. In fact, lack of cultural sensitivity can be more dangerous in small-group situations than in large-group ones. It is also one of the hardest areas to find out about. Few people are brave enough to challenge a group learning facilitator with this crime! It is useful for even the most skilled group-learning facilitators to undertake a regular self-audit on this issue. The following tactics can help:

- **Read about it.** There is no shortage of published material on equal opportunities, cultural issues and so on. Sometimes when reading this literature, one can be surprised by the thought, 'But sometimes I do this too'.
- **Watch other group learning facilitators, with this agenda in mind.** See what they do to avoid the pitfalls, and also notice when they fall into them. Work out alternative approaches which could have circumvented such problems.
- **Do not make assumptions.** It is particularly dangerous to bring to your role of learning facilitator any preconceptions about the different members of your groups, such as those based on gender, age, ethnic group, perceived social status and any other area where assumptions may be unwise and unfounded. Treating people with equal respect is an important part of acknowledging and responding to individual difference.
- **Talk to group members individually.** When you are working with a mixed group, for example, it is in your informal, individual conversations with members of the group that you are most likely to be alerted to anything which could be offending individuals' cultural or personal perspectives.
- **Ask directly sometimes.** It is important to pick your times wisely, and to select people who you believe will be willing to be frank with you if necessary. Rather than asking *too* directly (for example, 'What do I do which could be culturally insensitive?'), it can be useful to lead in more gently: for example, 'What sorts of learning experiences do you find can be damaged by people who are not sensitive enough culturally?', 'How does this happen usually?' and so on.

Facilitator favouring clones

This happens more often than most people imagine. It is noticed straight away by everyone *else* in the group. It can go entirely unnoticed by the perpetrator. It is, of course, perfectly human to have warmer or more empathetic feelings and attitudes towards someone who is more like oneself than other people, or who shares significant attitudes, values and even looks. In particular, teachers of any sort can be flattered and encouraged when they recognize a 'disciple' among a group of people. If you think you could be in danger of indulging in this particular behaviour, think about which of the following approaches may be most helpful to you:

- **Go clone detecting.** From time to time, think around the types of people who make up learning groups you work with, and test out whether any of them are more like you are (and particularly more like you *were*) than the others. Then watch out for any signs that you could be treating them differently (even if only slightly).
- **Do not over-compensate.** It is just as dangerous to be too hard on clones as to favour them. The person concerned may have no idea at all why you are being harder on him or her than on other people. The people you might (consciously or subconsciously) regard as clones may have no inkling that they are in this

special position. Subconsciously, you could be putting them under the same sort of pressures as you put yourself under long ago, and exacting of them the standards you applied to yourself.

Facilitator talking too much

This is one of the most common of all group-learning-facilitator bad habits. However, it is just about the easiest to do something about. The following suggestions should contain all you need to rectify this problem, if you own it:

- **Remind yourself that most learning happens by doing, rather than listening.** Concentrate on what your group learners themselves do during group sessions, rather than on what you do.
- **Do not allow yourself to be tempted into filling every silence.** In any group process, short episodes of silence are necessary components, space for thinking. When *you* happen to be expert enough to step in with your thoughts, before other people have had time to put theirs together, it is all too easy to be the one to break the silence. What seems to you like a long silence seems much shorter to people who are busily thinking. Let them think, then help them to put their thoughts into words. When they have ownership of putting together ideas and concepts, their learning is much deeper and more enduring.
- **Only say *some* of the things you think.** Being the expert in the group (you probably are!), you are likely to know more than anyone else about the topic being addressed. You do not have to reveal all of your knowledge, just some of it. Do not fall into the trap of feeling you have to defend your expertise, or that you need to justify your position.
- **Do not let *them* let *you* talk too much.** It is easier for group members to sit and listen to you than to get on with their own thinking. Sometimes they can encourage you to fill all of the time, and opt for an easy life.
- **Present some of your thoughts (particularly longer ones) in print.** Use handouts to input information to the group, but not at the expense of getting group members to think for themselves. You can convey far more information in five minutes through a handout than you could in five minutes' worth of talking. People can read much faster than you can speak, and in any case, they can read a handout again and again. They cannot replay you speaking (unless they are recording it – and even then, would they *really* replay it all again?).

Facilitator not providing clear objectives

In education and training it is increasingly accepted that objectives, or intended learning outcomes, have a vital part to play in ensuring that learning takes place successfully. This is no less true of small-group work than of lectures. Moreover, the *absence* of clear objectives for group work is only too readily taken by learners as a signal that the group work cannot really be an important part of their overall learning. The following suggestions may help you to put objectives or statements of intended learning outcomes to good use in facilitating group learning:

- **Work out exactly what you intend each group-learning session to achieve.** It is best to express this in terms of what you intend learners themselves to gain from the session. Make sure that the learning outcomes are expressed in language that learners themselves can readily understand, so that they see very clearly what they are intended to achieve.
- **Publish the learning outcomes or objectives in advance.** This allows learners to see where any particular group session fits in to the overall picture of their learning. It also helps them to see that their group learning counts towards their assessment in due course.
- **Maintain some flexibility.** For example, it is useful to have some further objectives for any group session, designed to cover matters arising from previous sessions, or to address learners' questions and needs as identified on an ongoing basis through a programme of study. These additional objectives can be added to the original intentions for the session, and re-prioritized at the start of the session if necessary.
- **Do not just write the objectives or outcomes – use them.** State them (or display them on a slide, or issue them on a handout) at the start of each and every group session, even if it is continuing to address a list of intended outcomes which were discussed at previous sessions.
- **Assist learners in creating their own objectives.** From time to time, ask them, 'What do *you* need to gain from the coming group session?', for example, giving them each a post-it on which to jot down their replies. Then stick the post-its on a chart (or wall, or door, or marker board), and ask the group to shuffle them into an order of priority, or to group them into overlapping clusters.

A closer look at tutorials

In this chapter so far, we have looked in general terms at the processes of students working together. In the next section, let us think of the most common small-group scenario: that of the academic tutorial, where a tutor is present alongside a small number of students. How many students make a tutorial? It used to be the case in many universities that a tutorial was either a one-to-one encounter between a student and a tutor, or a tutor working with a group of no more than four or five students. With present-day class sizes, elements that appear on the timetable as 'tutorials' can in some disciplines and in some universities involve significantly larger numbers of students than five.

The purpose of an academic *tutorial*

Everyone who is involved in tutorial work with students agrees that there is no clear dividing line between academic and personal tutorials. Academic tutorials are subject-related, while personal tutorials are normally thought of in terms of development of the 'whole student', but either kind of tutorial is likely to spill over into the other domain. In this chapter, I would like to flag this overlap now at the outset, but then focus on aspects of academic tutorials and other kinds of small-group teaching–learning situations, recognizing that quite a lot of the discussion can be translated to personal tutorials too.

There is no agreed definition of a tutorial, and this is probably wise, as tutorials should fulfil any one or more different roles. These may include:

- to provide students with opportunities to learn by doing, practising applying things that have been covered in lectures, handouts, and learning packages;
- to address students' motivation, helping to increase their confidence in their abilities to handle the curriculum successfully;
- to provide students with feedback, from each other as well as from the tutor, helping them to find out more about how their learning is progressing;
- to give teaching staff opportunities to find out what problems students may be encountering with the subjects they are learning;
- to help students digest or make sense of the concepts they are learning;
- to allow students to ask questions which they may not be able to ask in large-group sessions.

However, the above description does not amount to a definition of a tutorial, but only serves as a description of some of the processes likely to be involved in the sort of tutorials that help students to get to grips with the curriculum.

The purpose of a personal *tutorial*

These are usually regarded as one-to-one encounters between a student and a tutor, where the purpose is not to extend or deepen the academic understanding of the subjects being studied, but to support the student's learning in a much broader sense. The tutor may be one of the lecturers involved in the student's course, or may be a teaching assistant or research assistant with some tutorial duties. Students are often assigned a 'personal tutor' for the duration of a year of their course, or for their entire time at university. These tutors are normally expected to exercise a counselling or advising role when necessary, on the wide agenda of anything that may be causing concern to their respective students. However, the success of personal tutorial support is at best patchy. Some tutors take it very seriously, and put themselves out to get to know their students well, and to remain well briefed on the progress of each student. For many students, however, their personal tutor is just a name.

A result of this situation is that for most students, the majority of personal tutoring happens in the context of the contact they have with academic staff in those teaching–learning situations where the staff–student ratio is low enough for advice and counselling to be available, and that often means in what are intended to be academic tutorials.

What students can do before *academic tutorials*

It is often argued by teaching staff that a problem with tutorials is that students just do not do the preparatory work they were intended to undertake before attending tutorials. However well briefed students are, it seems inevitable that some will turn up without having done any such work, and others will decide to miss the tutorials altogether, feeling guilty that they have not put in sufficient time or energy into preparing for them.

These are some ways of maximizing the probability that students will engage with preparatory work:

- **Give work briefings in print rather than orally.** This increases the chance that students not present at the briefing will get copies of it.
- **Issue tutorial briefings on sheets of a particular colour rather than just on white paper.** This helps students not to lose such briefings amongst other papers.
- **Make briefings sheets interactive.** For example, include some structured questions with boxed spaces for students to write their answers or conclusions in. This makes it much easier to spot who has done some preparation and who has not – and students do not like to be *seen* not to have written something into the boxes.
- **Arrange that coursework to be handed in for assessment is gathered in at tutorials.** This can help to ensure that students attend, if only to hand in their work. It also allows tutorials to be used to discuss problems students may have encountered with the coursework, before they have forgotten exactly what the problems were.
- **Include in tutorial time activities such as student self-assessment and peer-assessment,** depending on preparation that students are required to have done before participating.

It can be worth exploring possibilities of students doing collaborative work before tutorials, such as meeting together (without a tutor) to help identify common problems and questions, to establish an agenda for forthcoming tutorials – or better still, perhaps, for forthcoming large-group sessions.

What students can do during academic tutorials

It is probably best to start by looking at things that students *should not* be doing in academic tutorials. These include activities with low learning payoff, including:

- making notes just by copying down things said by the tutor, or things written on the board or screen;
- spending most of the time listening passively, while one or two students dominate the discussion;
- pretending that they understand what is being discussed, rather than admitting to having problems with the material.

There are many varieties of activity with high learning payoff that students can engage in during academic tutorials. These include (but are by no means restricted to):

- solving problems or doing calculations, either individually or collaboratively;
- discussing different perspectives on an issue;
- working out different ways of approaching a problem or case-study situation;
- applying assessment criteria to their own or each other's work;
- marking examples of past students' assignments or exam answers;
- asking the tutor questions, or working out agendas of matters for future tutorial exploration;
- answering questions posed by each other and by the tutor;
- doing exercises helping them to apply, and make sense of, material covered in lectures;
- linking work they have done in practical sessions to underpinning concepts and models;
- making summaries and checklists to help them distinguish the main points of a subject from the background detail.

Practical pointers for making small-group teaching work

Already in this chapter there are many suggestions on recognizing and responding to some of the things that can go wrong with small-group teaching. The suggestions below are selected from *500 Tips on Group Learning* (Phil Race, Kogan Page, 2000).

Getting groups started

Once group work has gathered momentum, it is likely to be successful. The greatest challenge is sometimes to get that momentum going. The first few minutes can be crucial, and you will need all of your facilitation skills to minimize the risk of groups drifting aimlessly in these minutes. Take your pick from the following suggestions about getting group work going right from the start of a task:

1 **Foster ownership of the task.** Wherever possible, try to arrange that the members of the whole group have thought of the issues to be addressed by small-group work. When possible, allow members to choose which group task they wish to engage in. When people have chosen to do a task, they are more likely to attempt it wholeheartedly.

2 **Start with a short group icebreaker.** Before getting groups under way with the main task, it can be useful to give them a short, 'fun' icebreaker so that each group's members get to know each other, relax and become confident to work with each other. See the next section for some ideas about icebreakers.

3 **Keep the beginning of the task short and simple.** To Einstein is attributed 'Everything should be made as simple as possible, but no simpler.' Make sure that the first stage of each group task is something that does not cause argument, and does not take any time to interpret. Once a group is under way, it is possible to make tasks much more challenging.

4 **Do not rely only on oral briefings.** Oral briefings are useful, as they can add the emphasis of tone of voice, facial expression and body language. However, when *only* oral briefings are given for group learning tasks, it is often found that after a few minutes different groups are attempting quite different things.

5 **Use printed briefings.** It is useful to put the overall briefing up on an overhead transparency or Power-Point slide, but if then groups move away into different syndicate rooms, they can lose sight (and mind) of the exact briefing. It is worth having slips of paper containing exactly the same words as in the original briefing, which groups can take away with them.

6 **Visit the groups in turn.** It can make a big difference to progress if you spend a couple of minutes just listening to what is happening in a group, chipping in gently with one or two useful suggestions, then moving on. During such visits, you can also remind groups of the deadline for the next report-back stage.

7 **Clarify the task when asked.** Sometimes, groups will ask you whether you mean one thing or another by the words in the briefing. It is often productive if you are able to reply, 'Either of these would be an interesting way of interpreting the task; you choose which interpretation you would prefer to address.' This legitimizes the group's discovery of ambiguity, and can increase the

efforts they put into working out their chosen interpretation.

8 **Have an early brief report-back from groups on the first stage of their task.** This can help to set expectations that everyone will be required to be ready for later report-back stages at the times scheduled in the task briefing. Any group which finds itself unprepared for the initial report-back is likely to try to make sure that this position does not repeat itself.

9 **Break down extended tasks into manageable elements.** Often, if the whole task is presented to groups as a single briefing, group members will get bogged down by the most difficult part of the overall task. This element might turn out to be much more straightforward if they had already done the earlier parts of the whole task.

10 **Try to control the amount of time that groups spend on successive stages of each task.** It can be useful to introduce a sense of closure of each stage in turn, by getting groups to write down decisions or conclusions before moving on to the next stage in the overall task.

Icebreakers: some ideas

There are countless descriptions of icebreaking activities in books and articles on training; see particularly the books by Jaques and Brandes in 'Further Reading'. An icebreaker is most needed when members of a group do not already know each other, and when the group is going to be together for some hours or days. Most icebreakers have the main purpose of helping individuals get to know each other a little better. Here are some ideas to set you thinking about what the most appropriate icebreakers could be for your own groups. Some icebreakers can be very quick, acting as a curtain raiser for the next activity. Others can be extended into larger-scale activities at the start of a major group project. Do not try to rush these:

1 **Triumphs, traumas and trivia.** Ask everyone to think of one recent triumph in any area of their lives (which they are willing to share), a trauma (problem, disaster and so on), and something trivial – anything that may be interesting or funny. Then ask everyone in turn to share a sentence or so about each. Be aware that this activity often brings out a lot of deep feelings, so keep this for groups whose members need to know each other well, or already do so.

2 **What's on top?** This can be a quick way of finding out where the members of a group are starting from. Ask everyone to prepare a short statement (one sentence) about what is, for them, the most important thing on their mind at the time. This helps people to clear the ground, perhaps if they are (for example) worrying about a sick child or a driving test, and enables them then to park such issues on one side, before getting down to the real tasks to follow.

3 **What's your name?** Ask everyone in turn to say their (preferred) name, why they were called this name, and what they feel about it. This not only helps group members to learn each others' names, but also lets them learn a little about each others' backgrounds, views, and so on. Bear in mind that some people do not actually like their names much, so make aliases acceptable.

4 **Pack your suitcase.** Ask individuals to list ten items that they would metaphorically pack into a suitcase if they were in a disaster scenario. Emphasize that these items would not have to literally fit into a suitcase, and could include pets, but should not include people. Ask them to mill around a large room, finding a couple of others who share at least two items from their list. This enables them to get into groups of three or four, with plenty to talk about, before you get them started on the actual group work.

5 **What I like, and what I hate.** Ask everyone to identify something that they really like, and something they really loathe. Ask them then to introduce themselves to the rest of the group, naming each thing. This helps people to remember each others' names, as well as to break down some of the barriers between them.

6 **What do you really want?** Ask everyone to jot down what they particularly want from the session about to start, and to read it out in turn (or stick post-its on a flipchart, and explain them). This can help group members (and facilitators) to find out where a group is starting from.

7 **What do you already know about the topic?** Ask everyone to jot down, on a post-it, the single most important thing that they already know about the topic that the group is about to explore. Give them a minute or so each to read out their ideas, or make an exhibition of them on a flipchart. This helps to establish ownership of useful ideas within the group, and can help facilitators to avoid telling people things that they already know.

8 **Draw a face.** Ask everyone to draw on a scrap of paper (or a post-it) a cartoon 'face' showing how they feel at the time (or about the topic they are going to explore together). You may be surprised at how many 'smiley faces' and alternatives can be drawn.

9 **Provide a picture, with small cartoon figures undertaking a range of activities.** Then ask people to say which activity feels closest to the way they feel at the moment (for example, digging a hole for themselves, sitting at the top of a tree, on the outside looking in and so on). Use this as a basis for getting to know each other through small-group discussion.

10 **Discover hidden depths.** Ask people in pairs to tell each other 'one thing not many people know about me', that they are prepared to share with the group. Then ask each person to tell the group about their partner's 'hidden secret', such as

ballroom dancing, famous friends, ability to build dry-stone walls or whatever. This is a particularly good exercise when introducing new members to a group who already know each other, or when a new leader joins a well established group.

11 **Make a junk sculpture.** Give groups of four or five people materials such as newspaper, disposable cups, string, sticky tape, plastic straws and so on. Ask them to design and produce either the highest possible tower, a bridge between two chairs that would carry a toy car, or some other form of visible output. Ask them to think, while on task, about the group processes involved (who led, who actually did the work, who had little to contribute, and so on), then ask them to unpack these thoughts and share in plenary their summarized conclusions about the group processes.

12 **Develop verbal skills.** Ask students in pairs to sit back to back. Give one of each pair a simple line drawing comprising squares, triangles, rectangles and circles. Without letting their partner see the original, ask those holding the drawings to describe what is on the page, using verbal instructions only, so that their partners can draw the original on a fresh sheet of paper. After a fixed time, let them compare the originals with the copies, and ask them to discuss what the task showed them about verbal communication. A similar task can also be designed using plastic construction bricks.

13 **Make a tableau.** Ask groups of about seven or eight students to decide on a theme for their tableau (for example, the homecoming, the machine age, playtime) and ask them to compose a tableau using themselves as key elements. Ask each group in turn to present their tableau to other groups, and then to discuss how they went about the task. Polaroid or digital photos of the tableaux can add to the fun, but do not use this activity if you feel that group members are likely to be sensitive about being touched by others.

14 **Organize a treasure hunt.** Give each group a map of the training centre or campus, and a set of tasks to complete across the location. For example, task elements can include collecting information from a display area, checking out a reference item via the Internet, collecting prices for specific items from the catering outlet, drawing a room plan of a difficult-to-locate study area and so on. Different groups should undertake the tasks in a different order, so that individual locations (and people) are not mobbed by hosts arriving at the same time. Give a time limit for the treasure hunt, and award prizes for all who complete on time. This activity helps people to get to know each other and their learning environment at the same time.

15 **Which of these are 'you'?** Give everyone a handout sheet containing (say) 20 statements about the topic to be explored. Ask each participant to

pick out the three that are most applicable to them. Then ask everyone in turn to disclose their top choice, asking the rest to show whether they too were among their own choices.

16 **Interview your neighbour.** Ask participants in pairs to interview each other for (say) three minutes, making notes of key points that they may wish to report back in summary of the interview. Then do a round asking everyone to introduce their neighbour to the rest of the group.

Learning and using names

People in general tend to take more notice of people they know. Your students will take more notice of you if they feel that they know you, and above all that you know them. This is particularly important when you work with small groups of students, as they are much more likely to expect you to know who they are. Getting their names right is a useful step towards building up the sort of relationship which fosters learning. The following suggestions provide some general advice on how to improve your 'hit rate' of correct name-calling in small-group work:

1 **Learn all the easy names first.** If you have a group with three Peters in, make sure you know them first and which one is which! You then have a 3 in 20 (say) chance of getting the first name right.

2 **Make a conscious effort to learn three or four names a session.** This way you should build up a reasonable ability to talk to people by name within the first few weeks in small-group work.

3 **Take particular care with difficult names.** If you encounter names that you find difficult or unusual to say, write them out clearly and check how to say them, then write them phonetically in a way you will recognize over the top. Use the name as often as you can until you have mastered it, regularly checking that you have got it right.

4 **Consider students' feelings.** Think how you feel when someone gets your name wrong – especially someone you would have expected to know it. One of the problems with university teaching is that new students can feel quite anonymous and alone.

5 **Use preferred names.** At the beginning of the course, ask students, 'What do you want to be called?' The names they give you will be more accurate than your printed class lists, and you'll quickly find out whether Victoria wants to be called Vicky, Jaswinder, Jaz, Cedric, Rick and so on.

6 **Use labels.** At early stages it is useful to give students sticky labels to write their names on in bold felt-tip pen. This gives you the chance to call them by the name they prefer – and gives them the chance to start getting to know each other.

7 **Help students to learn each other's names.** In groups with up to about 20 students, try a round as follows: 'Tell us your name, and tell us something about your name.' This can be a good icebreaker, and can be very memorable too, helping people develop association-links with the names involved.

8 **Help students to get to know each other better.** An alternative round is to get the students sitting in a circle. Ask one to say his or her name, then the person to the left to say 'I am… and this is…'. Carry on round the circle, adding one name at each stage, till someone goes right round the circle correctly. A further alternative is to ask students to introduce themselves, stating first their names, and then two 'likes' and two 'dislikes', so some memorable details help associate the person with the name.

9 **Use your list of names to quiz students.** To help you to get to know their names, once you have a complete list of the names, ask people from your list at random some (easy) questions, not to catch them out, but to help you to put names to faces.

10 **Consider using place cards.** In places where small groups of students are sitting in particular places for a while, it is useful to give the students each a 'place card' (a folded A5 sheet of card serves well) and ask them to write their names on both sides of the card and place it in front of them. Cards can be seen at a distance much better than labels. This allows you to address individuals by name, and also helps them to get to know each other.

Home groups

Home groups are often used in colleges and universities where an ethos of group learning is being fostered intentionally and strategically. 'Home groups' is the term used to describe a relatively long-term group which stays together through thick and thin along a diverse learning pathway. Home groups come together all the way along a learning pathway, so that members can exchange experiences and learn from each other's triumphs and disasters alike. The following suggestions may help you to help students get the most from being members of home groups:

1 **Give home groups time for members to get to know each other.** Home groups are often intended to be safe, non-threatening environments, where group members can share their moans as well as their successes. It is important that members of home groups develop trust in each other, so that they relax and get the most from each others' support and help.

2 **Give home groups something interesting to do, to start them off.** It is not really important that this icebreaking task is relevant to the future work of the group. It is more important that it brings group members together well. It is therefore particularly important that the first home-group task is not threatening, and not assessed in any way.

3 **Decide carefully how you wish to constitute home groups.** Revisit the suggestions elsewhere in this book about forming groups, and decide whether you want to leave home-group membership entirely to students themselves, or to constitute the groups yourself strategically. Both extremes have their own advantages and drawbacks.

4 **Make sure that home groups are quite distinct from other group constitutions.** For example, it is important that a home group is quite different from an action-learning set, or syndicate allocated a particular learning objective. The major strength of a successful home group can be the disparity of its members' experiences.

5 **Cause home groups to get together quite regularly.** It is worth giving home groups tasks from time to time, which will then be followed up by members either individually or in completely different group settings. They then come to regard their time in home groups as feeding in substantially to the central parts of their learning.

6 **Think about your own level of facilitation in home groups.** You may wish to play a significant role in early meetings, to set the tone of the group and to underline its importance. However, it can be really useful to back off once the groups are working well, and give the groups the comfort of privacy in which to share and exchange members' experiences, problems and triumphs.

7 **Legitimize home groups as the place where members can be themselves.** For example, when other parts of their learning are proving difficult, home groups should be seen as a place where worries can be shared, and peer-support can take place quite informally.

8 **Set questions from other group contexts, to be taken back to home groups.** It is important that home-group time is seen by members as being well spent in the overall pattern of their learning, and that key questions and issues central to the learning programme are aired and debated in home groups.

9 **Set preparation for other group contexts, to be done in home**

groups. This helps to establish the place of home groups in the bigger picture. When home groups are working well, it leads to a lot of relevant preparation being achieved before other group settings, making them more productive and efficient.

10 **Make sure that home groups finish well.** Ideally, a good home group will want to (and may find ways to) continue after the official lifetime of the group. The group should not fizzle out when the learning programme is over. It is much better if the group is allowed to come to a resounding and memorable conclusion in one way or another.

Action-learning sets

Action-learning sets can have some things in common with home groups, not least effective peer support, and confidence-building processes. The difference is usually that action-learning sets have relatively prescribed learning outcomes, and the overall work of the sets is likely to be subject to some kind of formal assessment. The following suggestions may help to trigger your own ideas about how best to use action-learning sets in your own contexts:

1 **Do not make action-learning sets too big.** As with any other learning group, there is likely to be an optimum size, dependent on the nature of the tasks the group is intended to engage in. Four members is often a suitable minimum constitution, and six members may be a sensible maximum to avoid the likelihood of passengers or bystander behaviours.

2 **Think carefully *how* the membership should be established.** An action-learning set which has chosen its own membership is likely to have strengths regarding identity, but when free choice is used as the overall strategy, there are bound to be 'remainder' groupings, which set off to a much less happy start.

3 **Action learning is about achieving learning objectives.** Sometimes, these may usefully be prescribed by the facilitator or tutor. When possible, however, it is better to allow action-learning sets some freedom in their interpretation of the intended objectives.

4 **Action learning is about learning from experience.** This is just as much about learning from things that went wrong as from things where no problems were encountered. Help set members to value the business of 'what we learnt about ourselves from this', for both positive learning experiences and more traumatic ones.

5 **Consider setting the objectives, but allowing the group to determine the evidence they will furnish for**

their achievement. This allows the curriculum covered by action-learning sets to be reasonably closely defined, while still allowing the groups some freedom in their interpretation of how they will demonstrate that they have reached the specified targets.

6 **Suggest that the leadership of action-learning sets is rotated appropriately.** This can mean different members taking the lead for different tasks contributing to the overall work of the set.

7 **Consider allowing action-learning sets to negotiate their own learning outcomes.** Where particular standards are required to be evidenced, some care will need to be taken to assist action-learning sets to strike a sensible balance between over-ambitious outcomes and underachievement.

8 **Consider the scope for renegotiation of outcomes and evidence of achievement.** When action-learning sets have some freedom to adjust their targets, timescales and products, the increased ownership of their agenda that they develop manifests itself in better group learning.

9 **Help action-learning sets to track their own work.** For example, suggest that records are kept, such as the agendas for their meetings, the decisions they reached, the areas where consensus was achieved straight away and the issues that caused disagreement. These records, suitably prepared, can lend themselves to assessment of the work of the group, whether self-assessment by the group members themselves, or tutor assessment.

10 **Legitimize 'any other business'.** Action-learning sets should not just feel that they have to stick rigidly to their agreed or negotiated intended outcomes. Other useful learning that occurred on the way to their achievements can be every bit as important as the intended learning. Allow scope for sets to keep records of their own 'unexpected' learning as well as their intended learning.

Tutorless groups

Tutorless groups overlap with home groups and action-learning sets, both of which can function in a tutorless mode for at least some of their working lifetimes. It can also be useful to establish tutorless groups for particular purposes which are different from those of action-learning sets or home groups. The following suggestions (overleaf) may help you to think of how you may relinquish control of appropriate parts of group learning to your own students:

1 **Brief tutorless groups on the purposes of this way of learning.** Ensure that they understand the value of the process and do not just see it as tutor cop-out.

2 **Brief tutorless groups clearly.** Ensure they have clear guidance on the tasks expected of them, and the likely outcomes they should be aiming to achieve.

3 **Provide clear back-up.** Build in checkpoints at intervals, so tutorless groups do not feel they are struggling alone to make sense of their learning. However, ensure that in checking progress, you do not over-direct in developing group activities.

4 **Prepare for problems.** Let groups know how they can get help if they have genuine problems which they cannot solve themselves, but try to make sure that they set out to be as self-reliant as reasonably possible.

5 **Consider using tutorless groups for resource-based learning.** For example, rather than suggest that students undertake elements of open learning or computer-based learning individually, ask them to do these elements in small, specially-constituted groups. The peer-group learning which can occur when a small group works through an open-learning resource together is often far-reaching.

6 **Consider the most appropriate task size for tutorless groups.** The overall task needs to be big enough to be worthwhile, but not so big as to be crucial if the group fails to gel well. The tasks do need to be important, however, otherwise students may regard tutorless groups as a luxury rather than as a key part of their intended learning.

7 **Consider rotating the membership of tutorless groups.** While home groups and action-learning sets work best when their membership is constant over a significant time period, tutorless groups can be effective for much shorter tasks, with different membership for each task. Such rotating membership can actually add to the feeling of belonging to the other kinds of group.

8 **Make the most of students explaining things to each other.** Tutorless groups are particularly appropriate for situations when some students have already mastered a topic, but need consolidation by explaining it to others.

9 **Give tutorless groups the means to assess their own achievements.** When devolving the learning to people, it is appropriate to devolve the assessment too – at lest as far as allowing the groups to assess their own learning in privacy before any formal assessment of it is undertaken.

10 **Suggest that tutorless groups should accumulate evidence of their work.** If, for example, the product of a tutorless-group task is to be assessed in due course, the product itself will be evidence of the achievement of the group, but may not lend itself to being evidence of the processes that the group went through, or of the

relative contribution to the work of the group by individual members. It can be useful to suggest to groups that they should, in their own way, gather evidence of how they did what they did.

11 **Keep a safe distance from tutorless groups.** Tempting as it may be to test the temperature of the groups to see that they are working effectively, it is better to test the product of their learning in ways that do not interfere with the freedom of the groups to operate in their own way.

12 **Process is important, but should be free from interference from tutors.** While it may be appropriate from time to time for tutors to monitor the group processes which occur in home groups or even action-learning sets, in tutorless groups it could undermine the special responsibility which group members can have for making their own processes work well. Testing the

products of tutorless groups can in its own way be a sufficient incentive to group members to sort out their processes.

13 **Suggest that tutorless groups should rehearse for forthcoming assessments.** In the absence of an authority figure, the group can safely discuss views on likely tasks or exam questions, and can work out what needs to be done to prepare for these. When a tutor is present, there is a tendency for students to wish *not* to show what they do not yet know.

14 **Gather feedback about the value of tutorless groups.** Ask students what they found most useful about the process, and what they found least useful. Also ask them what they enjoyed most and least, and what they learnt about themselves from the process. Build on their feedback in your future design of tutorless group task briefings and processes.

Conflict in group work

Much has been written about the stages that are quite normal in group work. For example, it is common for groups to progress through stages of 'forming, storming, norming and conforming' – not necessarily in one particular order! The following suggestions (overleaf) may help you to minimize the dangers associated with conflict in group work, and to maximize the benefits that can be drawn from people who sometimes disagree:

Legitimize conflict. It is important to acknowledge that people do not have to agree all of the time, and to open up agreed processes by which areas of disagreement can be explored and resolved (or be agreed to remain areas of disagreement). Ensure, however, that the groups have ground rules for conflict resolution, so that they strive to avoid slanging matches and power games.

2 **Establish the causes of conflict.** When conflict has broken out in a group, it is easy for the root causes to become subsumed in an escalation of feeling. It can be productive to backtrack to the exact instance which initiated the conflict, and to analyse it further.

3 **Encourage groups to put the conflict into written words.** Writing up the issues, problems or areas of disagreement on a flipchart or marker board can help to get them out of people's systems. Conflict feelings are often much stronger when the conflict is still bottled up, and has not yet been clearly expressed or acknowledged. When something is 'up on the wall', it often looks less daunting, and a person who felt strongly about it may be more satisfied. The 'on the wall' issues can be returned to later when the group has had more time to think about them.

4 **Establish the ownership of the conflict.** Who feels it? Who is being affected by it? Distinguish between individual issues, and ones that affect the whole group.

5 **Distinguish between people, actions and opinions.** When unpacking the causes of conflict in a group situation, it is useful to focus on actions and principles. Try to resolve any actions which proved to cause conflict. Try to agree principles. If the conflict is caused by different opinions, it can help to accept people's entitlement to their opinions, and leave it open to people to reconsider their opinions if and when they feel ready to do so.

6 **Use conflict creatively.** It can be useful to use brainstorming to obtain a wider range of views, or a broader range of possible actions that can be considered by the group. Sometimes, the one or two strong views which may have caused conflict in a group look much more reasonable when the full range of possibilities is aired, and areas of agreement are found to be closer than they seemed to be.

7 **Capture the learning from conflict.** When conflict has occurred, it can be beneficial to ask everyone to decide constructive things they have learnt about themselves from the conflict, and to agree on principles which the whole group can apply to future activities to minimize the damage from similar causes of conflict arising again.

8 **Refuse to allow conflict to destroy group work.** You may wish sometimes to tell groups that achievement of consensus is an aim, or a norm, or alternatively you

may wish to ask groups to establish only the extent of the consensus they achieve.

9 **Consider arbitration processes.** When conflict is absolutely unresolvable, the facilitator may need to set up a 'court of appeal' for desperate situations. The fact that such a process is available often helps groups to sort out their own problems without having to resort to it.

10 **Make it OK to escape.** When people know that they can get out of an impossible situation, they do not feel trapped, and in fact are more likely to work their own way out of the conflict. It can be useful to allow people to drop out of a group and move into another one, but only as a last resort. Beware of the possible effects of someone who is seen as a conflict generator entering a group which has so far worked without conflict!

Gender issues in group work

When problems occur in groups due to gender issues, they can be felt more deeply than problems arising from almost any other cause. The following suggestions may help you to avoid some problems of this sort from arising in the first place, or to alert group members themselves to the potential problems, so that they can work round them in their own group work:

1 **Think about gender when forming groups.** There are advantages and disadvantages for single-sex groups, depending on the balance of the sexes, and other issues including culturally-sensitive ones. In some cultures females may be much happier, for religious reasons, working in single-sex groups. However, in other cases it may be helpful in terms of future employment to gently encourage them to get used to working with members of the opposite sex.

2 **Try to avoid gender domination of groups.** This can happen because of majority gender composition of groups. If it is inevitable because of the overall gender balance of the whole group, try to manage group composition so that minority participants do not feel isolated. If it is unavoidable, address the issue directly when setting ground rules.

3 **Decide when single-gender groups might be more appropriate.** For group work on gender-sensitive issues, such as child abuse, it can be best to set out to form single sex groups.

4 **Require appropriate behaviour.** For group work to be effective, all participants need to behave in a professional way, with standards that would be expected in an effective working environment. Outlaw sexist

or offensive behaviour, and emphasize that one person's 'joke' or 'tease' can be another person's humiliation.

5 **Decide when to stick with existing group compositions.** When a set of groups is working well, without any gender-related or other problems, do not just change the group composition without a good reason.

6 **Set ground rules for talking and listening.** It can be useful to agree on ground rules which will ensure that all group participants (irrespective of gender) are heard, and not talked down or over by other participants.

7 **Avoid setting up excessive competition between male groups and female groups.** When there are gender-specific groups, do not egg a group of one gender on, by saying words to the effect, 'Come on, you can do better than them', referring to groups of the other gender.

8 **Be sensitive about role assignment.** For example, try to raise awareness about the dangers of tasks being allocated within groups on the basis of gender stereotypes, such as typing or making arrangements being handled by females, and 'heavy' work by males.

9 **Alert groups to be sensitive to leadership issues.** It is often the case that, for example, male members of groups may automatically see themselves as stronger contenders to lead the group than their female counterparts, and put themselves forward. When group members are aware that this is an issue, they are more likely to agree on a more democratic process for deciding who will lead an activity, or who will report back the outcomes.

10 **Avoid sexual preference oppression.** When it is known that group participants have different sexual preferences from the majority of the group, there is a tendency for them to be oppressed in one way or another by the rest of the group. It can be delicate to raise this issue in general briefings, and it may be best to respond to it as a facilitator when it is seen to be likely to occur.

5: Resource-based learning

Intended outcomes of this chapter

This chapter is intended to help you to:

- decide what forms of resource-based learning relate best to your students' learning needs (for example, print-based, computer-based, online, and so on);
- set the terms 'open learning', 'distance learning' and 'flexible learning' in context;
- choose good reasons for developing resource-based learning components in your teaching;
- decide whether to adopt existing materials, or adapt them to your purposes, or compose new resource-based learning materials;
- choose an effective and efficient strategy for developing your own resource-based learning materials;
- interrogate print-based or computer-based learning resource materials using a checklist to find out how well they deliver learning payoff for your students;
- choose from a range of ways of helping students to develop appropriate skills to help them to learn successfully from resource materials;
- explore some suggestions regarding learning from electronic sources to help you decide which sources may be useful to your students.

This chapter is primarily about selecting from the wide range of learning resource materials which may be available in print, on CD ROM or online, some of which could be directly relevant to your students' needs. You may wish to employ resource-based learning materials directly within your own taught course, or turn them into flexible learning pathways for appropriate parts of your curriculum. You may also be considering implementing open or flexible learning as learning provisions in their own right. The chapter also includes some suggestions about how to go about designing new resource-based learning materials of your own, and how to adapt existing materials to be more appropriate for your students.

Resource-based flexible learning, in one form or another, is increasingly being used to provide learning pathways within higher education courses in universities, as well as to open up distance-learning pathways to students outside the universities. In the UK, the use of resource-based learning is increasing dramatically, as universities and colleges are required to cater for larger numbers of students, with increasingly diverse educational backgrounds, in an environment where communication and information technologies impact ever more greatly on teaching and learning. I will start the chapter, however, by reviewing what is meant by some of the principal terms involved in resource-based learning.

Some terms and buzz-phrases

There are several terms used widely in connection with resource-based, student-centred learning materials, reflecting the ways in which such materials are employed. There exist many definitions of these terms, so it is worth reviewing the meanings of them.

The term *distance learning* is used when students study at a distance from the provider of the materials. The Open University in the UK is a major provider of distance-learning programmes. Though the Open University is principally located in Milton Keynes, it is unusual for students actually to go there. Most students study at home (or at work, or at any other places of their own choices). The Open University provides tutor support for students, using a combination of full-time Open University staff based in various parts of the UK, and a much larger body of part-time tutors, who are often lecturers in conventional colleges and universities. These tutors are used both to provide ongoing support for students studying with the Open University, and to assess students' coursework. Assessment is usually scheduled to submission deadlines for assignments, and students take formal examinations set by the Open University, usually taking place in examination centres set up in other universities or colleges.

Although the Open University uses print-based learning resource materials widely, increasing use is being made of computer-based resources and online communication, with tutors giving feedback on assessed coursework. The Open University itself is responsible for setting the coursework and exams, moderating the assessment by part-time tutors, and awarding qualifications to students. Similar models of distance learning are extensively used in other parts of the world, notably Canada, Australia and New Zealand.

The term *open learning* is often used for study programmes involving distance learning, as described above. Implied in the concept of open learning is the opening up of some or all of the following aspects of freedom to students:

● when they do their learning;
● where they do their learning;
● at what pace they learn.

There are further degrees of freedom that vary considerably across the range of programmes operating under the umbrella term of open learning. These include whether students:

- need any qualifications before being accepted onto an open learning programme;
- learn completely independently, or can choose to make use of tutor support;
- have any formal mentoring provision to assist them during their studies;
- can start a particular study module or course at any time ('roll-on, roll-off') or have fixed start dates and completion dates (usually dictated by examinations arrangements);
- can select which parts of the programme they study, and in which (if any) of the assessed elements of the programmes they participate.

In some distance-learning programmes, particularly correspondence courses, some or all of these choices are available to students. In others, students are constrained by set start dates and assessment dates, and by the structure of the assessments leading to the award of degrees, diplomas or certificates.

The term *open learning* is therefore predominantly used to reflect the freedoms available to students regarding where, when, at what pace and how they actually undertake their studies. There are several other terms which overlap with open and distance learning, including *independent learning, individualized learning, self-study programmes, self-managed learning,* and so on.

The term *flexible learning* can be used in connection with all the kinds of study programme mentioned so far in this chapter. Flexibility is about when, where, at what place and by what processes the learning takes place. The concept of flexible learning extends, however, to the inclusion of open learning, or self-study elements within a conventional college-based programme. For example, students may be attending lectures, workshops, practical sessions and tutorials on a college campus, but at the same time studying selected elements of the curriculum more or less under their own steam, using learning packages (which may be print-based, computer-based or multimedia) to support those parts of their work. The assessment of the flexible-learning components may entirely be integrated into the overall assessment of their work, or may be done separately, or any combination of the two.

The term *resource-based learning* embraces the learning materials that are used in distance, open and flexible learning, but equally applies to the learning that is designed to occur *outside* formal lectures or classes in universities and colleges. The common factor is that the curriculum is packaged into learning resource materials, from which students learn either individually or in small groups, with some freedom regarding when, where and how fast. The learning resources themselves are designed in many formats, including:

- print-based interactive learning packages;
- traditional textbooks, journal articles and so on, addressed by interactive *study guides;*
- computer-based learning materials, supplied to students on disk;
- multimedia computer-based learning materials, using CD ROM, including video extracts, audio commentaries, and so on;
- online computer-based materials, with electronic communication through a local Intranet and/or globally through the Internet.

Reasons to use resource-based learning

Why move from traditional teaching or training processes towards resource-based learning? As you will probably know already, it takes a lot of skill, work and commitment to make the switch from something formerly taught and learnt in a traditional way, to a resource-based learning programme. It is all too easy to find reasons for not making such a change. Sometimes, the ethos of an institution may not accommodate such changes being implemented. There are, however, many factors that are causing institutions to review the potential of developing resource-based learning programmes, ranging from elements of the curriculum studied as flexible-learning components within traditional college-based courses, to whole programmes offered in parallel with, or as alternatives to, college courses. Some of the arguments supporting the development of resource-based learning by universities are summarized below.

- **There is increased attention to student-centred learning.** It is increasingly realized that in many disciplines, full-time higher education students are seriously over-taught (and over-assessed – see Chapter 4), and that this produces surface rather than deep learning, and limits students' development of highly valued transferable skills.
- **There is far more information than there used to be.** It is no longer possible to cover all of the information in a subject area in traditional lectures or classes,

and in any case information itself does not bring knowledge to students. The most productive way of providing students with information is through learning resource materials.

- **There is a strong drive towards greater use of information technology in curriculum delivery.** This, coupled with the use of communications technologies for both student–tutor and student–student communication, increases the usefulness of learning pathways that allow students to interact with the technologies at their own pace, and at times of their own choosing.

- **Electronic communication technologies make it faster, easier and cheaper to get information to students.** These technologies can also speed up student–tutor interactions – particularly assessment and associated feedback – and can be regarded as more environmentally friendly than consuming increased amounts of paper.

- **There is greater participation in higher education.** This leads to a greater diversity in the student population, and the need to accommodate a wider range of students' learning preferences. This is also coupled with the increase in the number of mature part-time students returning to learning.

- **There is less time to continue traditional practices.** Lecturers in higher education have much higher workloads than previously, and often are unable to keep up with the work involved in teaching – and particularly assessing – larger numbers of students. Lecturers may also be under considerable pressure to devote more time to research and publication, not least owing to the stronger links between research output and institutional funding. Therefore, flexible learning can be an attractive way of creating more opportunity for research, once the investment of time is made that allows flexible learning to happen effectively.

- **There is an increased expectation regarding collaboration between institutions.** With increased need for collaboration between providers of education and training, resource-based learning provides an easier basis for such collaboration. It would be unwise for every university to develop from scratch a whole range of learning resource materials, when there already exists a wide range of such materials which can be bought in, shared online or adapted.

- **Modular frameworks, and credit accumulation and transfer systems are now widespread.** The availability of a substantial proportion of the curriculum in packaged form significantly helps progress towards a modular structure, and allows students increased choice. More students are moving from one university to another during the course of their studies, or from one discipline to another. Resource-based learning provision can also help to overcome some of the timetabling problems that can be caused by the increasing proportion of students who wish to study unusual combinations of subjects.

- **There is increased pressure for cost-effectiveness.** Increased pressure on funding means that universities need to be able both to cater for larger class sizes in popular discipline choices, and to find and respond to new target groups of part-time and distant students. Flexible learning pathways can play a significant role in enabling universities to demonstrate cost-effective provision.

- **Students come from different backgrounds.** As the proportion of non-traditional-entry students increases, universities and colleges need to complement traditional teaching and learning approaches by creating additional flexible learning pathways, sometimes working in parallel with traditionally-taught programmes.
- **Students' expectations of higher education are changing.** With increasing use of computer-based learning and supported self-study in secondary education, students' expectations are changing from being taught mostly in lectures, towards taking more responsibility for managing their own learning.
- **There are increased levels of franchising of programmes.** With the increased franchising of university programmes in further education colleges and in in-company training departments, the availability of learning resource materials provides an excellent means of ensuring that the quality of learning is maintained and controlled.
- **Higher education is a more competitive business.** Increasing competition between institutions of higher education and training means that universities have to be able to cater more flexibly for a wide variety of student needs and expectations. The element of competition has been increased, with students (or their parents) increasingly paying towards the costs of tuition as well as living expenses.
- **The emphasis on learning skills development continues to grow.** Perhaps the most important outcome of higher education should be the development by students of their ability to manage their own learning. Key skills are being incorporated into a wide range of higher education programmes, and the attributes that are indicative of graduate status are increasingly given higher priority. Resource-based learning pathways develop such abilities. 'Being taught' often inhibits such development.

The main components of resource-based learning materials

The principal components of learning materials vary considerably, depending whether the materials are print-based, computer-based or multimedia, and on whether the materials are designed to be self-sufficient learning resources, or to refer out to existing books, papers and articles, or to be used in conjunction with face-to-face learning situations such as lectures, tutorials or practical sessions. However, it is possible to identify some elements which characterize modern resource-based learning materials, and which differentiate them from more traditional forms of print-based resources such as 'straight' textbooks. These elements include:

- statements of the intended learning outcomes or learning objectives;
- structured learning-by-doing elements such as self-assessment questions, tasks, exercises, quizzes and so on;
- feedback responses on-screen or in print, to the structured learning-by-doing elements;
- open-ended learning-by-doing activities, such as assignments, exercises, readings and practical tasks, to help students to consolidate the learning they are doing from the materials;
- a tone and style that is more user-friendly and informal than in conventional published books and articles;
- tutor-marked assignments, online or submitted on paper, often with details of the marking schemes and assessment criteria.

There may additionally be some of the following components:

- guidance regarding prerequisite knowledge or skills, to help students to judge for themselves whether they are equipped to start work with the learning materials;
- study-guide briefings to read other materials, such as particular sections or chapters of books, journal articles and so on, usually coupled with tasks for students to do while using these resources;
- pre-prepared feedback discussions on tasks which students have undertaken with learning resource materials;
- links to face-to-face elements of college-based courses, such as lectures, tutorial programmes, and so on;
- study-skills commentaries, to help students undertake their own study of the materials as effectively and efficiently as possible.

In well-designed resource-based learning materials, the content itself is broken up into manageable chunks by the interactive elements. It is important that the content is not simply presented in the same way as in a traditional textbook, but is punctuated by learning-by-doing and feedback episodes, and that this is done frequently throughout the materials rather than merely at the end of an element of learning. Tutor-marked assignments may be used when it is necessary to link students' work on resource-based learning materials into the assessment scheme of a whole course or module, with the purposes being formative, summative or both. There may also be formal exams, or some exam questions in a wider exam which covers the whole of the syllabus of which part is delivered by resource-based learning, to represent the summative assessment of the syllabus area addressed by the materials.

Adopting, adapting or starting from scratch

A wide range of resource-based learning packages already exists, spanning all levels of study from introductory to postgraduate. Many of these can be purchased from publishers and commercial materials providers, or accessed online (or downloaded) from the Internet. Many learning packages have also been developed in-house in particular university departments, or by specialist producers, and it is often possible to come to site-licence arrangements with the producers to purchase them with the view to adopting them as they stand, or to adapting them to fit a particular course or programme. The following checklist may help you to decide whether to adopt such packages, adapt them, or whether you may need to develop some completely new materials for resource-based learning by your students.

- **Are there relevant materials already available?** It is worth checking publishers' catalogues, and databases of learning materials, held in most university libraries or learning resources centres.
- **Are the intended learning outcomes of available materials sufficiently close to those of your course?** When the learning outcomes converge well, it is an indicator that it may be possible to use at least parts of the materials as they stand.
- **Will the 'not-invented-here syndrome' come into play?** When learning materials are brought in from external sources, it is sometimes the case that lecturers (or students) do not feel that the materials are as credible as in-house materials or programmes. Any dissatisfaction that lecturers may feel with the materials is quickly passed on to students, damaging in turn the students' trust in the materials, and their confidence in the processes of learning from resources.
- **Have you time to develop entirely new materials?** The short answer to this may be likely to be 'no!', but some of the ideas in this chapter may help you to see that resource-based learning materials can indeed be developed step by step, and that you may already have quite a lot to start from.

Materials that you can adapt

Lecturers usually have a wide range of materials that can be adapted to take their places in resource-based learning packages. The materials you already have available may include:

- your existing syllabus specification, including identified learning outcomes;
- your own lecture notes;
- handout materials you already use;
- tasks and exercises you already set your students;

- tutorial sheets;
- assignment briefings;
- model answers;
- case-study materials;
- test and exam questions.

In addition to some of these, you may already have some even more important things to draw on, including:

- your experience of teaching the subject involved;
- your knowledge of students' problems with the subject;
- your experience of helping students with particular problems;
- your experience of assessing students' learning in the subject.

Many learning resource materials are produced by people who may know the subject involved, but who may lack some of the vital experience regarding teaching, learning and assessing the subject. Not surprisingly, materials that are developed by writers or designers who are not involved directly in teaching a subject rarely work nearly as well as those developed by experienced lecturers.

A strategy for designing resource-based learning materials

The following ideas are adapted from a strategy I first developed in *The Open Learning Handbook: 2nd edition* (Kogan Page, 1994).

1 **Start with the intended learning outcomes.** Express these in a clear, friendly, jargon-free way. It is best to do this by addressing them directly to the students who will use the materials. For example, it is useful to use wording along the lines of:

When you've worked through Section 6 of this package, you'll be able to:
explain why ...
list five factors which influence...
predict when ... is most likely to occur.
design a process to enable ...

The main aim should be that students will know exactly what they are intended to be able to do when they will have completed their work on each flexible learning element. It is important to avoid words such as 'understand' or 'know', as these do not tell students enough detail regarding how they could be expected or required to *demonstrate* their understanding or knowledge.

2 **Think of tasks, activities and exercises which will give students learning-by-doing experience.** Try not to simply use tasks which require students to recall things they have just learnt, but rather use tasks which help them to extend and build on their learning as they work through the resource-based learning materials. It is better to draft out 20 tasks, then to use only three in the materials, than to try to make each task good enough at the outset to include in the materials.

3 **Decide which of the tasks you can already *respond to*.** For example, if you have thought of a multiple-choice question, you can probably respond separately to students choosing each of the options. A congratulatory response may be appropriate for students who choose the best option (often referred to as the 'key'). More importantly, for each of the other options (the 'distractors') you can probably respond with a direct message to students who make the mistakes or misunderstandings which may have led them to choose any of these distractors. The tasks where you can respond in print (or on-screen in computer-based packages) are the basis of structured self-assessment questions.

3 **Decide which tasks you cannot directly respond to.** These could be the tasks where the human judgement of a lecturer or tutor may be necessary to work out what help students may need, or where students will need detailed feedback on what they have done well and what they may have missed. These tasks may well be best as tutor-marked assignment questions.

4 **Write draft feedback responses to the self-assessment tasks.** You will almost certainly want to edit and polish these responses when you have feedback from students on your first draft of the learning materials, but it is well worth writing these responses in some detail if necessary before putting together the whole of an element of material.

5 **Link together self-assessment questions and feedback responses.** Check that your feedback responses address as many as possible of the problems which students may have when they attempt the questions.

6 **Link each feedback response to the next self-assessment question.** To move students on from your response to one particular self-assessment question, to be ready to attempt the next one, you will usually need to introduce some new ideas or information. This is an element of the content of your resource-based learning materials, but is best kept concise and relevant, so that it specifically serves to bridge only the gap between that response and the next question.

7 **Try out the self-assessment questions and feedback responses with 'live' students.** There is no quicker way of finding out whether the questions and responses will work well, than to use them as class-based exercises in lectures or tutorials, and find out how students react to them. This helps you to select those questions which will work effectively in resource-based learning materials, to adjust and improve the wording of those which can be made to work with a little

attention, and to discard those questions where it may not be straightforward to devise self-sufficient feedback responses.

8 **Develop the tutor-marked components (if you are using such components).** It could be useful here to devise marking schemes, aiming to make it possible for *any* lecturer to mark students' work on these components. Ultimately, you may be able to develop the marking schemes sufficiently to be able to get students to self-assess their own work (if you are not needing such assessment data as part of their coursework profiles).

Although the above steps are listed as a sequence, it is best to work on them iteratively, working on one facet of the learning package, then adjusting others to tune them in to what you have done. For example, you can fine-tune your developing learning materials by:

- adjusting learning outcomes to match the actual self-assessment questions that you devise;
- adjusting self-assessment questions when you have tried to write responses to them;
- adjusting the lead-in sections preceding self-assessment tasks when you have seen how the tasks work in practice;
- adjusting the feedback to self-assessment questions when you have seen how the questions work with some live students in a lecture or tutorial;
- developing the tutor-marked components when you see how students are getting on with the self-assessment elements, and so on.

There is no substitute for student feedback as an aid to developing effective flexible learning materials. However, in the next section of this chapter I present a checklist which you can use as you write your own materials, and also use to help gauge the quality of existing published materials.

A quality checklist for resource-based learning materials

Now that we have looked in some detail at what resource-based learning is and how it works, it is worth summarizing many of the main points with a checklist which can be applied to resource materials in a bid to ensure that their expressed intended learning outcomes are achieved effectively and efficiently. When selecting learning resource materials from the plethora which may be on offer, it is useful to know what questions to ask to ensure that they will serve their purpose well. Even more important, when designing new learning resource materials of your own, or adapting those which are already available, it is important to have in mind at all times the ways in which the materials are intended to function, and how students will react to them. In the section which follows, I have identified a series of questions to pose, and some clarifications or suggestions arising from many of the questions. Most of the questions which follow can be applied to all the interactive learning material formats, from print-based flexible learning packages to the various forms of computer-based learning formats.

Objectives or statements of intended learning outcomes

1 **Is there a clear indication of any prerequisite knowledge or skills?** If not, you may usefully compose a specification of what is being taken for granted regarding the starting point of the materials. It is particularly important that when flexible learning elements are being used within college-based traditional courses, students should know where the flexible learning outcomes fit into the overall picture of their courses.

2 **Are the objectives stated clearly and unambiguously?** This is where you may wish to 'translate' the objectives of particular learning packages, making them more directly relevant to the students who will use them. This can often be done by adding 'for example, …' illustrations of how and when the intended outcomes will be relevant to their own situations.

3 **Are the objectives presented in a meaningful and 'friendly' way** (in other words, *not* 'The expected learning outcomes of this module are that the student will…')? I suggest that it is preferable to write learning outcomes using language such as 'When you've worked through Section 3, you'll be able to …' It is important that students develop a sense of ownership of the intended learning outcomes, and it is worthwhile making sure that the outcomes as presented to them make them feel involved, and that the expressed outcomes do not just belong to the learning package.

4 **Do the objectives avoid jargon which may not be known to students before starting the material?** It is of course normal for new terms and concepts to be introduced in any kind of learning, but it is best if this is done in ways that avoid frightening off students at the outset. It may remain necessary to include unfamiliar words in the objectives of a learning package, but this can still allow for such words to be explained there and then, legitimizing a starting-point of not yet knowing such words. Adding a few words in brackets along the lines of 'This means in practice that…' can be a useful way ahead in such cases.

Structure and layout

5 **Is the material visually attractive, thereby helping students to want to learn from it?** It is not always possible to choose the materials that *look* best, however. Sometimes the best-looking materials may be too expensive, or they may not be sufficiently relevant to learning needs. At the end of the day, it is the materials that *work* best that are cost-effective, so compromises may have to be made on visual attractiveness.

6 **Is there sufficient white space?** In print-based materials this is needed for students to write their own notes, answer questions posed by the materials, do calculations and exercises which help them make sense of the ideas they have been reading about, and so on. A learning package which allows – or insists on – students writing all over it, is likely to be more effective at promoting effective learning by doing.

7 **Is it easy for students to find their way backwards and forwards?** This is sometimes called 'signposting', and includes good use of headings in print-based materials, or effective menus in computer-based materials. Either way, well-signposted materials allow students to get quickly to anything they want to consolidate (or digest), as well as helping them to scan ahead to get the feel of what is to come.

8 **Is the material broken into manageable chunks?** Students' concentration spans are finite. We all know how fickle concentration is at face-to-face training sessions. The same applies when students are learning from resource materials. If an important topic goes on for page after page, we should not be surprised if concentration is lost. Frequent headings, subheadings, tasks and activities can all help to avoid students falling into a state of limbo when working through learning packages.

9 **Does the material avoid any sudden jumps in level?** A sudden jump can be a 'shut-the-package' cue to students working on their own. It is just about impossible for authors of learning materials to tell when they have gone one step too far too fast. The first people to discover such sudden jumps are always the students who cannot understand why the material has suddenly left them floundering. In well-piloted materials, such difficulties will have been ironed out long before the packages reach their published form, but not all materials have waited for this vital process to happen.

Self-assessment questions and activities (learning by doing)

10 **Are there plenty of them?** For example, I suggest that there should be one in sight per double-page spread in print-based materials, or something to do on most screens in interactive computer-based packages. If we accept that learning mostly happens by practising, making decisions, or having a go at exercises, it is only natural that effective interactive learning materials should essentially be packaged-up learning by doing.

11 **Are the tasks set by the questions clear and unambiguous?** In live sessions, if a task is not clear to students, someone will ask about it, and clarification will follow. With packaged learning resources, it is crucial to make sure that people working on their own do not have to waste time and energy working out exactly what the instructions mean every time they come to some learning by doing.

12 **Are the questions and tasks inviting?** Is it clear to students that it is valuable for them to have a go rather than skip the tasks or activities? It is sometimes an art to make tasks so interesting that no one is tempted to give them a miss, especially if they are quite difficult ones. However, it helps if you can make the tasks as relevant as possible to students' own backgrounds and experiences.

13 **Is there enough space for students to write their answers?** In print-based materials, it is important to get students writing. If they just *think* about writing something, but do not *do* it, they may well forget what they might have written! In computer-based materials, it is equally important to ensure that users make decisions, for example by choosing an option in a multiple-choice exercise, so that they can then receive feedback directly relating to what they have just done.

14 **Collectively, do the self-assessment questions and activities test students' achievement of the objectives, and prepare them for any final assessments they may be heading towards?** Perhaps one of the most significant dangers of resource-based learning materials is that it is often easier to design tasks and exercises on unimportant topics, than it is to ensure that students' activities focus on the things that are involved in them achieving the intended learning outcomes. To eliminate this danger, it is useful to check that each and every intended learning outcome is cross-linking to one or more self-assessment questions or activities, so that students get practice in everything that is important. The self-assessment questions should collectively prepare students for any other assessments that they will experience after completing their open learning.

Responses to self-assessment questions and activities (feedback)

15 **Are they really *responses to what students will have done*** (and not just answers to the questions)? We saw earlier in this chapter how important it is for students to get the chance to learn through feedback on their efforts. If students cannot get the correct answer to a question, telling them the answer is of very limited value. They need feedback on what was wrong with their own attempt at answering the question. In face-to-face training, they can get such responses from their lecturer. In resource-based learning, such feedback needs to be available to them in predetermined ways, in print or in feedback responses which appear on their computer screens.

16 **Do the responses meet each student's need to find out:**
'Was I right?'
'If not, why *not?*'
When students get a self-assessment question or activity 'right', it is quite straightforward to provide them with appropriate feedback. It is when they get them wrong that they need all the help we can give them. In particular, they need to know not only what the correct answer should have been, but also what was wrong with their own answers. Multiple-choice question formats are particularly useful here, as they allow different students making different mistakes each to receive individual feedback on their own attempts at such questions.

17 **Do the responses include encouragement or affirmation (without being patronizing) for students who got them right?** It is easy enough to start a response with words such as 'Well done'. However, there are many different ways of giving praise. Saying 'Splendid' may be fine if the task was difficult and we really want to reward students who got it right, but the same 'Splendid' can come across as patronizing if students felt that it was an easy question.

18 **Do the responses include something that will help students who got it wrong *not* to feel like complete idiots**? Do the responses give them guidance on what an acceptable answer might look like? One of the problems of working alone with resource-based learning materials is that people who get things wrong may feel they are the only people ever to have made such mistakes. When a difficult question or task is likely to cause students to make mistakes or to pick incorrect options, it helps them a lot if there are some words of comfort, such as 'This was a tough one', or 'Most people get this wrong at first'.

Introductions, summaries and reviews

19 **Is each part introduced in an interesting, stimulating way?** There is no second chance to make a good first impression. If students are put off a topic by the way it starts, they may never recover that vital 'want' to learn it.

20 **Do the introductions alert students to the way the materials are designed to work?** Learning resource materials should not assume that all students have developed the kinds of study skills needed for flexible learning. It is best when the authors of such materials share with students the way in which they intend the optimum learning payoff to be achieved. When students know where they are intended to be going, there is more chance they will get there.

21 **Are there clear and useful summaries or reviews?** Do these help students to digest what they have learnt? In any good face-to-face session, lecturers take care to cover the main points more than once, and to remind students towards the end of the session about the most important things they should remember. When designing learning resource materials, authors sometimes think that it is enough to put across the main points well – and only once. Summaries and reviews are every bit as essential in good learning materials as they are in live sessions.

22 **Do summaries and reviews provide useful ways for students to revise the material quickly and effectively?** A summary or review helps students to identify the essential learning points they should have mastered. Once they have done this, it should not take much to help them retain such mastery, and they may well not need to work through the whole package ever again if they can polish their grasp of the subject just by reading summaries or reviews.

The text itself

23 **Is it readable, fluent and unambiguous?** When students are working on their own, there is no one to ask if something is not clear. Good learning resource materials depend a lot on the messages getting across. Those people who never use a short word when they can think of a longer alternative should not be allowed to create learning resource materials. Similarly, short sentences tend to get messages across more effectively than long sentences.

24 **Is it relevant?** For example, does the material keep to the objectives as stated, and do these fit comfortably into the overall picture of the course or module? It can be all too easy for the creators of learning resource materials to get carried away with their pet subjects, and go into far more detail than is reasonable.

25 **Is the tone 'involving' where possible?** Is there plenty of use of 'you' for the student, 'I' for the author, 'we' for the student and author together? This is a matter of style. Some writers find it hard to communicate in an informal, friendly manner. There is plenty of evidence that communication works best in learning materials when students feel involved, and feel that the learning package is 'talking' to them in a natural and relaxed way.

Diagrams, charts, tables, graphs, and so on

26 **Is each non-text component as self-explanatory as possible?** In face-to-face training sessions, there are all sorts of clues as to what any illustrations (for example overheads or slides) actually mean. Lecturers' tone-of-voice and facial expressions do much to add to the explanation, as well as the words they use when explaining directly. With learning packages, it is important that such explanation is provided when necessary in print.

27 **Do the students know what to do with each illustration?** They need to know whether they need to *learn it, label* or *complete it,* to *note it in passing,* or to *pick out the trend,* or even *nothing.* In a face-to-face session, when lecturers show (for example) a table of data, someone is likely to ask, 'Do we have to remember these figures?' If the same table of data is included in learning materials, the same question still applies, but there is no one to reply to it. Therefore, good learning resource materials need to anticipate all such questions, and clarify to students exactly what the expectations are regarding diagrams, charts and so on. It only takes a few words of explanation to do this, along such lines as, 'You do not have to remember these figures, but you do need to be able to pick out the main trend', or, 'You do not have to be able to draw one of these, but you need to be able to recognize one when you see one.'

28 **'A sketch can be more useful than 1,000 words': is the material sufficiently illustrated?** One of the problem areas with flexible learning materials is that they are sometimes all in words, at the expense of visual ways of communicating important messages. Sometimes the explanation is as simple as the writer of the materials not being confident about providing sketches or diagrams. However, good-quality materials overcome this weakness, by using the services of someone with the appropriate talents.

Some general points

29 **Does the material ensure that the average student will achieve the objectives?** This of course is one of the most important questions we can ask of any learning package. If the answer is 'No', it is probably worth looking for a better package.

30 **Will the average student *enjoy* using the material**? In some ways this is the ultimate question. When students 'can't put the package down, because it's so interesting to work through it' there is not usually much wrong with the package.

31 **How up-to-date is the material covered?** How quickly will it date? Will it have an adequate shelf-life as a learning resource, and will the up-front costs of purchasing it or developing it be justified?

32 **How significant is the 'not invented here' syndrome?** Can you work with the differences between the approach used in the material and your own approach? Can you integrate comfortably and seamlessly the two approaches with your students? (If you criticize or put-down learning resource materials your students are using, you are quite likely to destroy their confidence in using the material, and their belief in the quality of the content of the material as a whole.)

33 **How expensive is the material?** Can students realistically be expected to acquire their own copies of it? Can bulk discounts or shareware arrangements be made? If the material is computer-based, is it suitable for networking, and is this allowed within copyright arrangements?

34 **Can students reasonably be expected to gain sufficient access?** This is particularly crucial when large groups are involved. Could lack of access to essential resource materials be cited as grounds for appeal by students who may be unsuccessful when assessed on what is covered by the resource material? This particularly applies to information technology laboratories and personal computers, when they play an important part in flexible learning delivery. Are part-time students disproportionately disadvantaged in terms of information technology access?

35 **What alternative ways are there of students learning the topic concerned?** What complementary ways are there in which students can combine other ways of learning the topic, with their learning from the resource material in question?

36 **How is the resource material or medium demonstrably better than the cheapest, or simplest way of learning the topic?** There need to be convincing answers to this question, not least regarding expenditure.

37 **Will the material make students' learning more efficient?** How will it save them time, or how will it focus their learning more constructively? Or will students lose time waiting for access to the learning resources?

38 **Will the resource material or medium be equally useful to all students?** Will there be no instances of disadvantaging (for example) students learning in a second language, women students, mature students, students who are not good with computers and so on?

39 **What additional key skills outcomes will students derive from using the material?** For example, will they develop skills as independent or autonomous learners? Will they develop keyboarding skills, or electronic communication skills? Are these outcomes assessed? Could they outweigh the *intended* learning outcomes?

40 **How best can feedback on the effectiveness of the resource material be sought?** What part should be played by peer-feedback from colleagues, feedback from student questionnaires, observations of students' reactions to the material, and assessment of students' learning?

Learning from glass

Resource-based learning is increasingly dominated by computer-based learning packages, and on-line learning through Intranets and the Internet. In all these contexts, we need to explore how effectively 'learning from glass' is likely to take place. We are relatively accustomed to interrogating 'learning from paper' in the contexts of handouts, books, articles and so on, even when it is well known that unless there is substantial learning by doing and feedback, the learning payoff from paper can be all too minimal. The next section of this chapter looks critically at 'learning from glass', and particularly at some of the questions which can be in students' minds as they confront any particular screenful of a computer-based learning package, or online sequence.

Perhaps the most important indicator that learning from glass is *not* happening successfully is if the student at the keyboard looks for the 'print' command. In short, if someone learning from a computer-based package needs to print something, it is a signal that it was not possible to do everything that may have been intended with it on-screen.

Some advantages of glass over paper

These can include:

- **There can be instant feedback on-screen to pre-planned decision making.** For example, choosing an option in a screen-based multiple-choice question can lead to immediate feedback on whether it was the best option to select, and (more importantly), 'If not, *why* not?'
- **Feedback can be withheld on-screen until some learning by doing has happened.** For example, the feedback to a selection in a multiple-choice question can be withheld in computer-based learning until learners have made their selections. In print-based materials, it can be all too tempting to check out the feedback responses *before* having made a firm choice.
- **Computers can add sound to on-screen feedback.** Where students can use headphones, for example, the benefits of tone of voice can be exploited in feedback responses to students' keyboard choices.
- **Computers can route learners on to what they need next.** For example, if students have succeeded in several on-screen questions, they can be moved on to something which may be more challenging to them (some harder questions), or if they are struggling with the on-screen tasks they can be moved back to some further practice questions.
- **Computer screens are less likely to cause information overload.** Paper, whether in books, articles, or even handouts, tends to get filled up with print. The limit of screen size causes at least some economy of information presentation. However, this advantage can only too easily be thrown away by congested screens of information, especially when what is designed to appear on-screen is too closely linked to what might have otherwise been presented on paper.

Some disadvantages of glass compared with paper

- **'Now you see it, now it's gone!':** visual memory tends to be relatively transient. If something important is on-screen, there is every chance it will evaporate from students' minds after a few more screens of information.
- **Glass cannot be used everywhere.** Learning from glass is dependent upon being beside a computer and monitor.
- **Glass cannot be spread out around a teaching room or learning space as easily as paper.** This means that students cannot move around as freely as they could with print-based learning resources.
- **Computer-based learning resources are often less easy to navigate than paper-based learning resources.** With a book, handout or article, it is easy to flick backwards and forwards to consolidate what has already been learnt, and to spy out the landscape of what is to come. With computer-based learning, this is not always nearly so easy.

Is this screenful actually working?

Imagine a student looking at a single tiny element of a computer-based learning programme, or a single screen of information online on an Intranet or the Internet. Any, or all, of the following questions could go through the student's mind while looking at a single screen of information. In Table 5.1, I have linked these questions to the five principal processes underpinning effective learning, as outlined in Chapter 1 of this book:

- wanting to learn;
- needing to learn;
- learning by doing;
- learning through feedback;
- digesting (making sense) of what is being learnt.

Practical pointers on resource-based learning

The following sets of suggestions on resource-based learning have been adapted from relevant parts of *2000 Tips for Lecturers* (Phil Race, Kogan Page 1999).

Material that lends itself to resource-based learning

It is worthwhile to think about which parts of the curriculum best lend themselves to an open or flexible approach. It is useful to start your resource-based learning writing

Table 5.1 Interrogating a computer screenful: questions which could be in learners' minds

Questions which could be going through a student's mind	Links to the factors underpinning successful learning
Why am I seeing this particular screenful? Why is it there? Can I just skip it? Is it just padding? Can I move straight on from here?	**Wanting to learn**: could be damaged if there is not a good reason for the screenful being there. **Needing to learn**: the rationale for the screenful's existence should at least confirm what the student needs to get from its presence.
What are the intended learning outcomes associated with this particular screenful? If there are none, why is it there at all?	**Wanting to learn**: could be undermined if the purpose of the screenful is not self-evident. **Needing to learn**: if it is not linked to intended learning outcomes, the message could be that it is not needed, and not important enough to think about.
What exactly am I supposed to *do* with this bit? How am I supposed to handle it? Am I intended to be jotting down my thoughts? Are there on-screen tasks for me to do, such as picking options, entering text, entering numbers, clicking boxes, moving objects around on-screen and so on?	**Learning by doing**: this is addressed when the screenful is an *interactive* one, in one way or another. The *doing* could be practice, learning by mistakes, or more sophisticated, for example requiring quite a bit of thought *before* action.
Will I be able to get back to this bit if I want to, or need to? How important is this particular bit? If it is important, will I have another chance to think about it, without having to go backwards to find it?	**Digesting – making sense**: putting the screenful into perspective is an important part of making sense of it. If it is not clear from the screenful whether it will be important or not, the student may assume it is not important.
Where does this bit fit in to the big picture? Where does it fit in to the overall intended learning outcomes? How much will it count for in forthcoming assessments?	**Wanting to learn, needing to learn, digesting**: if the screenful does not clearly link to the overall learning programme, the student may decide it is just there 'in passing' and learn very little from it.
How will I tell whether, and when, I have succeeded with this bit? Will I get feedback from the computer itself? Will I have to write down, or key in, something that will lead to later feedback from a tutor? Will I be given something to compare to what I am asked to do with the screenful?	**Learning through feedback**: the availability of feedback to the student, after doing something with what is on the screen, gives the message that the screenful is important enough to be taken seriously.
Where is this bit leading me towards? Where is it taking me from? Can I tell where I am heading? Am I supposed to remember where I am coming from, and what I learnt from previous screenfuls?	**Digesting – making sense**: it is easy to get lost in computer-based scenarios. It is perfectly possible to ensure that each screenful has enough context-setting included, so that this danger is minimized. Unfortunately, this 'navigational' agenda is often not addressed well enough.
Who else is involved? Will someone be assessing what I have got out of this bit? Am I supposed to be doing this on my own, or am I expected to talk to other students about it? Is anyone watching me? Would I treat it differently if they were?	These questions can link to *all* **of the factors** underpinning successful learning. Feedback can be forthcoming on-screen, or from a tutor. Learning by doing can be coupled to discussing the screenful with fellow students. The additional interaction and feedback can enhance wanting to learn and consolidate the needing-to-learn agenda, and aid the making-sense process.

Table 5.1 *contd*

Questions which could be going through a student's mind	Links to the factors underpinning successful learning
What else should I be thinking about while this bit is on-screen? Should I be looking at printed resources as I go? Should I be looking at notes I am making as I go?	These questions can link to *all* **of the factors** underpinning successful learning, particularly digesting – making sense.
What else am I learning from this bit? What am I learning over and above what is on-screen at the moment? How important are these other things I am thinking about? Will they be assessed in some way and, if so, when, how and by whom? Will I get feedback on these other things I am thinking about?	These questions can link to all of the processes underpinning successful learning, particularly 'feedback' and 'digesting'. If the further agendas associated with the screenful are interesting, and seen as important, the 'wanting' and 'needing' to learn aspects are also enhanced.
What am I learning about myself? How is this bit helping me to develop as someone who can learn effectively and independently from a computer-based resource? How am I developing skills at managing my own learning?	Questions like these involve the **digesting – making sense** aspect of learning, as well as developing receptivity to feedback, and the ability to develop one's own motivation.
So what? If there have not been any good reasons for looking at the screenful after thinking through all of the questions above, is there any reason at all for it being there?	**Cut**! Or present the information in another way, such as on a handout, or in an accompanying manual. If the screenful is not addressing at least some of the questions listed above, it may as well be deleted from the on-screen agenda of the learning package.

with such parts, and perhaps better still to experiment with adapting existing resources covering such curriculum areas towards a resource-based learning format first. The following suggestions show that such starting-points can be based on several different considerations, and are often linked to ways in which resource-based learning can augment face-to-face college-based programmes.

- **Important background material.** In face-to-face programmes, a considerable amount of time is often spent near the start, getting everyone up to speed with essential knowledge or skills, to the annoyance of the students who already have these. Making such information the basis of a resource-based learning package can allow those people who need to cover this material before the whole group starts, to do so in their own time and at their own pace, without holding up the rest of the group.
- **'Need to know before…' material.** For example, when different students will be attempting different practical exercises at the same time, it could take far too long to cover all the prerequisite material with the whole group before introducing practical work. Designing separate short resource-based learning elements to pave the way to each practical exercise can allow these to be issued to students so that the practical work can be started much earlier.

- **Remedial material.** In many courses, there are problem topics which can hold up a whole class while the difficulties are addressed by lecturers or tutors. This can lead to time being wasted, particularly by those students for whom there are no problems with the parts concerned. The availability of resource-based learning packages addressing such areas can allow such packages to be used only by those students who need them, in their own time, so that the progress of the whole group is not impeded. Do not, of course, use a term as insulting as 'remedial' in the title of your package!

- **'Nice-to-know' material.** While 'need-to-know' material is more important, resource-based learning elements can be particularly useful for addressing 'nice-to-know' material, and giving such material to students without spending too much face-to-face time on it. This allows contact time to be saved for helping students with the really important material, and for addressing their problems.

- **Much-repeated material.** If you find yourself often covering the same ground, perhaps with different groups of students in different contexts or courses, it can be worth thinking about packaging up such material in resource-based learning formats. If you yourself get bored with things you often teach, you are not going to pass much enthusiasm for these topics on to your students, and it can be mutually beneficial to invest your energy into creating an alternative resource-based learning pathway to cover such material.

- **Material which is best learnt by doing.** Resource-based learning is based on students answering questions, and doing tasks and exercises. Therefore it can be a useful starting point for a resource-based learning package to base it on the sorts of activity that you may already be giving your face-to-face students. Standard assignments and activities already in use in traditionally-delivered courses and programmes may be adapted quite easily for resource-based learning usage, and have the strong benefit that they are already tried and tested elements of the curriculum.

- **Material where students need individual feedback on their progress.** A vital element of resource-based learning is the feedback that students receive when they have attempted to answer questions, or had a try at exercises and activities. The kinds of feedback that you may already give your face-to-face students can be packaged up into resource-based learning materials.

- **Material that you do not like to teach.** It can be tempting to turn such elements of the curriculum into resource-based learning materials, where students can work on them individually (or in untutored groups), and use face-to-face time more efficiently to address any problems that students find, rather than teach them from scratch.

- **Material that students find hard to grasp first time.** In most subjects there are such areas. Developing resource-based learning materials to address these means that students can go through them on their own, as many times as they need. Effectively, the resource-based learning material becomes their teacher.

Students can then work through such materials at their own pace, and can practise with the learning materials until they master them.

■ **Material which may be needed later, at short notice.** It is often the case that some topics are only really needed by students quite some time after they may have been covered in a course or programme. When such materials are turned into resource-based learning formats, students can polish up their grip on the topics involved just when they need to.

Students who are particularly helped

All sorts of people use resource-based learning in distance-learning mode. The following categories of students can be helped particularly in different ways. Many parallels can also be drawn to the use of resource-based learning elements in college-based programmes, where similar benefits can be delivered to a variety of constituencies of the student population.

■ **High fliers**. Very able students are often frustrated or bored by traditional class-based programmes, as the pace is normally made to suit the average student and may be much too slow for high fliers. With resource-based learning, they can speed through the parts they already know, or the topics they find easy and straightforward. They can work through a package concentrating only on the parts that are new to them, or which they find sufficiently challenging.

■ **Low fliers.** The least able students in a group are often disadvantaged when the pace of delivery of traditional programmes is too fast for them. They can be embarrassed in class situations by being seen not to know things, or not to be able to do tasks that their fellow students have no difficulty with. With resource-based learning, they can take their time, and practise until they have mastered things. They have the opportunity to spend much longer than other students may take.

■ **Anxious students.** Some people are easily embarrassed if they get things wrong, especially when they are seen to make mistakes. With resource-based learning, they have the opportunity to learn from making mistakes, in the comfort of privacy, as they try self-assessment questions and exercises, and learn from the feedback responses in an interactive learning package.

■ **Students with a particular block.** Students who have a particular problem with an important component of a course can benefit from resource-based learning, in that they can work as often as they wish through materials designed to give them practice in the topic concerned. It can be useful to incorporate self-assessment exercises, with detailed feedback specially included for those students who have problems with the topic.

■ **Students needing to make up an identified shortfall.** For example, in science and engineering programmes, it is often found quite suddenly that some students in a group have not got particular maths skills. Rather than hold up the progress of a whole class, self-study components can be issued to those students who need to get up to speed in the areas involved. When the students have a sense of ownership of the need that these materials will address, they make best use of the materials.

- **People learning in a second language.** In class situations, such students are disadvantaged in that they may be spending much of their energy simply making sense of the words, with little time left to make sense of the ideas and concepts. With resource-based learning materials, they can work through them at their own pace, with the aid of a dictionary, or with the help of students already fluent in the language in which the materials are written.

- **Part-time students.** These are often people with many competing pressures on their time, or with irregular opportunities for studying, perhaps due to shift work, work away from home, or uneven demands being normal in their jobs. Resource-based learning materials allow them to manage their studying effectively, and to make the most of those periods where they have more time to study.

- **People who do not like being taught.** Surprisingly, such people are found in college-based courses, but there are many more of these who would not consider going to an educational institution. Resource-based learning allows such people to have a much greater degree of autonomy and ownership of their studies.

- **Students who only want to do part of the whole.** Some students may only want to – or need to – achieve a few carefully-selected learning outcomes that are relevant to their work or even to their leisure activities. With a resource-based learning package, they are in a position to select those parts they want to study, whereas in face-to-face courses they may have to wait quite some time before the parts they are really interested in are covered.

- **Students with special needs.** For example, people with limited mobility may find it hard to get to the venue of a traditional course, but may have few problems when studying at home. Students with other problems may be able to work through resource-based learning materials with the aid of an appropriate helper or supporter. Open and flexible learning is increasingly being used to address the particular needs of diverse groups including carers, prisoners, mentally-ill people, religious groups and socially excluded people.

Writing new resource-based learning materials

The most difficult stage in starting out to design a learning resource can be working out a logical and efficient order in which to approach the separate tasks involved. These suggestions (overleaf) should help you to avoid wasting too much time, and particularly aim to help ensure that the work you do is directly related to composing learning material rather than writing out yet another textbook:

1 **Think again.** Before really getting started on designing resource-based learning materials, it is worth looking back, and asking yourself a few basic questions once more. These include:

- Am I the best person to write this material?
- Is there a materials production unit in my institution which can help me?
- Are there any experienced materials editors there whose expertise I can depend upon?
- Is there graphics design help and support?
- Is there already an institutional house style?
- Can someone else produce the resource-based learning materials, while I simply supply the raw material and notes on how I want it to work in flexible-learning mode?

If, after asking these questions, you decide to press ahead with designing your own materials, the following steps should save you some time and energy.

2 **Do not just start writing subject material.** A resource-based learning package is much more than just the subject matter it contains, and is something for students to *do* rather than just something to read.

3 **Get the feel of your target audience.** The better you know the sorts of people who will be using your resource-based learning material, the easier it is to write for them.

4 **Express your intended learning outcomes.** It is worth making a skeleton of the topics that your material will cover in the form of learning outcomes, at least in draft form, before writing anything else. Having established the learning outcomes, you are in a much better position to ensure that the content of your resource-based learning material will be developed in a coherent and logical order.

5 **Seek feedback on your draft learning outcomes.** Check that they are seen by colleagues to be at the right level for the material you are designing. In particular, check that they make sense to members of your target audience of students, and are clear and unambiguous to them.

6 **Design questions, tasks and activities, firmly based on your intended learning outcomes.** Some of the outcomes may require several tasks and activities to cover them. It is also useful to plan in draft form activities that will span two or three learning outcomes simultaneously, to help pave the way towards integrating your package and linking the outcomes to each other.

7 **Test your draft questions, tasks and activities.** These will in due course be the basis of the learning by doing in your package, and will set the scene for the feedback responses you will design. It is extremely useful to test these questions and tasks first, with anyone you can get to try them out, particularly students who may be close to your anticipated target

audience. Finding out their most common mistakes and difficulties paves the way towards the design of useful feedback responses, and helps you adjust the wording of the tasks to avoid ambiguity or confusion.

8 **Plan your feedback responses.** Decide how best you will let your students know how well, or how badly, they have done in their attempts at each of your tasks, activities and questions.

9 **Think ahead to assessment.** Work out which of the questions, tasks and activities you have designed will be self-sufficient as self-assessment exercises, where feedback responses can be provided to students in print in the learning package, or on-screen if you are designing a computer-based package. Work out which exercises need the skills of a tutor to respond to them, and will usefully become components of tutor-marked assignments.

10 **Map out your questions, tasks and activities into a logical sequence.** Along with the matching learning outcomes, this provides you with a strong skeleton on which to proceed to flesh out the content of your resource-based learning material.

11 **Work out your main headings and subheadings.** It is wise to base these firmly on the things that your students are going to be doing, reflecting the learning outcomes you have devised. This is much better than devising headings purely on the basis of the subjects and topics covered, or on the original syllabus you may have started out with.

12 **Write 'bridges'.** Most of these will lead from the feedback response you have written for one question, task or activity, into the next activity that your students will meet. Sometimes these bridges will need to provide new information to set the scene for the next activity. It is important to ensure that these bridges are as short and relevant as you can make them, and that they do not run off on tangents to the main agenda provided by the skeleton you have already made. This also ensures that you make your writing really efficient, and save your valuable time.

13 **Write the introductions last.** The best time to write any introduction is when you know exactly what you are introducing. It is much easier to lead in to the first question, task or activity when you know how it (and the feedback associated with it) fits in to the material as a whole, and you know how and why you have arranged the sequence of activities in the way you have already devised. Although you may need to write draft introductions when first putting together your package for piloting, it is really useful to revisit these after testing out how students get on with the activities and feedback responses, and to include in the final version of each intro-duction suggestions to students about how to approach the material that follows, based on what was learnt from piloting.

Choosing computer-based learning resources

Computer-based packages are widely used in teaching, and play a valuable part in resource-based learning programmes. There may well exist computer-based packages which will be helpful to your own students, and it could be more cost-effective to purchase these and adopt them as they stand (or adapt them) than to design new materials of your own. The following suggestions may provide you with help in selecting computer-aided learning packages for your students:

1 **Remember that it is harder to get a good idea of the effectiveness of computer-based materials than of paper-based ones.** This is not least because it is not possible to flick through the whole of a computer-based package in the same way as is possible with a printed package. It can be quite hard to get a feel for the overall shape of the learning that is intended to accompany a computer-based package.

2 **Choose your packages carefully.** The best computer-based learning packages are not always those which look most attractive, nor are they necessarily the most expensive ones. The best indicator of a good package is evidence that it causes learning to be successful. Where possible, try packages out on students before committing yourself to purchasing them. Alternatively, ask the supplier or manufacturer for details of clients who have already used the packages, and check that the packages really deliver what you need.

3 **Prepare your own checklist to interrogate computer-based materials.** Decide the questions that you need to ask about each possible package,

before committing yourself to purchase. Questions could include:

- Are the materials supplied with workbook elements?
- Do students themselves *need* these elements?
- Can support materials be freely photocopied?
- What is the standard of the equipment needed to run the packages effectively?
- What level of technical support and backup will be required?
- Does the software include individual student progress monitoring and tracking?
- Do the materials make good use of pre-test and post-test features?
- Can the materials run effectively on a network?
- Are there licensing implications if you wish to run the package on more than one machine?
- Can you afford multiple copies if the materials are multimedia, single-access packages?

4 **Try to establish the pedigree of the software.** Some computer-based packages have been thoroughly tested and developed, and have been updated and revised several times

since their launch. Such packages normally give some details of the history of their development. Beware of packages, however well presented, that have been published or disseminated without real trialling.

5 **Find out about packages from colleagues in other institutions.** Use your contacts. Ask them what packages they know of, which work well and really help students to learn. Also ask them about packages that they do not rate highly, and about the factors that led them to this conclusion.

6 **Try before you buy.** Computer-aided learning packages can be quite expensive, especially if you need to purchase a site licence to use them on a series of networked computer terminals, or to issue students with their own copies on floppy disk. If you are considering buying a particular package, try to get a sample of your students to evaluate it for you. Their experience of using it is even more valuable than your own, as only they can tell whether they are learning effectively from it.

7 **Look at how the medium is used to enhance learning.** If the material does no more than to present on glass what could have been presented equally well on paper, it is probably not worth investigating further. The medium should do something that helps learning, such as causing students to engage in interaction that they might have skipped if the same tasks or questions had been set in print.

8 **Get familiar with the package, before letting your students loose with it.** There is a learning curve to be ascended with most computer-based packages, and it is best if *you* go up this ahead of your students. They will need help on how to make best use of the package, as well as on what they are supposed to be learning from it. Find out what it feels like to use the package. By far the best way to do this is to work through the package yourself, even if you already know the subject that it covers. Find out what students will *do* as they use the package, and check whether the tasks and activities are really relevant to your students, and pitched at an appropriate level for them.

9 **Check the intended learning outcomes of the computer-based package.** The best packages state the intended learning outcomes clearly within the first few screens of information. The intended outcomes, and the level that the package is pitched at, should also be spelt out in supporting documentation which comes with the package. The main danger is that such packages address a wider range of intended outcomes than is needed by your students, and that students may become distracted and end up learning things that they do not need to learn, possibly interfering with their assessment performance.

10 **If necessary, rephrase the learning outcomes associated with the package.** It may be useful to tell your students exactly what the learning outcomes mean in the context of their particular studies. You may well need to redefine the standards associated with the outcomes.

11 **Think about access to equipment and software.** Some packages come with licence arrangements to use the package with a given number of students, either allowing multiple copies to be made, or the package to be used over a network. Ensure that the software is protected in order to prevent unauthorized copying, or unlicensed use on more than one machine.

12 **Think how students will retain important ideas from the package after they have used it.** Make sure that there is supporting documentation or workbook materials, as these will help students to summarize and remember the important things they gain while using computer-based packages. Where such resources do not already exist, you should consider the benefits of making a workbook or an interactive handout, so that students working through the package write down things (or record them) at important stages in their learning.

13 **Ensure that learning by doing is appropriate and relevant.** Most computer-based packages contain a considerable amount of learning by doing, particularly decision making, choosing options and entering responses to structured questions. Some of the tasks may not be entirely relevant to the intended learning outcomes of your programme, and you may need to devise briefing details to help students to see exactly what they should be taking seriously as they work through the package.

14 **Check that students will get adequate feedback on their work with the package.** Much of this feedback may already be built in to the package as it stands. However, you may need to think about further ways of keeping track of whether your students are getting what they should from their use of the package. It can be worth adding appropriate, short elements to tutor-marked assignments, so that there is a way of finding out whether particular students are missing vital things they should have picked up from the package.

15 **Check how long the package should take.** The time spent by students should be reflected in the learning payoff they derive from their studies with the package, and this in turn should relate to the proportion of the overall assessment framework that is linked to the topics covered by the package.

16 **Think ahead to assessment.** Work out what will be assessed that relates directly to the learning that is to be done using the computer-based materials. Express this as assessment criteria, and check how these link to the intended learning outcomes. Make sure that students, before working through the computer-

based materials, know *what* will be assessed, *when* it will be assessed, and *how* it will be assessed.

17 **Explore software that tracks students' progress.** This can involve pre-testing and post-testing, and storing the data on the computer system, as well as monitoring and recording the time taken by each student to work through each part of the package. Such data can be invaluable for discovering the main problems that students may be expe-riencing with the topic, and with the package itself.

18 **Seek feedback from your students.** Ask them what aspects of the package they found most valuable, and most important. Ask them also what, if anything, went wrong in their own work with the package. Where possible, find alternative ways of addressing important learning outcomes for those students who have particular problems with the computer-delivered materials.

The Internet: the greatest learning resource?

Students may be able to use the Internet at times of their own choice, in their own ways, at their own pace, and from anywhere that access to it is available to them. That said, it is not automatically a vehicle for productive and effective learning. Indeed, it is very easy to become side-tracked by all sorts of fascinating (or inappropriate!) things, and to stray well away from any intended learning outcome. The following suggestions may help you to help your students both to enjoy the Internet, *and* to learn well from it:

1 **Play with the Internet yourself.** You need to pick up your own experience of how it feels to tap into such a vast and varied database, before you can design ways of delivering with it some meaningful learning experi-ences to your students.

2 **Decide whether you want your students to use the Internet, or an Intranet.** An Intranet is where a networked set of computers talk to each other, while using Internet conventions, but where the content is not open to the rest of the universe. If you are working in an organization which already has such a network, and if your students can make use of this network effectively, there will be some purposes that will be better served by an Intranet. You can also have *controlled* access to the Internet via an Intranet, such as by using hot links to predetermined external sites.

3 **Use the Internet to research some-thing yourself.** You may, of course, have done this often already, but if not, give it a try before you think of setting your students 'search and retrieve' tasks with the Internet. Set yourself a fixed time, perhaps half an hour or even less. Choose a topic that you are going to search for, preferably something a little offbeat. See for yourself how best to use the search engines, and compare the relevance and efficiency of different engines.

Find out for yourself how to deal with 4,593 references to your chosen topic, and how to improve your searching strategy to whittle them down to the ten that you really want to use.

4 **Do not just use the Internet as a filing cabinet for your own teaching materials.** While it is useful in its own way if your students can have access to your own notes and resources, this is not really *using* the Internet. Too many materials designed for use in other forms are already cluttering up the Internet. If all you intend your students to do is to download your notes and print their own copies, sending them e-mailed attachments would do the same job much more efficiently.

5 **Think carefully about your intended learning outcomes.** You may indeed wish to use the Internet as a means whereby your students address the existing intended outcomes associated with their subject material. However, it is also worth considering whether you could add further outcomes, to do with the processes of searching, selecting, retrieving and analysing subject material. If so, you may also need to think about whether, and how, these additional outcomes may be assessed.

6 **Give your students specific things to do using the Internet.** Make these tasks where it is relevant to have up-to-the-minute data or news, rather than where the answers are already encapsulated in easily accessible books or resources.

7 **Consider giving your students a menu of tasks and activities.** They will feel more ownership if they have a significant degree of choice in their Internet tasks. Where you have a group of students working on the same syllabus, it can be worth letting them choose different tasks, and then communicating their main findings to each other (and to you) using a computer conference or by e-mail.

8 **Let your students know that the process is at least as important as the outcome.** The key skills that they can develop using the Internet include designing an effective search and making decisions about the quality and authenticity of the evidence they find. It is worth designing tasks where you already know of at least some of the evidence you expect them to locate, and remaining open to the fact that they will each uncover at least as much again as you already know about.

9 **Consider designing your own interactive pages.** You may want to restrict these to an Intranet, at least at first. You can then use dialogue boxes to cause your students to answer questions, enter data and so on. Putting such pages up for all to see on the Internet may mean that you get a lot of unsolicited replies.

10 **Consider getting your students to design and enter some pages.** This may be best done restricted to an Intranet, at least until your students have picked up sufficient skills to develop pages that are worth putting up for all to see. The act of designing their own Internet material is one of the most productive ways to help your students develop their critical skills at evaluating materials already on the Internet.

Helping students to learn from the Internet

The Internet is the electronic highway to the largest collection of information, data and communication ever constructed by the human species. Playing with the Internet is easy, but *learning* from it is not always straightforward. The following suggestions may help you to point your students in directions where they will not only enjoy playing with the Internet, but also develop their techniques so that they learn effectively from it too. Some of these suggestions may also help *you* to learn more from it:

1 **Consider starting small.** For example, you might be able to download selected information from the Internet onto individual computers, or a locally networked series of terminals. You can then give your students specific 'search' tasks, where it will be relatively easy for them to locate specific information.

2 **Get your students to induct each other.** Learning from the Internet need not be a solo activity. Indeed, it can be very useful to have two or three students working at each terminal, so that they talk to each other about what they are finding, and follow up leads together. Encourage them to take turns at working the keyboard, so that they all develop their confidence at handling the medium, and are then equipped to carry on working on their own.

3 **Give your students exercises that help them to improve their selection of search words.** Show them how choosing a single broad search word leads to far too many sources being listed, and makes it very slow and boring to go through all of the sources looking for the information they really want. Get them to experiment with different combinations of search words, so that the sources located become much more relevant to their search purposes.

4 **Allow your students to find out about the different speeds at which information can be found on the Internet.** For example, let them experiment at different times of the day, so they can see when the Internet is heavily used and slower. Also let them find out for themselves how much slower it can be waiting for graphics to be downloaded than for mainly-text materials. Help them to become better at deciding whether to persist with a source that is highly relevant but slow to download, or whether to continue searching for sources which may download more quickly.

5 **Remind your students that finding information is only the first step in learning from it.** It is easy to discover a wealth of information during an Internet search, only to forget most of it within a very short time. Encourage your students to download and edit the materials that

they think will be most relevant, or even to make conventional hand-written or word-processed notes of their own while they use the Internet.

6 **Help your students to learn to keep tabs on what they have found.** Entering 'bookmarks' or 'favourites' is one of the most efficient ways of being able to go back easily to what may have turned out to be the most relevant or valuable source of information during a search. Get your students to practise logging the sites that could turn out to be worth returning to. Also help them to practise clearing out bookmarks that turn out to be irrelevant, or that are superseded by later finds.

7 **Give your students practice at recording things they have found during searches.** It can be useful to design worksheets to train them to note down key items of information as they find it, and to train them to be better at making their own notes as a matter of routine when exploring a topic using the Internet.

8 **Consider getting your students to experiment with a learning log.** This can be done for a few hours of work with the Internet, and then looked back upon for clues about which tactics proved most successful. It can be even better to get students to compare notes about what worked well for them, and where the glitches were.

9 **Help your students to develop their critical skills.** For example, set them a task involving their reviewing several sources they find on the Internet, and making decisions about the authenticity and validity of the information that they locate. Remind them that it is not possible to tell whether information is good or bad just by looking at the apparent quality of it on the screen. Remind your students that information on the Internet may not have been subjected to refereeing or other quality-assurance processes normally associated with published information in books or journal articles.

10 **Remind students to balance playing with the Internet and learning from it.** It is perfectly natural and healthy to explore, and to follow up interesting leads, even when they take students far away from the purpose of their searches. However, it is useful to develop the skills to ration the amount of random exploration, and to devote 'spurts' of conscious activity to following through the specific purposes of searches.

6: Looking after yourself

Intended outcomes of this chapter

When you have dipped into the suggestions offered in this chapter, I hope you will feel able to take more control of – or to *manage* more successfully – some of the following aspects of your overall life in higher education:

- workload management;
- stress management;
- working well with academic colleagues;
- managing your meetings;
- building your teaching portfolio;
- preparing for appraisal;
- putting together your application for Membership of the Institute for Learning and Teaching (if you work in the UK, and have three or more years experience of teaching in higher education);
- managing your feedback from students.

While other chapters in this toolkit have been directly or indirectly about looking after your students, most of this one is about ensuring that *you* survive! I am only too aware of the levels of stress that are experienced by many lecturers, owing to all manner of causes, many of which are beyond their control, and I hope that the suggestions in this chapter will contain something for everyone, and help to reduce – or at least enable you to *manage* – some of the causes and effects of stress. That is why all the sections in this chapter are entitled 'Managing your…'

The first part of the chapter offers selected practical suggestions on a wide range of administrative, personal and interpersonal aspects of surviving in higher education today. The remainder of the chapter offers more detailed discussion of four dimensions of higher education in the UK in particular, which may well impact on your own work: appraisal, subject review, professional accreditation and gathering feedback from students. I continue with a fairly detailed discussion about appraisal – how to prepare for it, and how to approach getting the most from it. Next, I discuss external quality assurance, and in particular the 'subject review' presently operated by the Quality Assurance Agency for Higher Education (QAA) in the UK. The chapter continues with some suggestions for UK higher education readers with three or more years of teaching experience in higher education, about how – if you wish – you can put together your application for Membership of the Institute for Learning and Teaching in Higher Education (ILT), on the 'experienced staff' route (often called 'fast-track' route) to membership, which is available at the time of writing this edition of the toolkit. Finally, I have included a range of suggestions about how you may go about getting feedback from your students, and analysing it to your (and their) advantage.

Managing your workload

Heavier workloads have become a fact of life for most lecturers. It seems highly unlikely that this situation will change. Managing your workload may increasingly seem like a balancing act between teaching, research and administration. I hope the following suggestions will help you to adjust your balance if necessary:

1 **Do not waste energy on trying to turn the clock back.** What some people affectionately refer to as 'the good old days' are very unlikely to return. One danger is that we spend so much time talking about how much better things once were, that we put even more pressure on the time and energy we have to face today and plan for tomorrow.

2 **Prioritize your own workload.** It is useful to go through all the tasks and roles that you undertake, asking yourself which are the *really* important ones, and which are the ones that would not have significant effects on your students if you were to prune them or abandon them.

3 **Cut your assessment workload.** This does not mean reduce the quality of your assessment. It is widely recognized that over-assessment is bad for students, and in former times it was all too easy for such patterns of over-assessment to be established. Now may be the time to think again about how much assessment your students really

need, and to improve the quality of this, but at the same time significantly reduce its volume.

4 **Look for more efficient ways of giving feedback to your students.** Many colleagues find that e-mailed feedback communications end up saving a lot of time, particularly when you can develop your own electronic bank of 'frequently needed responses' and paste them in as needed in individual e-mails.

5 **Make good use of learning resource materials.** Students nowadays learn a great deal more from computer-based and print-based materials than once was the case. The quality of learning resource materials is improving all the time, and such materials are getting steadily better at giving students opportunities to learn by doing, and to learn from healthy trial and error. Materials are getting much better at providing students with feedback on their individual progress and performance. Making the most of such materials can free up valuable face-to-face

time with students, so you can deal with their questions and problems rather than merely impart information to them.

6 **Make good use of your administrative and support staff.** It is easy for us to find ourselves doing tasks which they could have done just as well, and often they could have done them more efficiently than ourselves.

7 **Make better use of feedback from students.** Listen to their concerns, and focus on them, making your own work more useful to them at the same time. They know better than anyone else where their problems lie, so it is worth making sure that your valuable time is spent addressing the right problems.

8 **Do not carry your entire workload in your mind.** We can only do one thing at a time, so when doing important work such as teaching and assessing students, do not get side-tracked into worrying about the numerous other tasks jostling for your attention.

Managing your stress levels

The lecturer's job can be extremely stressful as staff are put under increasing pressure to teach longer hours and in possibly unfamiliar ways, and to spend longer hours on assessment and record-keeping as well as research. At the same time, students are becoming more diverse and have an ever-widening range of requirements and expectations. An increasing proportion of staff in higher education are becoming physically ill as a result of stress. There may indeed be very little you can do about many of the causes of stress, but you could be surprised at how much it is possible for us to adapt our responses to stressors. These tips cannot eliminate your stress, but may suggest some strategies to help you deal with it:

1 **Get better at recognizing the physical signs of stress.** These include raised heart rate, increased sweating, headaches, dizziness, blurred vision, aching neck and shoulders, skin rashes and lowered resistance to infection. When people are aware that such symptoms may be caused by stress, it helps them to look to their approaches to work to see if the causes may arise from stress.

2 **Get better at recognizing the behavioural effects of stress.** These include increased anxiety, irritability, increased consumption of tobacco or alcohol, sleep disturbance, lack of concentration and inability to deal calmly and efficiently with everyday tasks and situations.

3 **Increase awareness of how the human body reacts to stress.** Essentially this happens in three distinct stages. The 'alarm reaction'

stage causes defences to be set up and increased release of adrenalin. The 'resistance' stage is when the body will resist the stressor, or adapt to the stress conditions. The 'exhaustion' stage results when attempts by the body to adapt have failed, and the body succumbs to the effects of stress.

4 **Do not ignore stress.** There are no prizes for struggling to the point of collapse: indeed, this is the last thing you should be doing. As the symptoms of stress become apparent to you, try to identify the causes of your stress and do something about them.

5 **Get over the myths surrounding stress.** Research has shown that stress should not be regarded as being the same as nervous tension, and is not always a negative response, and that some people do indeed survive well and thrive on stress. In an education organization, it is more important to manage stress than to try to eliminate it.

6 **Look to the environmental causes of stress.** These include working or living under extremes of temperature, excessive noise, unsuitable lighting, poor ventilation or air quality, poorly laid-out work areas and even the presence of vibration. In your own institution, finding out what people think of such environmental conditions is a good first step towards adjusting them.

7 **Look to the social causes of stress.** These can include insufficient social contact at work, sexual harassment, racial discrimination, ageism, inappropriate management approaches, unhealthy levels of competition, and conflict between colleagues. Any or all of these, when present, can be discovered and identified by asking people about them.

8 **Look to the organizational causes of stress.** These include inappropriately heavy workloads, ineffective communication, excessive supervision or inadequate supervision, lack of relevant training provision, undue concern about promotion or reward systems and unsatisfactory role perceptions. Once identified, all of these causes can be remedied.

9 **Cultivate the right to feel stress, and to talk about it.** Stress is at its worst when it is bottled up and unresolved. It should be regarded as perfectly natural for people's stress levels to vary in the normal course of their work. When stress is something that can be discussed, it is much more likely that the causes will be addressed. Talk about your problems. Actually voicing what is stressing you to a colleague, a line manager, the person you are closest to or even your cat can sometimes improve the situation. Bottling it all up through a misplaced sense of fortitude can be dangerous.

10 **Do not be afraid to go to the doctor.** The worst excesses of stress can be helped by short-term medication and medical intervention of some kind. People are often unwilling to resort to a visit to their GP for

matters of stress when they would not hesitate to seek help for a physical ailment. Do not let such feelings get in the way of finding the kind of support you need.

11 **Take a break.** Often our panics over time management are caused not so much by how much we have to do, as whether we feel we have sufficient time to do it in. Try to take a real break from time to time, so as to help you get your workload into proportion. A little holiday or a whole weekend without college work occasionally can make you better able to cope with the onslaught on your return.

12 **Overcome powerlessness with action.** When you are stressed out, it is often because you feel totally powerless in the situation. It can be useful to look at the areas you do have some control over and try to do something about them, however minor. This may not change the overall picture very much, but will probably make you feel better.

13 **Try counselling.** Many colleges have someone to whom staff can turn for trained counselling in times of great stress. Otherwise you could look elsewhere through your GP or in the phone book under 'therapeutic practice' or 'alternative medicine' to find someone who can guide and support you through the worst patches. This is often more productive than piling all your stress onto your nearest and dearest who usually have problems of their own!

14 **Try not to personalize a situation into hatred and blame.** It is easy to fall into the trap of seeing all your stress as being caused by an individual or group of people who have it in for you. Of course it may be the case, but usually high stress situations are caused by cock-up rather than conspiracy.

15 **Avoid compounding the problem.** If things are pretty stressful at work, try to avoid making important life changes at the same time, such as moving to a larger house or starting a family, if these can be deferred for a while.

16 **Try to adopt a long-term perspective.** It can be really hard to project into the future and to review current stress as part of a much larger pattern, but if you can do it, it helps. Much of what seems really important now will pale into insignificance in a few weeks, months or years.

Managing your colleagues

Working in an educational institution can be really miserable if the people around you are not supportive and helpful. Try to start by ensuring that the people around you find *you* a helpful and supportive colleague, and you may be delighted at how the condition can spread (see overleaf):

1   **Help out when the going gets tough.** If someone in your team is struggling, it makes a big difference if you are prepared to roll up your sleeves and lend a hand, whether it is in collating marks, stuffing envelopes or preparing for an important event. With luck they will reciprocate when you are having a tough time too.

2   **Do not spring surprises on colleagues unnecessarily.** If you know you are going to be away for an extended period, or if you cannot fulfil your obligations, try to give as much advance notice as possible. This will enable colleagues who have to fill in gaps for you to build it into their own schedules.

3   **Keep to deadlines, especially when they impact on others.** If you are late doing your own marking, for example, or in putting together your section of a report, it will often affect others whose own time management will be thrown out of kilter. Try as far as humanly possible to do what you have said you will within the time available.

4   **Keep track of what your colleagues really appreciate in what you do.** Try to do more of these things whenever you can. It can also be worth working out what a 'terrible colleague' might be like, maybe by making a word-picture of a hypothetical case, and avoiding doing the sorts of things that may be brought to mind by such a picture.

5   **Find out how colleagues feel.** Do not just wait for them to tell you how they feel, and do not keep informal conversations to work-based topics. 'How are you feeling today?' or 'What's on top for you just now?' can be open-ended questions which allow colleagues to share with you things that are important to them at the time, but which would just not have arisen in normal work-oriented discussions.

6   **Be considerate when sharing an office.** Often staff workrooms are extremely cramped for space, and colleagues who leave papers all over a shared desk and who hog all available storage space make life difficult for others. Do not leave dirty cups around, clear up your own mess and be thoughtful about noise. If students need to be seen privately, try to agree times when fellow tutors can have uninterrupted use of the space.

7   **Be punctual for meetings.** Everyone slips sometimes, for very good reasons, but as a rule, try to ensure you are always spot on time for meetings, so other people are not kept waiting for you while you make a last-minute phone call or a cup of tea.

8   **Keep colleagues informed about what you are doing.** People need to know what you are up to when this impacts on their work. If, for example, you know you will be filling the office with a lot of bulky portfolios to mark, it might be a good idea to tell colleagues before they fall over the boxes coming into the room. Tell them also when you will have visitors, when you will be away and

when you expect to have a lot of students visiting you.

9 **Be gracious when rooms are double-booked.** This inevitably happens from time to time and can be the cause of much disagreement. Colleagues with two or more groups of students needing to use the same room should tackle the problem together, rather than having a slanging match over who booked the room first. It makes sense for the group in situ or the largest group to occupy the available room with their tutor, while the other group is asked to wait somewhere like the refectory or quietly in the corridor until another room is found.

10 **Leave teaching spaces as you found them (or better!).** If you move furniture or use the walls for display, try to leave the room fit for use by others when you leave. Encourage students to clear their own litter and leave the space tidy.

Managing your meetings

Many lecturers find that meetings become the bane of their lives, and seriously erode the time available for research and teaching. Committee work and meetings can take many different forms, ranging from course boards and exam boards to a host of other kinds of meeting. Most of the suggestions below are aimed at colleagues who are relatively new to participation in committee work, and who may find their first experiences of such work daunting, impenetrable, frustrating or confusing:

1 **Decide whether you are sure you need to attend.** Life is too busy to attend irrelevant meetings. If you find that you do not participate at a meeting, you probably should not have gone to it.

2 **If chairing the meeting, ensure that the agenda has timings on it.** People need to be able to plan when to start the next thing they will do after your meeting, so a realistic finishing time should be worked out and published. Also, separate agenda items should be timed appropriately, so that all can be discussed adequately and fairly in the time available, and so that it can be clear to everyone when the time available for a particular item is about to be used up.

3 **Take the right paperwork with you.** It is also useful to find time before the meeting to read the paperwork – or at least to scan it – highlighting points where you may wish to make a contribution, and jotting down keywords which will help you to remember what you want to say.

4 **File your papers appropriately.** It helps you to keep on top of the paperwork and enables you to find what you need for the next meeting without stress.

5 **Read the last set(s) of minutes.** This is especially important if you are new to a group, as it helps you to get a feel for what is going on. It also helps you to feel clued-up, even if you have met the group several times before.

6 **Try to provide documentation in advance of the meeting.** Do this for key issues you wish to raise. What you have to say is likely to be taken more seriously if it is available on paper. It also means that there is less chance of your points being left until 'any other business' when they are more likely to be ignored.

7 **Make supporting papers short, precise and readable.** Try making an A4 summary if the information is detailed or contains support data or statistical information. List action points. It helps considerably if it is clear at the meeting exactly what decisions are intended to be taken, and spelling these out boldly and concisely in committee papers can help to ensure that these decisions are addressed.

8 **Work out who is at the meeting, and make yourself a seating diagram so that you know who is saying what.** When names are not displayed on the table already, and if you are new to a committee, it can help you to pick up the threads of the different contexts and positions of contributors. Having people's names helps you to put names to faces in the future, and to connect what you have already heard about people to their behaviour and interests as seen at the meeting.

9 **Carefully note any action points down to you, and act on them.** You can wait to see the minutes to check what exactly your action points are, but make sure that you can be seen to have taken action before the next meeting. If you are unsure what you are expected to do, or do not think it will be feasible, make sure that you speak about it at the time during the meeting, or approach the chair as soon as you see what the minutes have listed for you to do.

10 **Jot down your own notes at the meeting.** The minutes of a meeting may be minimal and focused on decisions rather than discussions, and may not cover all the detail that you need to remember.

11 **Watch out for hidden agendas.** An astute meetings-watcher may be able to discern all kinds of hidden currents and covert politics which may influence outcomes more significantly than the actual contributions to the meeting. You may need to keep your eyes and ears open, particularly for subtle nuances.

12 **Do not let conflict in meetings rattle you.** Often you will find that postures are adopted and sabres are rattled, while the participants themselves often emerge from the meeting seemingly as the best of friends. Remember that behaviour in meetings can often be strategic and theatrical.

13 **If a meeting is irrelevant to you, consider leaving.** There is little point; storming out, simply slip

away quietly and with minimum disruption at a natural pause, so long as the conventions of the context do not make this seem hopelessly discourteous.

14 **Consider attending only parts of a meeting.** This is especially possible when there is timed business, and you can judge when to arrive and depart from the meeting according to when the items you need to attend for are timed. However, it is a fair assumption to expect most timed business to overrun.

15 **If you are asked to do the minutes of a meeting, or to chair a meeting,** **find out how to do it well.** The difference between a good minute-taker or chair and a poor one is often about whether the people involved understand their roles and have had relevant training on how best to approach the role.

16 **Take all your relevant paperwork with you.** You are likely to need class lists, for example, at exam boards, together with exam regulations, papers, copies of coursework mark schemes and so on. Do not be embarrassed by having insufficient material to answer searching questions.

Managing your teaching portfolio

A teaching portfolio is one of the most successful ways of demonstrating the quality and range of your teaching. If you are a new lecturer doing a staff development programme as part of your conditions of appointment, you may be required to build a teaching portfolio as part of the evidence required for (for example) a Postgraduate Certificate Academic Practice. Building one could be regarded as the start of something to continue throughout your university career. It can also provide a useful compendium of information to have available for a variety of occasions, including appraisal, formal 'subject review' inspections, and applications for promotion or for posts elsewhere. Having a well-filed collection of evidence of the quality of your teaching is a good start towards assembling your actual teaching portfolio. The danger is that putting it all together seems like an enormous task, and tends not to get started. The following suggestions should help you go about building up a representative portfolio of your work (see overleaf):

1 **Remind yourself *why* you want to build a teaching portfolio**. It is best that you *want* to build one, rather than simply that you are required to build one by your institution's staff development programme.

2 **Check carefully any specific format suggested for your teaching portfolio.** It helps to keep it firmly in mind both while collecting evidence, and when annotating it with your own reflective commentaries.

3 **If your portfolio will be assessed, keep the assessment framework in sight.** While you can put anything *else* that you think is relevant into your portfolio if you want to, you *need* to include evidence which relates to the assessment framework.

4 **Decide what sorts of evidence you will need.** The exact nature of your own evidence will depend upon the kinds of work you do with students in your job. Make a list of the main things that you do in your job, and alongside each of these write down a few words about the sort of evidence you could collect to prove that you do it well.

5 **Start collecting evidence straight away.** Much of the content of your teaching portfolio will come from your everyday work with students. The most efficient way of starting off a teaching portfolio is to start collecting examples of this evidence as a normal part of your everyday work.

6 **Collect evidence of your curriculum design work.** This can include examples of a syllabus area you have planned, intended learning outcomes or objectives you have formulated or adapted, and plans for how you structure your delivery of a syllabus area. You can also include changes you make to existing programmes, with your rationale and justification for such changes.

7 **Collect evidence of your teaching itself.** This can include examples of lesson plans, course plans, and examples (not too many!) of the materials that you use in your teaching, such as handout materials, overhead transparencies and other learning resources that you devise or adapt.

8 **Make sure that you have enough evidence of peer feedback.** Make good use of any observation checklists you are provided with. You can also include examples of video recordings of actual teaching sessions, ranging through large-group lectures, small-group sessions and one-to-one encounters with students. Remember to be highly selective. A good teaching portfolio includes many *kinds* of evidence, but only a few examples of each kind.

9 **Collect evidence of student feedback on your teaching.** This can include examples of feedback questionnaires completed by students, along with your own analysis of the overall findings from the feedback. Include in your portfolio reflective comments about changes that you have made, or will make, as a result of feedback from students.

10 **Collect evidence of your assessment work.** This can include examples of tests and exercises that you set students, and a breakdown of how each test performed in practice. It is useful to link the content of each of the tests and exercises to the intended learning outcomes as expressed in the syllabus areas within which you are working.

11 **Collect evidence of your feedback *to* students**. This can include photocopies of typical assessed work, showing how you give students feedback on their written work. You can also include assignment return sheets that you have devised, copies of e-mails you send to students, and an account of other ways in which you ensure that students receive feedback on their progress and performance.

12 **Collect evidence of your collegiality.** Such evidence can arise from your participation in course teams, committees and assessment boards. You can also include evidence relating to work you undertake jointly with other staff, showing how well you can work with colleagues.

13 **File your evidence systematically.** Do not put it all in a file or a drawer. Sort it first, according to the particular sections of your portfolio that the evidence will go into. It is worth starting up a number of parallel files, to make sure you make it easy to decide where each element of your evidence should be stored.

14 **Decide on the physical form of your portfolio.** For example, you may decide to use a ring binder for your main evidence (your reflections, peer-observation details, and other important evidence) and lever-arch file for your appendices (examples of handouts, overheads, assessment tasks, feedback to students and so on). Such formats make it much easier to adjust the contents of your portfolio, or to rearrange the order in which you present sections. They also allow you to use punched, plastic wallets to collect together samples of papers such as feedback questionnaires and marked student work.

15 **Do not use plastic wallets for things which need to be easy to read (or assess).** While it is fine to use such wallets to keep together sets of similar papers in appendices (such as handouts, overheads and questionnaire responses), it is very frustrating for a reader (or assessor) to have to take out individual primary evidence sheets to read them.

16 **Make a draft index.** Decide in which order you wish to present evidence of the quality of your teaching. There is no 'right' order for headings and subheadings, even when the overall structure of the sections of the portfolio is laid down. The order of your headings and subheadings will depend on the nature of your work, and the range of evidence you wish to present for the quality of your work. It is, however, very useful to have this order sorted out in your

mind before you start to put together the 'front-end' of your portfolio, in other words, your reflections and commentaries *about* your evidence.

17 **Think of your target audience.** Who is going to read your portfolio? More importantly, who will perhaps make judgements on it? The people who are most likely to look at it in detail are those whose responsibility includes teaching quality and appraisal.

18 **Do not write the introduction too soon.** The introduction to a portfolio is extremely important. There is no second chance to make a good first impression. You can only write a really good introduction when you know exactly what you are introducing, so leave the introduction till you have more or less finished everything else in your portfolio. You can, of course, write a *draft* introduction, but this is probably best as a bullet-point list, or a mind-map sketch.

19 **Get other people to give you feedback about your portfolio.** Another pair of eyes is always useful. Show bits of your portfolio to your mentor, colleagues, friends and even contacts in your field in other institutions if you can. Ask them to scribble liberally over anything where it could be worth your having second thoughts, or giving further explanations. Ask them also not to hesitate in pointing out typographical or grammatical errors: it is always easier for someone else to find them than for us to spot our own.

Managing your appraisal

Most universities and colleges in the UK have in place appraisal programmes that link directly into the overall mission of the institution, the local plans of the school or department, and the needs of each individual. For people who have never been appraised, the process may seem intrusive and threatening. Yet other people may look forward to appraisal as an opportunity to get some feedback on how they are doing. Many people coming into universities, especially from industry, may have very negative experiences of appraisal, which in some contexts is used very much as a management tool to control staff.

How appraisal is organized

Often the person chosen to appraise you will be your nearest line manger. Ideally it will be someone who knows your work and the context you work in, and is also in a position to make decisions and act on the agreements you make within the performance review process. In some universities, it is possible for you to choose your own appraiser; in others you are allocated an appraiser and it is then not normally possible for you to reject the institution's choice. As far as possible, many institutions try to respect specific requests for you to be appraised by someone of the same gender or ethnic group as yourself, but this is not always feasible or seen to be desirable. Often there is a pre-appraisal meeting lasting 10 to 15 minutes in which appraiser and appraisee have the chance to set the agenda for the actual appraisal, which then allows time for the appraisee to think about the desired focus of the meeting and to prepare some pre-appraisal documentation.

The sorts of questions you may be asked

Many universities have a standard pro forma which can be used in preparing for appraisal. Questions could include:

- What areas of your work do you feel you can associate with a sense of achievement?
- What evidence can you supply to demonstrate your achievements (such as student evaluations, comments from peer observations or reports from external assessors)?
- Which activities and goals that you had planned to undertake have fallen by the wayside?
- What are the particular reasons for these unfulfilled aims?
- What support have you received from your line manager and other colleagues during the period under review?

You are also likely to be asked to look forward to the next year and identify:
- your provisional goals for the next 12 months;
- your developmental needs over this period;
- any training or special support you are likely to require to enable you to fulfil your plans;
- what might interfere with your plans to achieve, and what strategies you can adopt to prevent this happening.

If no appraisal pro formas are supplied, it is still a good idea for the appraisee to prepare a short report under these headings to provide areas for discussion.

Your appraisal interview

During your appraisal you should try to review as honestly as you can how well you feel you are doing and where you need to develop. You should not try to sweep your problems away under the carpet, nor should you be afraid to blow your own trumpet about the things of which you have a right to be proud. At the end of the interview, the appraiser should draw the process to a close by summarizing briefly what has been said, then should guide you towards drawing up a set of realistic, specific and measurable goals for the next year, with timescales attached and recognition of the training, support and resources that are likely to be needed to help you to achieve them. If your appraiser does not do this for you, then you will need to make sure that you do it anyway.

In many institutions it is normal for a report to be written on the appraisal meeting. Often, this is written by the appraisee and then signed with or without comments by the appraiser. After the appraisal interview, the appraisal report will then provide a useful reference document for the work of the year to come. There is also normally a system in place by which training needs identified during the process are fed into an institution-wide staff development programme.

General suggestions on preparing for your appraisal

Appraisal can be a strong positive power for the good when it is used developmentally to ensure that individuals and groups review their own achievements, set realistic goals for the future and think about how what they are doing fits into their whole institutional programme. The following tips aim to guide you away from allowing appraisal to become merely a tiresome formality, and towards it being an active and dynamic means of coordinating your work and getting the best from yourself and the institution:

1 **Prepare thoughtfully for your review.** Try to ensure that you have a clear idea prior to the review of the areas you aim to focus on. After all, it is your appraisal and it is up to you to get the most you can out of the occasion. If you skimp on the preparation, your appraiser may well take cues from you and also take the process less seriously than it deserves.

2 **Try to see both sides of the process.** If you are preparing for review, think about how it feels to be in your position, so that you can help your appraiser to make the process positively developmental. See the appraiser as a guide and support for your process of self-review, rather than as an interrogator who is trying to catch you out.

3 **Collect evidence of achievement.** Bring to the review, or make a list of, concrete examples of outcomes that you have achieved, so that any successes or progress you claim can be backed up with examples. For example, you might bring along student feedback data; print-outs of your students' achievements; examples of your effective organizational and administrative skills; and letters and memos from internal and external colleagues who have acknowledged your efforts. You can

also tell your reviewer about examples of your dealing with problems; your contributions to strategic decisions; your promotion of the effective work and reputation of your college. You might like to collect these in a loose-leaf folder, with material easily referenced so you can refer to specific elements within the appraisal without too much difficulty in finding them.

4 **Regard the review as an opportunity.** Make it an occasion where you can raise all the important issues you have not had time to discuss earlier. Have a mental shopping list of training you would like agreement that you can undertake, or aspects of your job description that you would like to develop further. You may be able to negotiate time or resources for professional training of various kinds. You might wish to gain approval for your participation in local or national activities relevant to your work. Remember that professional development need not involve high expenditure. Opportunities exist for you to undertake personal development through work-shadowing, self-instruction and the use of staff development resource materials without large outlays of cash.

5 **Review your own performance objectively.** Do not over-claim success, or downgrade your own achievements. Try to analyse what has gone well, and why, as well as what has been less successful, and why. In your preparation, ask colleagues who are not involved in your appraisal to help you evaluate realistically how you are doing. Ask them to help you remember the good parts that might have slipped your memory, as well as to give you dispassionate accounts of the perhaps traumatic occurrences that you regard as having gone badly.

6 **Do not be artificially modest.** Without being boastful, you can use appraisal as an opportunity to celebrate the things of which you are proud. Often people are not fully aware of what individuals have done, and how much of a cooperative activity has in fact been the responsibility of one person. It is amazing how often an appraiser will say, 'I never realized that you are involved in so many areas.'

7 **Be realistic about your part in areas that have not been successes.** There is no need to shoulder all the blame, but the performance review is a chance to analyse how much responsibility you bear for the projects that have not succeeded, or for the deadlines that have been missed. This is the time for you to learn from the mistakes of the past and look forward to the next era. Avoid seeing your review as raking over old ground or digging up past errors and mistakes. Use it as a chance to reflect and to learn from what went wrong or did not work. Do not use this part of your review to criticize other colleagues or dwell on things over which you (or your manager) have little control (particularly a lack of resources).

8 **Write your own private reflective log after your appraisal.** Even if you have already produced a more formal report for your appraiser to sign off as part of the appraisal process, it can be helpful to have a more personal record of your own to refer back to. This can include how you felt when discussing your successes or failures, and notes to yourself about how you will go about following up your commitments arising from the review.

9 **Remember that it is *your* review.** Do not allow it to become a one-way process, with your reviewer doing most of the talking. Use it as a proactive opportunity to affect your own working life. See your review as the most appropriate occasion to renegotiate your job description and make it more interesting or rewarding. If you regard the staff review process as a tokenistic activity in which your manager is simply going through the motions, then that is what it is likely to become.

10 **Use a part of your review to discuss institution-wide issues that concern you.** These might include equal opportunity matters, health and safety issues, or your concerns about teaching, learning and assessment. The review process provides a rare chance for you to have the undi-

vided attention of your line manager.

11 **Try to think of appraisal as a process and not an event.** Do not regard the date of your appraisal interview as the be-all and end-all of appraisal. It may be quite a crucial date, but it is only a milestone on a continuing journey.

12 **Finish the review with an agreement as to what will happen next.** Normally this will involve a confidential written record of the review, together with an agreed action plan which includes deadlines and responsibilities for both you and your line manager. Make sure that you know who is doing what before the end of the meeting. Make notes in your diary so you can follow up agreed actions in due course. Contact your reviewer if you do not feel an agreed activity has actually been set in train or had any outcome.

13 **Review the review process.** If you feel that you have been short-changed by your reviewer because you felt rushed, not listened to, or not taken seriously, say so and do not countersign the formal record of the review or action plan. If you are happy with the way things have been done, make this clear too so that your reviewer in turn can use your satisfaction as evidence in his or her own review.

Managing your subject review

Quality assurance has different names and different processes in different countries. In higher education in the UK the process is currently called 'subject review'. It uses a peer-review system based on a self-assessment document (SAD) in which the subject team identify the aims and objectives against which their provision will be judged under six key headings:

- curriculum design, content and organization;
- teaching, learning and assessment;
- student support and guidance;
- student progression and achievement;
- learning resources;
- quality management and enhancement.

In the UK the system is being developed further into a broader, somewhat 'lighter-touch' version, with 'academic reviewers' undertaking much of what is presently being done by 'subject reviewers' on behalf of the Quality Assurance Agency for Higher Education (QAA). At the time of writing this edition, the new methodology is being piloted in Scotland.

In further education in the UK a comparable system is used, again making use of self-assessment and peer-review. There are many elements of common ground between the different external scrutiny systems, and the processes that can be used to maximize the chance that such reviews will produce successful outcomes. The sections which follow give some practical suggestions based on UK experience, to help prepare for quality reviews of various kinds, the self-assessment process (upon which the quality review will be strongly based), and offer some tips for ensuring that quality is evident during the review visit:

Preparing for quality visits

1 **Recognize the importance of making sufficient time available for preparation.** It is all too easy to be so busy with everyday matters that it is tempting to take the attitude 'They'll just have to take us as they find us'. Sound preparation pays dividends in terms of both staff confidence and good outcomes.

2 **Prepare well in advance.** It is never too early to start. As soon as you get advance warning of your dates, devise a strategy and action plans, working out target dates for each major task, and spreading responsibilities in ways that help to ensure that staff take on ownership of the processes.

3 **Do not grumble about 'waste of time'.** Try instead to see review as a chance to overhaul your teaching programmes. While it is natural (and often justified) to complain about valuable time being taken away from teaching and research, both could be damaged even more by the effects of quality being found to be lacking. Various studies on QAA review have emphasized the long-term benefits that have accrued to involvement in a process that foregrounds teaching, learning and assessment.

4 **Regard review as an ongoing process, not a one-off event.** When the sorts of action that are involved in preparing for quality visits are not special, but are part of the normal day-to-day life of an institution, the distance between 'where you are' and 'where you want to be seen to have reached' is narrowed continuously, and the anxiety that can be caused by an impending spotlight is reduced.

5 **Work from the outset at making the statistical information as accurate as possible.** In most institutions, you will not just be able to rely on centrally-collected data, which is rarely completely accurate at a local level. Use standard procedures to provide statistical information where these exist, but check and double-check these against staff perceptions. Remember too that it is normally possible to provide statistical updates close to the visit, so you can present the most accurate picture possible based on live data.

6 **Think about how best to present your statistical information.** UK systems with tight word counts and restrictions on available pages mean that statistics need to be accurate, self-explanatory and well presented. Flow diagrams and charts can be used to represent student progression data, for example, more effectively than mere description.

7 **Promote peer observation and review well in advance of the visit.** Teaching staff may feel very apprehensive about being observed teaching, and may need practice if they are to be confident under external scrutiny. Set up support groups and encourage discussion of the advantages of peer observation. Instituting peer-observation cells can be really beneficial, particularly if staff involved are trained to make it part of routine enhancement activities, not something just set up prior to the visit.

8 **Make full use of people with experience of your kind of external review.** In large universities and colleges, there are likely to be colleagues who have been involved in previous subject reviews, or who are trained assessors with experience of review elsewhere. They are far too valuable to waste and can be co-opted to comment on draft self-assessment documents, take part in staff briefing sessions and to help run rehearsals, all aimed at helping teams present themselves in the best possible light.

9 **Nominate your own staff to be involved in the review process nationally.** Many have reported that

subject groups which have the benefit of having trained assessors among their number tend to have a better understanding of the process and to do better than those in which staff stand aloof from the process. It is a good idea to get insider knowledge by participation.

10 **Avoid complacency based on past success.** Even if past reviews in your subject or institution have resulted in very positive outcomes, the next round will almost certainly involve different people, and a new process, since the way in which review is undertaken is being modified continuously.

11 **Avoid despair based on previous failures.** Even when a previous review has been traumatic, this does not necessarily mean that the next one will be a disaster. Many things are likely to have improved since that time, and because this can happen gradually, the home team may not be aware of the scale of the advances made.

12 **Work with your team on developing a collaborate approach.** When colleagues are pulling together constructively, the impression they create is always much more favourable than when there are conflicting attitudes and approaches in an institution. It is important that everyone feels part of the team, and that there is not a top–down ethos where colleagues may lose any sense of ownership of their responsibility for ensuring that the outcomes are favourable.

13 **Involve students in preparations at a very early stage.** They are important partners and need to be consulted on the self-assessment documentation, for example. If students do not recognize the subject provision as described in the paperwork, they may not support staff with the right kinds of comments when reviewers talk to them. That is not to say they need coaching before a visit, but they do need careful briefing.

14 **Use external scrutiny as a lever to ensure improvement to the learning environment.** In some institutions, Estates Services departments target funding on areas about to undergo external scrutiny, and this is often a good chance for teams to negotiate to upgrade the teaching accommodation. In addition, teams can do a lot themselves to produce a good impression. Clutter can be disposed of in classrooms and staff work rooms, student work can be displayed on walls and in corridors, and relevant posters and pictures can be hung to soften the atmosphere.

15 **Do your research on the process.** Read past overview reports, which are available for example in the UK on the World Wide Web. Look for areas that have excited comment in previous review rounds and make sure that any gaps and problems identified do not recur in your own subject provision.

16 **Do your research on your external scrutineers.** Once you have the names of the team who will visit

you, check out their CVs so you have an idea of their areas of interest. It is not a bad idea, if they have publications themselves that are relevant to your students, to make sure these are available and prominently displayed in the library and on reading lists.

17 **Do not get the whole process out of proportion.** It is unwise to have endless, long meetings about preparing for a visit so far in advance of the visit that staff get sick of the process before it looms close. Frequent very short meetings at regular intervals throughout the preparation period work better, especially when they identify responsibility and lead to action. Make sure each meeting has a small but definite purpose, rather than having meetings with so much on the agenda that nothing actually gets achieved.

18 **Do not try to solve every problem overnight.** Externals scrutineers

expect there to be some problematic areas and get suspicious if none are apparent. It is far better, once problems have been identified, to be relatively open about them, but to be able to demonstrate that an action plan has been devised to address them.

19 **Make good use of briefings and rehearsals.** It is said that 75 per cent of the success of an event is achieved before the arrival of the visiting reviewers. Brief students, former students, employers and all categories of staff who are likely to come into contact with the externals. Do not give them a pre-prepared script, but do provide guidance on the importance of the visit, and use briefings to try to identify in advance what issues are likely to arise, so that you can have in place strategies to combat difficulties.

Writing a self-assessment document

The UK system of quality assessment requires subject groups which are to have the quality of their teaching and learning reviewed to produce a self-assessment document (SAD) outlining the nature of the curriculum provision. This provides the basis for a quality assessment visit by a team of reviewers, who judge the provision against what is claimed in the SAD. The following tips are designed to help departments about to be reviewed to write such a document effectively:

1 **Think carefully about the picture you want to paint of your department.** The self-assessment document provides an opportunity for departments to make a case for what they do. In a strictly prescribed format, it enables those who know best the courses and modules being assessed to provide a basis for evaluation. Assessment is made against the institution's own aims and objectives.

2 **Remember that the self-assessment document will set the agenda for the visit.** Whatever you claim will provide the framework of what quality reviewers will review. They are likely to look for gaps, inconsistencies, problems and places where key issues are raised.

3 **Start data collection early.** Writing the necessary documentation can be a gruelling task, and one of the biggest jobs can be actually locating all the figures and information needed. Use existing data wherever possible as a basis for the paper, but do not assume that centrally-provided figures will be accurate at a local level.

4 **Aim to write very concisely.** Be prepared to be very selective about what you include, and use tables and graphs in the annexes where possible, to cover detail that cannot be fitted into the word count.

5 **Stick to the guidelines.** Do not exceed (or undershoot) the word length, as the documentation will be sent back for revision if the guidelines are not strictly adhered to.

6 **Make sure aims and objectives are really clear.** If objectives are not written in terms of what students will achieve by the end of a programme, they will be rejected.

7 **Do not give the task of preparing the SAD to one person alone.** An individual is likely to be too close to the task and may not have a clear overview. A working group with shared responsibilities and duties is best suited to the task.

8 **Get feedback on the document throughout its development.** The more people you can involve in polishing and tuning (but not lengthening!) the SAD, the less likely it is that you will be surprised or dismayed by the reactions of the document's intended recipients in due course. Seek feedback from colleagues, student reps and employers where relevant.

9 **Let one person have final responsibility for the ultimate version of the document.** One person needs to ensure a single authorial voice throughout the paper.

10 **Use someone outside the preparation process to review your documentation once it is written.** Brief this person to look for areas which are not fully explained or documented. Remedy them if possible within the limits of space in the documentation, or note them carefully to help you prepare for questioning on the day of the visit.

11 **Make sure that the documentation is impeccably produced.** Typographical

errors, poor layout and discontinuities will all give a poor impression of the department even before the quality reviewers visit.

12 **Be aware that reviewers will have available to them documentation other than the self-assessment.** All data published by the institution is likely to be scrutinized by the reviewers. It is therefore important that they are not faced with contradictory claims.

13 **Start with the mission statement of your institution.** Whatever your institution claims to be and do should be reflected in your SAD. This can provide difficulties when there is a published mission statement that is unwieldy or imprecise, but it should provide your starting point. Quality reviewers are not in the business of judging mission statements: their task is to judge how well these have been interpreted locally into teaching and learning provision.

14 **Make clear links between the different elements of the documentation.** It should be possible to see how the institution's mission statement, subject rationale, subject aims, subject objectives, course aims and course objectives all link together. These in turn should link to session aims and learning outcomes when individual classes are observed.

15 **Define your subject rationale.** This is likely to be fairly brief and should clearly articulate the reasons why the subject is being taught here and in

this particular context. If the rationale does not address all aspects of the mission, (as, indeed, it often would not be expected to) you should clarify why this is the case.

16 **Define your subject aims.** These should be a statement of the broad direction to be taken in the teaching and learning process, which is directly linked into the module/course/programme rationale. Aims are usually expressed in terms of the sorts of abilities, knowledge and attitudes that can normally be expected of a student who successfully completes a course of study in this area.

17 **Outline your subject learning outcomes.** These tend to be more specific and tend to be closely linked to separate components of the teaching and learning experience. They relate to the acquisition of knowledge, development of understanding, conceptual, intellectual and subject-specific skills, the development of generic transferable skills, the development of values, of motivation and positive attitudes to learning.

18 **Link these to your course aims and outcomes.** It should be evident in your documentation that the mission, rationale, aims and objectives of the institution and department are clearly translated into what you actually teach and assess. Inevitably there will be overlap between course and subject aims and objectives, so care will be needed in the writing of them so that there is not repetition.

19 **Draw clear links between learning outcomes and assessment processes and instruments.** Quality reviewers will need to be able to see clearly how you assess whether students have achieved what you claim they will. Discrepancies between the teaching and learning processes and the ways in which they are assessed will be unhelpful to your case. In my own training as a QAA Subject Reviewer, the emphasis on looking for the linking between learning outcomes and assessment criteria was particularly strong.

20 **Identify and assess what is distinctive about your subject.** If you claim in your documentation, for example, that you have a distinctive international focus for your teaching, this should be clearly evidenced in the curriculum as well as the prospectus.

21 **Provide profiles of staff and students and information about learning resources available.** These can be supported by tables, graphs and other data in the annexes at the end of the document.

22 **Provide documentary evidence of your achievements.** It is not enough merely to claim that your teaching in the department is underpinned by world-class research. Evidence for this should be provided in the form of specific examples. You can also provide employment statistics, student and employer feedback and so on.

23 **Do not try to hide the problems.** By the time quality reviewers have read all your documentation and talked to staff and students, they are likely to have a clear idea of anything that might be going wrong in your department, so it is futile to pretend problems do not exist. Subject reviewers are trained to sniff out 'fresh paint'!

24 **State clearly what you plan to do about any areas of difficulty.** Quality reviewers are likely to be more impressed by proposals of action to be taken on problem issues and areas of difficulty than by head-in-the-sand attitudes which ignore difficult areas.

Preparing for the week of the visit

The following suggestions (overleaf) may help make a quality visit go that little bit more smoothly, and can certainly make the visitors feel more welcome:

1 **Prepare the base rooms.** A welcoming, well-equipped base room for the reviewers will certainly help. It needs to be private, well stocked with drinks (hot and cold) and snacks. Such a room needs a telephone, computer, e-mail facilities, printer, photocopier, surfaces to write on, boxes with the information to peruse and space to lay out samples of students' work.

2 **Look after creature comforts.** Make sure the base room is warm enough in winter, or well ventilated (or air-conditioned) in summer. Make sure the reviewers' travel arrangements home are catered for. (Have timetables and taxi numbers to hand.)

3 **Plan for emergencies.** Such things as train strikes, go-slows, broken lifts, ill relatives and headaches can all disrupt a visit. All these are traumatic – almost as much as a photocopier which breaks down! Check whether any other special events are happening on the day. Make arrangements to cover equipment failures and so on.

4 **Keep the channels of communication going.** Events can change suddenly – be prepared for this. You may need to reschedule staff because of changing circumstances. The reviewers may realize that they have sufficient information on a topic and wish to change the focus. Additional paper information may be sought, or a request be made to interview a particular member of staff.

5 **Offer a support mechanism.** Occasionally things may not go according to plan. Someone may feel unwell but struggle on. A lecture may go badly or students may be unusually quiet. A sympathetic ear and a strong cup of tea may do the trick.

6 **Make sure that internal visits run smoothly.** Plan so that subject reviewers' visits to the library, IT centre, educational development service and other venues run smoothly as part of the quality appraisal event. Involve staff from Central Services (for example Student Services, Library, IT department) in your preparations. They often have valuable experience from previous visits to other subject areas.

7 **Make good use of your institutional facilitator.** This person is trained to make good links between the visiting panel and the subject team. Listen to the institutional facilitator's advice and act upon it.

8 **Keep an eye on loose cannons.** If you feel you have people who are likely to be destructive on the day, do not try to hide them or over-compensate for their actions or views, or send them off on a field trip! Quality reviewers are not fools and will be able to tell the difference between those with a genuine grievance or problem, and troublemakers.

Managing your ILT application

The Institute for Learning and Teaching in Higher Education (ILT) was set up in 1999, aiming to become the professional body for teachers in higher education in the UK. For the first years of its existence, membership is gained either by successful completion of an accredited staff development programme run by a university or college, or for staff with three or more years of teaching experience, by an 'experienced staff' route. This route is often called the 'fast-track' route, as it is probable that in due course it will be replaced by a portfolio-based route (which could be thought of as much slower, considering how long it takes to build up a teaching portfolio). The 'fast-track' route involves completing an application form, outlining your experience of teaching, learning and assessment in five reflections on your own work. Each section asks for a response of not more than 500 words. The applications are judged by appointed accreditors.

If you are a new (or indeed experienced) member of staff working your way through your own institution's Postgraduate Certificate of Academic Practice (or equivalent), and if that programme is already accredited by the ILT, you will be eligible for ILT membership as soon as you are awarded the certificate by your own institution. My suggestions below are therefore directed primarily to experienced staff who are not undertaking such a programme, and who may wish to apply directly to ILT using the 'fast-track' route.

Although I myself am a member of ILT, and an ILT accreditor, my suggestions in this section are not to be interpreted as indicating official ILT policies or practices in processing fast-track applications. At the time of writing this edition, I am just one of 5,000 members (the numbers are rapidly increasing), and one of 50 or so accreditors. These tips therefore are my personal suggestions to colleagues making such applications, as used at institutions where I happen to be running preparation workshops for applicants.

How ILT accreditation works

Your application will be judged by two accreditors, working side by side. At present, accreditors' panels are held regularly at the ILT offices in York, with 8 to 12 accreditors working as a panel, and considering individual applications in pairs.

Accreditors have been appointed from a wide range of subject disciplines. Normally, at least one of your accreditors will be working in higher education in a discipline area close to your own. Most of the accreditors are themselves working in higher education institutions, and many are themselves members of the ILT.

The accreditors see both parts of your application, but make recommendations based almost entirely on Part 2. They are required to make individual recommendations to 'accept' or 'refer' on what you put forward for each of the sections in Part 2, and then come to an overall recommendation. If both accreditors agree that your application should be accepted, your application will normally have succeeded straight away. The application and recommendations may be checked by ILT staff, and you will normally hear of the decision quite quickly thereafter.

If both accreditors agree your application should be referred, it is then passed to two further accreditors to confirm or debate the decision. If all four agree it should be referred, all four are involved in working out what feedback should be sent to you. Typically, such feedback takes the form of requests for specific further information in support of your application. If there is a split decision between the four accreditors, the application is held over till a later panel, and reconsidered by different accreditors.

If the first two accreditors cannot agree whether to accept or refer your application, it is passed to a further pair for review. Much more time, and discussion, is given at accreditor panel meetings to those applications that are not accepted immediately.

If you put important information in the 'wrong' section

Accreditors are briefed to look at applications holistically, and will do everything possible to give you credit for every element of your claim, wherever it happens to lie in your application. It does, however, make accreditors' work more straightforward if they can find the information they are looking for in each section straight away.

Overall suggestions

- **Do it now.** Putting together your fast-track application need not take you more than two or three hours, especially if you have done most of the thinking involved during a session on such applications, and have the benefit of feedback from other people on your draft ideas relating to the five main areas you need to address.
- **Do not put it off.** It is best to get your application at least into its first draft right away, rather than let this task sink down your in-tray.
- **Repeat: do it now.** As with any other procedure, it can be expected that the standard of applications will continue to improve, as people become more familiar with the process and the agenda, and as word spreads about exactly what has already constituted the basis for successful claims for fast-track accreditation. Do not wait for the standard to become even higher.
- **Do not spend too much time putting together your first draft.** It is easier to make good use of constructive and critical feedback from colleagues (and from your referees) if you have not spent so long on your early drafts that you have become over-protective about your words.
- **Get the tone right.** I have included a whole section of tips on tone and style for your application, and it is best to start writing in the most appropriate way

right from the start. Save yourself time: do not write anything until you have had a look at these suggestions.

■ **Choose your referees wisely.** I have put further suggestions about this later in this chapter. Meanwhile, take note of the fact that you need to get your referees to send their references back to you, in sealed, signed envelopes, for you to enclose (still sealed, of course) with your completed application.

■ **Work collaboratively.** The more pairs of eyes you get onto your draft application, the more you will benefit from other people's suggestions and feedback. Obviously, at the end of the process your application needs to be a snapshot of your work in teaching, supporting learning and assessment, but other people's ideas and attempts can help you decide how best to present your own case.

■ **Word process your application.** You are allowed up to 500 words to put your case regarding each of the five areas included in Part 2 of your application, and experience shows that it is best to use these (plus or minus 10 per cent). It is difficult to adjust and edit handwritten applications, and the boxes on the printed pro formas do not give you enough space to make as good a case for yourself as you can by using 500 words or so for each application. Do use your word processor to count your words for you, but try to resist putting (for example) '498 words' at the end of a particular section.

■ **Think ahead to the application as a whole.** The five areas addressed by Part 2 of the form overlap significantly, and it is likely to be the case that some thoughts you initially draft with one section in mind could end up better placed in a different section. Word processing allows you to cut and paste towards the final stages of putting together your application.

■ **Try making the first draft of your application in a single hour or two.** This helps you to make good decisions about which aspects of your work you wish to include in your application, and where you will provide details of your chosen aspects. Doing the early work in a single sitting also helps you to make the overall application more coherent and balanced. Where you have the opportunity to participate in a group workshop on making these applications, regard this as the single sitting where you can do most of your preliminary thinking at once.

■ **Keep reminding yourself that your application is your *claim*.** You do not have to send supporting evidence (other than that provided by your referees), so your claim about each of the areas of your work needs to be self-explanatory and self-sufficient.

■ **Stick to the brief.** Your application for membership of the ILT is about your work relating to teaching, learning and assessment. Many other aspects of your professionalism may be highly significant and worthy, but not relevant to this particular application.

■ **Do not repeat yourself.** You need to put your five sets of 500 words to good use, and it is worth making sure that you are not making the same points in different parts of your application. You can where necessary cross-reference your responses to the five sections, but it is best not to do this too much.

Tone and style suggestions

- **Make your application a personal claim.** Your application should be written for the eyes of fellow practitioners in higher education. If it is a strong application, it will only be studied in detail by two accreditors, so it is a relatively private, informal document. There is no need to use the same sort of language that you might normally use for a scholarly paper – indeed such language could dampen the impact your application could have.
- **Make your application sufficiently reflective.** This is most easily achieved through a relatively informal tone. In one section of your application in particular, your accreditors will be looking specifically for evidence that you reflect on your work, and act on feedback about it. In practice, it is best to include your personal reflections in all sections of Part 2 of your application.
- **Blow your own trumpet, softly!** In effect, your application is a self-assessment claim, written by yourself but corroborated by your peers, about how your work addresses and embraces the five key areas addressed by Part 2 of the application pro forma. Do not leave it to the accreditors to deduce how relevant or good your work is, make this clear in your claims. Obviously, avoid your claim coming across as pompous, but equally avoid understating your case too much.
- **Your referees can blow your trumpet more loudly.** The primary purpose of having referees is so that the details included in your application are authenticated by people who know your work well enough to do so. That said, referees often add significantly to applicants' claims, by adding further supportive information relevant to your claim.
- **Do not try to put your whole life's work into five sections of 500 words each.** You are likely to have far more to say about your teaching, learning and assessment-related activities than could possibly be summarized on five pages or so of typescript.
- **Be selective regarding what you do, and give 'rationale' details.** Your application should focus on particular cross-sections of your work, and illustrate these with brief descriptive details. It is much more important to say a little about *why* you do something the way you do, than to expend a lot of words describing *what* you do.
- **Do not aim for a 'perfect' application.** There is no single ideal way to state your claim to be worthy of membership of the ILT. All you need is for what you choose to say, about what you do, to be seen to address the principal areas covered by Part 2 of your application sufficiently well for your accred-

itors to vote to accept your application. The decisions are taken on a 'met' or 'not yet met' basis, and there are no prizes for distinguished or wonderfully eloquent applications, however much your accreditors may enjoy studying these.

■ **Get feedback on your drafts, and make good use of it.** Ideally, your two referees should be the sort of people who can give you feedback on the final (or near-final) version of your application. In any case, your referees are expected to have read your application carefully, and to offer comments on it in their references. However, informal feedback from colleagues and indeed fellow-applicants is invaluable in helping you to make your claims fluently, convincingly and effectively.

Claim 1   Teaching and the support of learning

Accreditors are looking for *what* you do, *why* you do it, and *how* you know it works for you:

■ **Think about *what* you teach**. Jot down notes of the main courses or programmes on which you teach. You will need to show that your teaching is at an appropriate level for higher education (for example, part of a degree course), and illustrate the subject areas your teaching addresses. This is the 'what?' dimension for this section. In your final application, however, do not just list all the programmes and subjects you teach. What you will say next about *how* and *why* is much more important to your accreditors.

■ **Think about two or three of the teaching *processes* you feel that you use well**. Jot these down. Choose processes you use regularly, and feel comfortable with. Make sure if you can that you will be able to show that you do not just use one process in your work, but that you select from a range of teaching processes on the basis of what will be best to help your students to gain an understanding of your particular subjects and topics.

■ **Next make brief notes about *why* you feel that you use your selected processes well**. How would you explain that each of these processes is appropriate for your students' learning?

■ **Think of how you could illustrate the quality and appropriateness of your teaching.** It is usually best to think of two or three 'snapshots' of particular things you do (and are proud of) in your teaching, and to write two or three sentences about each, to set the scene, and to justify your rationale for choosing the particular methods for the individual contexts in which you use them.

■ **Jot down any main features of your work which relate to leading a course, or being responsible for a subject area.** It will be useful for you to include such details in your claim for this section.

- **How do you *know* you are using your selected approaches well**? You may need to hold on to the answer to this question for use in a later section of your application, but it is worth establishing this straight away. For example, you may have solid evidence of your success from peer observation of your teaching (if your university has a policy regarding this), or your feedback may come mainly from student evaluations of your teaching.
- **Make sure that your claim in this section will relate clearly to your wish to enhance students' learning.** It is best to check that you have mentioned 'students' often enough in this section to show that your are concerned to help them to learn as well as you can, and that you are tuning your approach to the particular needs of your students.

Claim 2   *Contribution to the design of learning activities*

- **Think of one or two specific examples of curriculum development that you have been involved in.** Make brief notes about how you have planned learning activities for the students you teach.
- **Have you been involved in course or programme validation?** Whether this is at your own institution, or you have been involved as an external reviewer elsewhere, this can add to your claim for this section. If you have not yet been involved in this kind of work, do not worry, it just means that you will need to say a little more about how you have developed the curriculum of your own courses, and your own way of handling that curriculum.
- **Have you been involved in giving feedback to colleagues on their teaching?** This too can form useful evidence for your claim somewhere in your overall application. Such commentary may turn out to be best placed in one of the other sections, but if you find that the present section is somewhat 'thin', you could include it here.
- **Have you been involved in designing resource-based learning elements for your students?** This could include open or flexible learning materials or computer-based materials. This could be part of your claim for this section.
- **How would you demonstrate your concern for the appropriateness for the learning activities you have designed?** It is important for this concern to shine through the wording you use in this section of your application. Think of how you could justify your choice of approach to your students' effective learning of the subjects or topics involved, and write one or two short paragraphs as case studies of the rationale of your choice of teaching approaches for particular specific contexts.

Claim 3   Assessment and giving feedback to students

- **Are you responsible for the design (and implementation) of some assessment elements?** If so, it is worth addressing the following questions about them. If not, you may be better advised to concentrate on the feedback side of the agenda for this section.

- **What is the range of formal assessment processes you use?** List two or three different assessment processes if you can. Some processes may be summative (such as exams) and others may be primarily formative in nature (perhaps essays). For each of these, think about how you will explain *why* you use (or have chosen) that process for your particular students in your subject area.

- **What is the range of informal assessment processes you use?** You may or may not be able to use such processes in your work, but if you do, work out how you would illustrate *why* you use them, and *how* they help to deepen your students' learning, and help your students to benefit from feedback.

- **What assessment approaches do you use?** For example, do you make use of student self-assessment, or peer-assessment, or are you involved in the assessment of group work rather than just individual work? If you are involved in a range of assessment approaches (as well as using a range of assessment processes mentioned above), it will be useful if your 500 words in this section can show the breadth of your assessment-related work, as well as describing two or three chosen highlights in a little more detail.

- **How about giving feedback to students?** Particularly if your work does not include significant responsibility for designing and/or implementing assessment, you will need to say more in this section about the ways in which you give students feedback on their progress. Try to think of at least three different ways in which you give feedback to students, and think about how best you could justify your choice of each of your feedback methods, for the particular situations in which you use them.

- **Think of how you can relate assessment and feedback to helping students to learn successfully.** How can you justify your claim to be using assessment and feedback with your students' learning in mind?

Claim 4   Developing effective learning environments and student support systems

- **Note first that the briefing for this section covers a wide range of possibilities.** Therefore, here more than anywhere else in your application you are likely to need to be particularly selective, and to concentrate on *illustrating* a very few chosen scenarios relating to your work with students.

- **Note that the focus of your response to this section is about making a *range* of learning environments *responsive* to students' needs.** You are likely to have plenty to choose from, ranging from your possible involvement in organizing laboratory work, or preparing and giving tutorials, one-to-one supervision and so on. Try to decide which of these will not only illustrate your range of work, but also leave you room to give some detail about your concern that students benefit as much as possible from the chosen aspects of your work.

■ **Keep your accreditors' briefing in mind.** They are required to look for how you make 'reasoned and informed choices' about the evidence you cite in this section of your application. Do not forget to link your reasons to the intended quality of your students' learning.

Claim 5 *Reflective practice and personal development*

■ **Note that this is an important section.** I have already stressed that accreditors are briefed to look for indications that you are a reflective practitioner in your approach to teaching, learning and assessment. As mentioned earlier, the quality of your reflection should come through, just as much from *how* you make your claim, as from *what* you cite as evidence for your claim.

■ **Start with how you evaluate your teaching.** Jot down some details of how you collect and *use* feedback from students (and indeed feedback from peer observers if available) as a basis for the ongoing improvement of your teaching.

■ **Next, think of how you update yourself about teaching, learning and assessment.** You may well have listed relevant staff development activities in Part 1 of your application, but you may need to remind your accreditors here that you take such activities seriously.

■ **Do not forget your conferences.** Even those which are primarily about updating your subject expertise can have their own payoff in terms of helping you to reflect on your teaching and assessment processes.

■ **You may be able to include links here about how your research helps you to develop your teaching.** This is not the place to go into subject-specific detail about your research, but to make your case about how your research continues to make you a better teacher.

■ **Your accreditors will be looking for *commitment* to continuing professional development.** Choose your words carefully to make it clear that you seek actively to continue to develop your teaching, rather than participate reluctantly in programmes to that end.

■ **What if you do not teach directly?** This section is then the place where you give your most reflective words about how in your own way you contribute to supporting students' learning, and how you review the success of your efforts to this end.

Claim 6   Other information in support of your application

- **You have another 500 words in which to round off your claim.** Although you do not *need* to say anything else, if you have already made a solid and comprehensive claim in the previous five sections, it somehow looks a little half-hearted when applicants do not have anything to add. Do not necessarily aim to use the full 500 words this time, but look for important relevant information to add here to strengthen the case you have already made.
- **Your accreditors are briefed to look for any further relevant strengths.** That means, relevant to teaching, learning and assessment. However, you can use this section, in particular, to address any of the following areas.
- **Are you involved in mentoring new lecturers?** If so, whether formally or informally, it is worth mentioning this in this section.
- **Are you a member of any professional bodies?** If so, mention these briefly, especially if such membership has direct links to your teaching.
- **Do you do research which feeds into your teaching?** If so, mention this, but do not go into too much detail about the research itself. It is the fact that you bring it to bear on your teaching which is likely to interest your accreditors most.
- **Are you involved in team teaching, or other forms of group working?** If so, this could be worth mentioning in this section.
- **You may already have 'used up' some of the suggestions in the briefing for this section.** If so, do not repeat here the information already given earlier in your application, but look for further things to add to your claim. Alternatively, use your word processor to divert one or two relevant parts of your claims in earlier sections to this 'other information' section, especially if you found yourself rather tight for words in those earlier sections, and would benefit from being able to expand a little more on the most important of the claims you made there.
- **Try to make a good last impression.** Although this is not crucial here, as your accreditors will have made decisions on each of the five areas earlier in your Part 2, it does no harm to end with something that shows you are an enthusiastic and committed practitioner in higher education.

Choosing and briefing your referees

Accreditors read your references carefully. If your own application is really strong, not much then depends upon what your referees say about your work, providing of course their comments are not critical. It is when there are gaps in your claims in the main sections of Part 2 of your application that your references will be studied really carefully. In such cases, extra detail supplied by your referees may be used by your accreditors to compensate for information you did not include yourself (see overleaf):

- **Read carefully the information supplied about choosing your referees.** The main thing is that they should be in a position to corroborate the details in your application, which means that they should know sufficient about the teaching side of your work to make comments authoritatively.

- **Choose supportive referees.** That may seem obvious, but accreditors are asked to decide whether your references are 'strongly supportive', 'mildly supportive', 'neutral' or 'hostile'! Obviously, do not choose people who might be hostile, or even just neutral.

- **Read carefully the information *for* referees.** Make sure that you copy this and send it to both of your referees. If necessary, remind them that their main job is *not* to give you a 'normal' reference, but to confirm that what you have said about yourself in your application is true, *and* to expand on your strengths in their own way.

- **Make sure that you have filled in Part 1 of your application, with details of your referees.** Put in full contact details. It is possible that ILT may wish to follow up things your referees say about you, or check that your referees are who you say they are. Do not forget to include a few words where asked in Part 1 about the capacity in which your chosen referees can comment on your work.

- **Your referees can blow your trumpet for you, more loudly.** Your own words in your application are essentially 'blowing your own trumpet', but modesty usually necessitates doing this relatively gently. Your referees can, if they wish, say just how outstanding your teaching actually is.

- **Send your referees copies of your draft application, and ask for feedback from them.** They are very likely to be able to help you choose what you include, and remind you of important aspects of your work you may not yet have included. Make good use of any feedback you receive from your referees, and send them a revised copy of your application, if you have made any substantive changes.

- **Suggest to your referees that they may choose to use the five main section headings to structure their references.** This helps your accreditors, who may be able to draw from your references additional information about your work which they were looking for (but did not find) in your own words.

- **Suggest to your referees that they make it clear that they are indeed *supporting* your application.** Some referees simply do the corroboration, but forget to make it clear that they believe you are very suitable to be a member of the ILT.

- **Remind your referees that they need to send *you* their reference, in a sealed, signed envelope.** They may or may not choose to send you a further copy. Most referees find it embarrassing to send colleagues a copy of a document where they have waxed lyrical on your behalf, so do not think that it is bad news if they do not want you to read their words about you.

Managing your feedback from students

The consumer's view is being sought more and more, and with students increasingly paying for their tuition, their views need to be taken into account more than ever. Evidence of student feedback is one of the things that anyone reviewing the quality of your teaching is certain to ask to see.

The most serious danger is that from the students' point of view, giving feedback can become a chore. It is then not taken seriously. The value of obtaining feedback is undermined whenever there is a feeling that the purpose is merely 'to be seen to be obtaining feedback'. The purpose of feedback should not merely be to make things better next time round. Giving feedback can itself be turned into part of the learning experience, particularly when feedback is the result of group discussions. In this section, I would like to point to four questions we should be asking ourselves at each stage of feedback processes:

- **Are students developing a feeling of ownership of the feedback they give** (or is it just ticks and jottings on someone else's questionnaire)?
- **Are we getting the feedback we need from students** (or are we only getting the answers to *our* questions, rather than the things that students need to be telling us)?
- **Is giving feedback a learning experience in itself** (in other words, are students led into some deep and useful thinking about their studies, in the process of providing us with feedback)?
- **How are we planning to give students the results of their feedback?** (If they see that we are not actually taking any notice of their feedback, they are not likely to cooperate with our future attempts to procure feedback from them.)

Feedback on your lectures

In Chapter 1 I have already stressed how important feedback is as part of the processes by which people learn successfully. It is equally important for us as lecturers to get feedback about how we are doing, to help us to learn productively from our triumphs and our mistakes. There are many ways of getting feedback about the effectiveness of your lecture programme. Some are very simple, and require no special effort on your part.

Body language

You can find out a great deal about how your lectures are going by keeping an eye on the ways your students are behaving. You can easily tell the difference between eyes glazing over (or asleep!) and eyes which are interested and alert. However, you cannot always tell. Some students develop the art of appearing to be interested and alert when they are actually neither! There are, of course, body language traits that can alert you to unproductive processes: shuffling, chattering, fidgeting and so on.

Coursework

Often it is only when you assess the coursework associated with a particular topic that you fully discover how the students' learning *really* went. This can give you the opportunity to use further large-group teaching occasions to address what you have found out about the general state of the group's learning achievements. (It will be too late, of course, to do anything about discoveries about your students learning which will become all too apparent when you mark their exam scripts.)

Informal comments from particular students

Often you will have opportunities to talk informally to some of the students – for example, those who happen to come up and ask you questions. However, the feedback you get from these students may not be representative of the feelings of the whole group – the students who ask you questions may be the keenest ones, or the boldest. Any students experiencing real problems with the content of your sessions may not wish to give you any clue that they are not yet with you.

Peer feedback

Until relatively recently, there used to be too much privacy attached to our performances with large groups in lecture rooms. Now, most institutions of higher education have some sort of policy on peer observation, sometimes quite informal, but still very useful. Sitting in regularly on colleagues' sessions is one of the most productive ways to gain ideas to use in your own approaches to working with large groups. You will find things they do well which you would like to try, and (just as useful) you will notice things they do less well which you will decide to avoid if at all possible. It is really useful if you can identify one or two colleagues where you can develop peer feedback into something really useful, where you mutually give each other honest and constructive comments about how the sessions are going. Many universities now use peer observation of lectures to help lecturers not only to develop their teaching, but also to prepare themselves for the external review of the quality of their teaching.

If you are heading towards a teaching quality assessment of the sort where someone from another university may observe you at work with large groups, it can be very useful to rehearse the situation by getting one or two other lecturers – maybe from other disciplines – to observe you quite formally as preparation. This helps you to become accustomed to the presence of outsiders, and also to become more aware of the things that you do that are most effective and interesting.

Feedback from seeing yourself teach

Making your own video is easier than you may think. You can choose the room, time, class and position in which you place the camera, and when you switch it on and off, and no one but you needs to see the video (though it is even more useful if you get a colleague or friend to watch it with you). It can be even better to get a colleague, or a student, to operate the camera, and follow you around and zoom in to show details of your expression or of the visual aids you may use. You can derive a substantial amount of feedback about your own performance just by watching yourself.

Structured questionnaires

These have the advantage that they can be quite quick to complete, and they can be filled in anonymously by students. (This spares the feelings of those who may wish to be critical, and also spares *your* feelings towards those whose feedback you consider to be unkind or unjust.) Questionnaires are most easily made quick and anonymous if they are of the tick-box or ratings-scales varieties. It is worth reminding you that you should not be *upset* by negative feedback. Use it as useful information rather than criticism. With a questionnaire, do not regard every 'useless to me' tick as a stab in the back. As long as a majority of students are choosing favourable boxes you should be satisfied. Students who give very hostile feedback may be doing so because of reasons far beyond your control. It can be useful to tot up the scores in each box onto a master copy of the questionnaire, then compare your results again in a month or two, when you have tried to tackle some of the issues to which the feedback may have alerted you. Also, show your master copy to colleagues who use similar questionnaires, and discuss the outcomes.

Open-ended questions

These can be combined with structured questions, or can be used on their own. The feedback gained through open-ended questions is necessarily less anonymous, as (especially with small groups) students may feel that you will be able to trace them through their handwriting. Some possibilities for open-ended questions are listed below. It is best to use no more than two or three such questions at a time, otherwise it becomes too much of a chore for students to complete your questionnaire, and the feedback becomes stinted:

- What do you like most about this lecture programme?
- What do you like least about this lecture programme?
- What do you find most interesting?
- What do you find most difficult?
- What suggestions can you offer for improving the programme in future?

Stop, start, continue

A quick and versatile method of gaining feedback – especially from large groups of students – is to give them post-it slips, and ask them to write the three headings 'stop', 'start', and 'continue' on them as follows:

Stop...   Start...   Continue...

You can then ask the class a question along any one of the following lines:

- Under each heading, jot down what you would like *me to* do in future lectures on this course.
- Tell me what *you would* like to stop doing, start doing, and continue doing as we go further in this course.
- Simply write down anything you would like to tell me under each of the three headings.

A variety of feedback mechanisms

Feedback can be gathered from students in many different ways, including:

- from interviews with individual students;
- from feedback activities with groups of students, for example using nominal group technique sessions;
- from solicited feedback from large groups of students (for example using the 'stop, start, continue' agenda on post-its in large-group lectures, as mentioned above);
- from questionnaires of various types;
- from student representation on programme boards;
- informally (for example through tutorials, seminars, one-to-one chats with students and laboratory work);
- from students' exam performance (but then it is too late for some!);
- from students' coursework performance (and particularly from *their* reactions to our own feedback to them);

- from information that may be forthcoming from external observers who may be able to discuss with students their experience of courses, such as moderators and examiners.

This chapter continues with some illustrations of the advantages and disadvantages of a number of approaches to eliciting feedback from students.

Some limitations of questionnaires

Because it is easy to administer, the questionnaire has become the dominant method of seeking feedback. Unfortunately it is also easy to fall into the temptation to produce statistics based on questionnaire responses. If 84 per cent of students think Dr Smith's lectures are brilliant, we are inclined to ignore the 16 per cent who don't – but they may have very good reasons for disliking the lectures. The problem is not so much with gathering feedback by questionnaire, but with the ways feedback is processed and collated. Some of the factors which limit the value of questionnaire feedback are listed below:

- **The 'ticky-box' syndrome.** People become conditioned to make instant responses to questions. Getting through the questionnaire quickly becomes a virtue. Responses are made on a surface level of thinking rather than as a result of reflection and critical thinking. (This is not a problem on those occasions where instant reaction is what is wanted, but the feedback we gather is not usually analysed on that basis.)
- **'Performing dogs' syndrome.** Many people filling in questionnaires tend to want to please. They can usually tell which responses will please the people giving them the questionnaire, and the people whose work is involved in the issues covered by the questionnaire. If they like the people, they are likely to comment favourably on things, rather than use them to show their real views.
- **Lost learning opportunities.** Questionnaires are often used after an event rather than during it. This tends to minimize any real learning outcomes of the process of completing questionnaires. The sense of ownership is reduced when students do not see how their responses will be of any direct benefit to themselves, and assume they will only help their successors.
- **The 'WYSIWYG' syndrome (what you see is what you get).** Questionnaires produce feedback on the particular issues covered, but often *not* on other important issues. There is a tendency to design questionnaires which will give positive feedback, and to avoid asking those questions where there is every possibility of critical replies.
- **'Blue, rosy and purple' questionnaires.** A major limitation of most questionnaires is that responses are coloured by how people feel at the moment of filling

them in. If the same questionnaire were used a few days later, some responses might be completely different. Yet the results are often statistically analysed as though they reflected permanent, considered reactions to questions and issues, rather than fleeting, transient reactions.

■ **'Conditioned response' questionnaires.** When the same questionnaire format is used repeatedly, students can become very bored, and may revert to answering many of the questions in the same way as they have often done previously. Feedback then is not specific to the particular occasion when the questionnaire is being used, and at best represents overall feelings rather than specific responses.

■ **'Death by questionnaire'.** This happens when there are too many, too often, they are badly designed, and nothing ever happens as a result of the feedback that is given.

Some advantages of questionnaire feedback

Despite the reservations presented above, there are some significant advantages associated with gathering student feedback through questionnaires. The best ways of using questionnaires therefore depend on using the advantages deliberately, while at the same time minimizing the effect of the drawbacks:

■ **Feedback from questionnaires can be anonymous.** This allows students the chance at least of giving negative feedback without the embarrassment of giving it publicly.

■ **Feedback from questionnaires can be quick.** Many things can be covered in a few minutes.

■ **Feedback from questionnaires is amenable to statistical analysis.** This is an advantage – but as I've mentioned, a dangerous one!

■ **Feedback from questionnaires can be fed into institutional review and quality procedures.**

■ **Questionnaires can be used on a deeper level**. It is possible, for example, to get students to go through a questionnaire twice. The first time they can be briefed to respond as they feel, the second time they can be asked to respond as they would *like* to feel. This can help to get over the problem of different students preferring different things. The gap between 'how it is' and 'how you'd like it to be' is often more important – and more revealing – than students' reactions to 'how it is'.

Some ideas on structured questions

Structured (or 'closed') questions are of several types including the following:

Ticking boxes or putting marks on scales

This can be done with contrasting dimensions at opposite sides of a form:

interesting	boring
too fast	too slow
approachable	unapproachable

Alternatively, the terms can be included in a table, for example:

Interesting	Boring
Too fast	Too slow
Audible	Inaudible
Visual aids easy to read	Visual aids hard to read
Aims made clear	Aims hard to work out
I learnt a lot	I did not learn anything
My questions answered	My questions unanswered
Enjoyable	Not enjoyable

Table 6.1

One of the things that can go wrong with such scales is that the factors at each end turn out *not* to be opposites. Furthermore, if an odd number of columns is used, the middle column represents 'safe middle ground', and students tend to put their responses there when they cannot decide whether something is interesting or boring, and so on. It can be argued that it is better to force them to make a decision by having an even number of columns. Then, those students who *really* think that something is midway between the extremes have to make a conscious decision, for example to put their tick or cross on the central line.

'Usefulness' measures

Various features of the teaching methods or processes can be mentioned at the left-hand side of a pro forma, with boxes for 'very useful', 'quite useful' and 'not useful' to tick. The features can include such things as handout materials, visual aids and worked examples done in class. For example:

Feature	Very useful	Quite useful	Not useful
Handouts			
Seminars			
Slides in lectures			
In-class exercises			
Independent study tasks			

Table 6.2

Statements with 'agreement' measures

A series of statements can be checked against boxes such as 'strongly agree', 'more or less agree', 'disagree' and 'strongly disagree'. The statements can usefully be both positive and negative, to ensure that respondents do not fall into the pattern of agreeing (or disagreeing) with everything they see. Part of such a questionnaire could be as follows:

	Strongly agree	Quite agree	Disagree	Strongly disagree
I find your lectures stimulate me to further work				
I remain switched-off for most of my time in your lectures				
I am clear about the intended learning outcomes of each part of this module				
I do not really know what is expected of me in this subject				
I find it easy to ask questions in your lectures				
I find parts of this subject very hard to understand				

Table 6.3

Number gradings

This is another form of structuring students' responses, by asking them to enter numbers to indicate their feelings with regard to a statement or an issue. For example, the scale might be: 5 = most useful, 4 = very useful, 3 = quite useful, 2 = of limited use, 1 = of little use, 0 = of no use.

'More' 'Just right' and 'Less' boxes

These could be used for students to record their feelings about the things they do in tutorials, for example:

Processes used in tutorials	More of this please	Just right, thanks	Less of this please
Practising problem solving			
Seeing worked examples done			
Working through case-study materials			
Asking questions of the lecturer			
Being asked questions by the lecturer			
Having marked homework discussed individually			
Having marked practical work returned and discussed			
Seeing examples of assessment criteria			
Using assessment criteria directly to mark own (or other's) work			
Practising addressing previous exam questions			

Table 6.4

Prioritizing

This sort of structure helps overcome the 'ticky-box' syndrome, as it causes students to think more deeply about issues. For example, they can be asked to enter '1' against the best feature of Dr Smith's classes, '2' against the next best, and so on. My recommendation regarding getting students to prioritize teaching attributes remains: keep it as simple as possible. Questions and choices need to be clear and unambiguous. This can also be used to find out which topics in a subject area students find the most difficult, for example:

Physical chemistry: rank the topics below from '1' (the one you find most straightforward) to '8' (the one you find most difficult)	Your ratings
Electrochemistry	
Chemical kinetics	
Thermodynamics	
Phase equilibria	
Colloid chemistry	
Spectroscopy	
Photochemistry	
Mass transfer	

Table 6.5

Some ideas for open questions

Open questions allow each student to respond freely to set areas. While such questions can overcome some of the limitations I have mentioned regarding structured questions, the fact that students are entering their responses in their own handwriting can be a deterrent against their expressing negative or critical views, where they may feel that they could be traced and maybe even penalized as a result.

The two most useful features of your lectures are:

1

2

The two least useful features of your lectures are:

1

2

Suggestions for improvement:

The three topics I found most difficult to make sense of in this module are:

1

2

3

Computer-analysed feedback

Several software packages exist which allow student feedback to be gathered and statistically analysed. Students can be asked a series of multiple-choice or multiple-response questions, and their choices of entry can be recorded by the computer, enabling statistical analysis to be done on the responses from large groups of students. The feedback can be made anonymous, or students' names can be used. It is probably best to use such feedback approaches where a record is kept of which students have given their feedback, but the individual responses are analysed on an anonymous basis.

Students are more likely to give feedback using such software than by other methods, particularly if the process of gathering the feedback can be made more interesting for the students giving it, for example by providing responses back to each student on the basis of each choice he or she makes.

Computer-gathered feedback is not restricted to multiple-choice questions. Open-ended questions can also be included, and the software can sort and print out lists of the responses of a whole class of students to any particular question. Open-ended feedback of this sort, when gathered by computer, may be more reliable than when given in handwriting, as students may feel less under threat that their views will be noticed and used against them.

When very large numbers of students are involved, and sufficient access to computers is difficult to arrange, it is possible to retain the benefits of computer *analysis* of feedback choices by using paper-based questionnaires designed for optical mark reading.

Suggestions on ways of using questionnaires

So far, I have been quite critical about some of the most common methods used to seek and analyse student feedback, and have referred to many of the things which can go wrong with such methods. Next, however, I offer a range of suggestions for developing some of these methods further, taking into account the risks, and aiming to optimize the potential benefits, both to ourselves and to our students:

1 **Consider making the use of questionnaires private to individual members of staff.** For feedback about lectures (or tutorials, or lab work) I think it best that each lecturer designs and uses his or her individual questionnaire, and obtains feedback for his or her private use. This does not mean, however, that the forms are to be filled in 'privately' by students. It may well be better to use them as an agenda for group feedback.

2 **Make questionnaires 'short and often, not long and once'.** Any feedback form should be short enough not to bore or alienate students. A good guide may be that it should be possible for a group to complete the form in a few minutes. This means separate forms for lectures, tutorials and so on.

3 **Use questionnaires for formative rather than summative feedback whenever possible.** Seek feedback during a programme, so that something can still be done about matters emerging. Feedback after completion of a programme is still useful, but is not seen by students as being as valuable as when they have the chance to suggest changes they themselves will benefit from directly.

4 **Employ questionnaires for a wide range of matters to do with presentation, style and approachability.** These aspects of, for example,

lecturing, can be gathered in the private mode suggested above. Individual questionnaire components can be selected/composed by each staff member to search for comment about issues that may be of particular concern to the lecturer concerned.

5 **Consider more 'public' questionnaires for general issues, and for summative feedback.** These can be used to measure feedback relating to non-personal variables such as:

- relative workload of different topics or modules;
- relevance of topics as perceived by students;
- relevance of practical work to theory, as seen by students;
- balance of lectures, tutorials, and other teaching/learning situations.

The more 'public' sort of questionnaire is more likely to have value when used towards the end of a course or module, and to gather summative feedback, which can be used in reviewing the course or module prior to the next time it will be delivered.

6 **Structured questionnaires can have the advantage of anonymity.** Even if you are using a mixed questionnaire containing open-ended questions as well, you may decide to issue the structured and open-ended parts separately because of this factor.

7 **Try to avoid surface thinking.** Students – and any other people involved – get bored if they have long questionnaires to complete, and the decisions or comments they make become 'surface' rather than considered ones. Even though students may be able to respond to a structured questionnaire of several pages in relatively few minutes, the fact that a questionnaire *looks* long can induce surface response behaviour.

8 **Consider the visual appearance of your questionnaires.** Go for a varied layout, with plenty of white space, so that it does not look like a solid list of questions. Use a mixture of response formats, such as deletions or selections from lists of options, yes/no choices, tick-boxes, graduated scales, and so on. Make it *look* interesting to complete.

9 **For every part of the questionnaire, have definite purposes, including positive ones.** Do not ask anything that could prove to be superfluous or of passing interest only. Ask about positive experiences as well as searching for weaknesses.

10 **Plan your evaluation report before you design your feedback questionnaire.** It helps a great deal if you know exactly how you plan to collate and use the responses you will get from your questionnaires. Working out the things you hope to include in your report often alerts you to additional questions you may need to include, and (particularly) to superfluous questions which would not actually generate any information of practical use to you.

11 **Make each question simple and unambiguous.** If students' interpretations of the questions vary, the results of a survey will not be valid enough to warrant statistical analysis

of any sort. In particular, it is worth ensuring that in structured questions, students are only required to make decisions involving a single factor.

12 **Ask yourself, what does this question really mean?** Sometimes, your reply to yourself will contain wording which will work better in your questionnaire than the original idea you started with.

13 **Avoid a safe middle ground in scales.** For example, the scale 'strongly agree, agree, undecided, disagree, strongly disagree' may give better results if the 'undecided' option is omitted, forcing respondents to make a decision one way or the other (or to *write* 'can't tell' on the questionnaire, which then has the validity of a conscious decision).

14 **Be aware that some respondents will make choices on the basis of those they think they are expected to make.** Many respondents set out to please the person gathering the feedback, possibly thinking of possible recriminations if critical selections may be traced back to their authors.

15 **Keep prioritizing questions short and simple.** For example, if students are asked to rank seven factors in order of value (or importance), it may be easy enough to analyse the best and worst choices, but difficult to make a meaningful analysis of middle ground.

16 **Pilot your draft questionnaire.** There is no better way to improve a structured questionnaire than to find out what students actually do with it. Use short print runs for questionnaires, and edit between each use.

17 **Remember that students' responses can be influenced by their mood at the moment of answering the question.** Ideally, you may wish to balance this source of variation out in one way or another, for example by issuing a similar questionnaire at another time, and comparing responses, or by including some alternative questions in other parts of your questionnaire which 'test' the same agenda so you can be alerted to inconsistency in responses due to swings of mood.

18 **Do not leave big spaces for students to fill in their replies.** You can compensate for this restriction later with an 'Any other comments?' space. If students' responses are necessarily short, you are more likely to get easily-interpreted answers to your questions, which helps make statistical analysis more fruitful.

19 **Decide whether you want the questionnaire to be anonymous, optional or respondent-known.** With responses involving handwriting, there is always the possibility of tracing respondents, and students may respond differently with this possibility in mind. With computer-based open-ended questionnaires, this dimension is simplified, but not entirely overcome if log-in data could be used to trace respondents.

20 **Resist pressures to over-use standard questionnaires.** This applies equally to structured, to open-ended and to mixed-mode questionnaires. Students quickly get bored with identical questionnaires, and are likely to fall into a standard mode of response, where there is

considerable 'echo effect' carried forward from previous decisions and responses. The most useful feedback data is normally generated by specially-produced questionnaires relating to a specific course or subject, or a particular aspect of the teaching and learning in that subject.

21 **Try to get a good response rate.** When questionnaires are filled in during contact time, you are more likely to get everyone's views. If questionnaires are taken away by students to be sent back later, there is a tendency to get lower response rates, and the students who actually go to the trouble of responding may not be representative of the whole group.

22 **Give students some free-ranging questions.** For example, it is worth considering asking them, 'What other questions should be included in future editions of this questionnaire?' and inviting them to supply their own answers to the questions

they think of. Such data is unsuitable for any statistical purposes, but is valuable in qualitative analysis of feedback from students.

23 **Work out how you are going to analyse the data from open-ended questions.** Sometimes a transcript collecting all responses to a question is necessary before the gist of the feedback can be discerned accurately. In other circumstances, counting the number of times something is mentioned in students' responses can be a valuable process.

24 **Do not accumulate piles of uninterpreted questionnaire data.** It is best to make a deliberate effort to produce a summary report (even if only for your own private use) for each set of data. A pile of feedback responses quickly becomes out of date as new developments are implemented in courses. Also, it is worth showing students that you take the data seriously enough to analyse it straight away.

Feedback from interviews with students

Interviews with students can be a valuable source of feedback. However, interviewing students is costly in terms of time and effort. The following suggestions may help you to make it a cost-effective process:

1 **Prepare your agenda carefully.** To enable you to analyse and collate the feedback you get from students, it is important that they are all asked the same questions in the same way. It is all too tempting to develop the agenda on the basis of the replies of the first few students, so it is usually worth piloting your question list on a few students (not

necessarily from the group to be targeted) before starting on a set of 'real' interviews'.

2 **Link interviews with other means of getting feedback from students.** If you are already using (or planning to use) structured or open-ended questionnaires, you may find it worthwhile to work out what *else*

you will be particularly looking for in feedback from interviews.

3 **Consider the merits of using interviews to follow up questionnaire feedback.** When you have already analysed questionnaire responses by students, you may be able to pinpoint a few issues where you want to ask students more detailed or more personal questions about their experiences with a subject or a course.

4 **Consider the alternative possibility of using preliminary interviews to establish the agenda for feedback questionnaires.** This would probably not take the form of interviews with the whole group, but with a representative selection of students.

5 **You may not be able to interview the whole group.** Decide how you are going to select the students you choose to interview. There are many possibilities, each with its own advantages and drawbacks. For example, you could select randomly by name or student number, or you could make a representative selection including high performers, middle-range performers and low achievers in related assessments, or you could ask for volunteers (not, however, the most representative of the possibilities).

6 **Remember that students may be anxious.** Any kind of interview may feel to students as if there is an assessment dimension present, and this may cause them to be restrained, especially when it comes to expressing dissatisfaction.

7 **Ask questions which lead students to answer rather than to refrain from comment.** For example, asking students, 'Was there anything you found unsatisfactory?' may be less fruitful than asking, 'What was the thing you liked least about the way this module was taught?'

8 **Do not lead your witnesses.** It is one thing to ensure that students feel free to answer questions, but another to lead them towards the answers you want, or the answers they may think you want. 'Do you like the way I used coloured overheads in my lectures?' is an obvious example of a leading question.

Feedback from groups of students

Students may be more forthcoming in a group, and you could consider posing the questions (maybe as a handout), leaving the group to come to decisions about how the students wish to answer them, then return to hear their answers. Students have the safety of being able to report minority views or controversial views, without the student who actually speaks such responses having to 'own' the view reported. Group interviews can actually save a considerable amount of time compared to solo interviews, and allow students to compare and contrast their own perspectives. Students in groups can also be helped to prioritize or sequence in order of importance their responses, making their feedback even more valuable. Group interviews can also be used to get students to clarify or explain issues or responses which at first may be unclear.

This can be more useful than feedback from individuals, for the following reasons:

- **Feedback from groups captures discussion, reflection and debate.** This is more useful than only having the reactions of individual students.
- **A group can present negative feedback with less embarrassment than an individual.** Individuals can be more forthcoming in making inputs in a group, when their feedback is rendered more or less anonymous within the group.
- **Group feedback is likely to range more widely.** Where a questionnaire is used as an agenda for group feedback, the group is more likely to be willing to go beyond the agenda.

It is essential to make good notes when interviewing groups of students. After four or five interviews, you may have a good idea of the general nature of responses to your questions, but you could have lost a lot of the specific detail. More recent interview happenings tend to 'drown' earlier ones in one's memory.

Feedback from student representatives

Most institutions have policies on student representation on decision-making committees and boards. Student representation is, however, not without its problems. The following suggestions may help you to make the most of having student reps on committees:

1 **Try to ensure that the right person is chosen to represent student views.** Too often, the duty is thrust upon the first student who shows interest, or who is too polite to refuse. It can be worth allowing a class a period of time in which to choose who will represent them, and providing some contact time to discuss what is involved, and maybe to facilitate a ballot or election.

2 **Remember that the student(s) chosen may be somewhat in awe of the committee.** Students can feel uncomfortable in a gathering of so many highly-qualified academics, and this can lead them to be observers rather than true participants in the processes of meetings.

3 **Take care when putting student representatives 'on the spot'.** They will not necessarily be able to speak at once on behalf of their classmates. They may be able to give their own personal views (which of course are valuable in their own right), but you may need to allow them time to find out the opinion of their colleagues before reporting back to a future meeting of the committee or board.

4 **Allow student representatives to contribute to the agenda-forming process.** When they are given time to supply suggestions for the agenda of a future meeting, they have the chance to discuss the matter with fellow students, and the ownership of the representation is duly enhanced.

5 **Be prepared to give student representatives responsibilities for researching particular views of their classmates.** It is important that this does not become burdensome to them. It helps, however, when they have definite purposes underpinning each stage of their liaison with their fellow students. Student reps can, for example, have more success at getting a good response rate from a questionnaire to the class, especially if entrusted and briefed to make their own preliminary analysis of the findings *before* giving in the completed questionnaires.

6 **Treat student representatives as full committee members.** This means (for example) ensuring that they receive notice of meetings, agendas and minutes in the same ways as academic members of the committee. They should also feel at liberty to show any of the documentation to fellow students.

7 **Make sure student reps' comments and contributions are minuted accurately.** Even if they make controversial comments, the fact that they *are* being minuted acts as an appropriate restraining process. Also, this helps the student reps themselves prove to the students they are representing that they have indeed followed through matters at the committee.

8 **Do not cut student reps off in mid-flow.** It may have taken them considerable courage (maybe backed by substantial preparation or research) before they make an impassioned plea or complaint or suggestion. Courtesy demands that they are given at least as much chance to have their say as anyone else.

9 **Do not let student reps become overburdened with duties and commitments.** Remember that they are also studying, and it is tragic if their studies suffer significantly as a result of the energies and time they put into representing fellow students.

10 **Consider ways in which student reps may gain academic credit for their role.** For example, this could be done as a project module in an independent studies pathway. Many Student Union branches are looking at accreditation of the student representative role. Alternatively, consider finding ways of including the service of student reps into student profiles or records of achievement.

11 **Remember to thank student reps for their time and their work.** It is important that they feel that their role is valued, and not just a ritual for appearance's sake. As well as verbal appreciation at meetings, it is worth sending each student representative an official 'thank you' letter when terms of office are completed.

References and further reading

Andressen, L, Nightingale, P, Boud, D and Magin, D (1989) *Strategies for Assessing Students – Teaching with reduced resources*, SEDA Paper 78, Staff and Educational Development Association (SEDA), Birmingham, UK

Ausubel, D P (1968) *Educational Psychology: A cognitive view*, Holt, Rinehart and Winston, New York

Baume, C and Baume, D (1986) Learner know thyself – self-assessment and self-determining assessment in education, *New Era*, **67** (3), pp 5–67

Beaty, L and McGill, I (1992) *Action Learning: A practitioner's guide*, Kogan Page, London

Bell, C and Harris, D (1994) *Evaluating and Assessing for Learning*, 2nd rev edn, Kogan Page, London

Biggs, J (1999) *Teaching for Quality Learning at University*, Open University Press/SRHE, Buckingham

Biggs, J B (1989) Approaches to the enhancement of tertiary teaching, *Higher Education Research and Development*, **8**, pp 7–25

Bloom, B S, Engelhart, M D, Furst, E J, Hill, W H and Krathwohl, D R (1956) *Taxonomy of Educational Objectives: Cognitive domain*, McKay, New York

Boud, D (1986) *Implementing Student Self-Assessment*, HERDSA Green Guides vol 5, University of New South Wales, Australia

Boud, D (1992) The use of self-assessment schedules in negotiated learning, *Studies in Higher Education*, **17** (2), pp 185–200

Boud, D and Lublin, J (1983) *Self-Assessment in Professional Education*, University of New South Wales, Australia

Bourner, T and Race, P (1995) *How to Win as a Part-Time Student*, 2nd edn, Kogan Page, London

Bourner, T, Martin, V and Race, P (1993) *Workshops that Work*, McGraw Hill, Maidenhead

Brandes, D and Norris, J (1998) *The Gamester's Handbook 3*, Stanley Thomas, Cheltenham

Brandes, D and Phillips, H (1990) *The Gamester's Handbook 1*, Stanley Thomas, Cheltenham

Brandes, D and Phillips, H (1990) *The Gamester's Handbook 2*, Stanley Thomas, Cheltenham

Brown, G and Atkins, M (1988) *Effective Teaching in Higher Education*, Routledge, London

Brown, G with Bull, J and Pendlebury, M (1997) *Assessing Student Learning in Higher Education*, Routledge, London

Brown, R (1988) *Group Processes – Dynamics within and between groups*, Blackwell, Oxford

Brown, S and Glasner, A (eds) (1999) *Assessment Matters in Higher Education – Choosing and using diverse approaches*, Open University Press, Buckingham

Brown, S and Knight, P (1994) *Assessing Learners in Higher Education*, Kogan Page, London

Brown, S and Race, P (1994) *Assess Your Own Teaching Quality*, Kogan Page, London

Brown, S, Rust, C and Gibbs, G (1994) *Strategies for Diversifying Assessment in Higher Education*, Oxford Centre for Staff Development, Oxford Brookes University, Oxford

Brown, S, Race, P and Smith, B (1995) *500 Tips on Assessment*, Kogan Page, London

Brown, S, Race, P and Smith, B (1997) *500 Tips on Quality Enhancement*, Kogan Page, London

Brown, S (1996) The art of teaching in small groups – 1, *The New Academic*, **5** (3), SEDA, Birmingham

Brown, S (1997) The art of teaching in small groups – 2, *The New Academic*, **6** (1), SEDA, Birmingham

Brown, S and Race, P (1997) *Staff Development in Action*, SEDA Paper 100, SEDA Publications, Birmingham

Conway, R *et al* (1993) Peer assessment of an individual's contribution to a group project, *Assessment and Evaluation in Higher Education*, **18** (1), pp 45–56

Coulson, A (1994) *Objective Testing*, Red Guide Series 11 No 4, University of Northumbria at Newcastle

Cox, K R and Ewan, L E (1988) *The Medical Teacher*, Churchill Livingstone, Edinburgh

Crooks, T (1988) *Assessing Student Performance*, HERDSA Green Guides, vol. 8, University of New South Wales, Australia

Daniel, J S (1996) *Mega-Universities and Knowledge Media: Technology strategies for higher education*, Kogan Page, London

Ellington, H I and Race, P (1993) *Producing Teaching Materials*, 2nd edn, Kogan Page, London

Fry, H, Ketteridge, S and Marshall, S (1999) *A Handbook for Teaching and Learning in Higher Education – Enhancing academic practice*, Kogan Page, London

Gibbs, G (1992) *Assessing More Students*, Oxford Centre for Staff Development, Oxford Brookes University, Oxford

Gibbs, G (1994) (ed) *Improving Student Learning: Theory and practice*, Oxford Centre for Staff and Educational Development, Oxford Brookes University, Oxford

Gibbs, G (1994) *Learning in Teams: A student guide*, Oxford Centre for Staff and Learning Development, Oxford Brookes University, Oxford

Gibbs, G (1994) *Learning in Teams: A student manual*, Oxford Centre for Staff and Learning Development, Oxford Brookes University, Oxford

Gibbs, G (1995) *Learning in Teams: A tutor manual*, Oxford Centre for Staff and Learning Development, Oxford Brookes University, Oxford

Gibbs, G (1999) Using assessment strategically to change the way students learn, in *Assessment Matters in Higher Education – Choosing and using diverse approaches*, ed S Brown and A Glasner, Open University Press, Buckingham

Gibbs, G (with various co-authors) (1994) *Course Design for Resource-Based Learning*, separate volumes covering *Social Science, Education, Technology, Accountancy, Built Environment, Art and Design, Business, Humanities, Science*, Oxford Centre for Staff and Learning Development, Oxford Brookes University, Oxford

Gibbs G, Habeshaw, T and Jaques, D (1992) *Teaching More Students 3: Discussion with more students*, Oxford Centre for Staff and Learning Development, Oxford Brookes University, Oxford

Gibbs, G and Rust, C (1997) (eds) *Improving Student Learning through Course Design*, Oxford Centre for Staff and Educational Development, Oxford Brookes University, Oxford

Griffiths, S and Partington, P (1992) *Enabling Active Learning in Small Groups*, Universities Staff Development Unit (USDU), Sheffield

Habeshaw, S and Steeds, D (1987) *53 Interesting Communication Exercises for Science Students*, TES, Bristol

Hardingham, A (1998) *Working in Teams*, IPD Books, London

Heron, J (1989) *The Facilitator's Handbook*, Kogan Page, London

HM Government (1997) *Higher Education in the Learning Society*, Report of the National Committee of Enquiry on Higher Education ('The Dearing Report'), HMSO, London

Jaques, D (2000) *Learning in Groups*, 3rd edn, Kogan Page, London

Johnson, D W and Johnson, F P (1991) *Joining Together: Group theory and group skills*, Prentice Hall, Englewood Cliffs, NJ, USA

Knight, P (ed) (1995) *Assessment for Learning in Higher Education*, Kogan Page SEDA Series, London

Kolb, D A (1984) *Experiential Learning: Experience as the source of learning and development*, Prentice-Hall, Englewood Cliffs, NJ, USA.

Laurillard, D (1993) *Rethinking University Teaching*, Routledge, London

Leigh, D (1996) *Designing and Delivering Training for Groups*, Kogan Page, London

Lewin, K (1952) Field theory in social science, in *Selected Theoretical Papers* ed D Cartwright, Tavistock, London

Matthews, L (1994) *Managing Dissertation Supervision*, Red Guide Series 8 No 5, University of Northumbria at Newcastle

Matthews, L (1994) *The Range of Marks in Assessment*, Red Guide Series 8 No 4, University of Northumbria at Newcastle

Northedge, A (1990) *The Good Study Guide*, Open University Press, London

Pask, G (1976) Styles and strategies of learning, *British Journal of Educational Psychology*, **46**, pp 12–25

Race, P (1992) *500 Tips for Students*, Blackwell, Oxford

Race, P (1993) *Never Mind the Teaching, Feel the Learning*, SEDA Paper 80, SEDA, Birmingham

Race, P (1994) *The Open Learning Handbook*, 2nd edn, Kogan Page, London

Race, P (1999) *How to Get a Good Degree*, Open University Press, Buckingham

Race, P (ed) (1999) *2000 Tips for Lecturers*, Kogan Page, London

Race, P (2000a) *How to Win as a Final-Year Student*, Open University Press, Buckingham

Race, P (2000b) *500 Tips on Group Learning*, Kogan Page, London

Race, P and Brown, S (1993) *500 Tips for Tutors*, Kogan Page, London

Race, P and Smith, B (1995) *500 Tips for Trainers*, Kogan Page, London

Ramsden, P (1992) *Learning to Teach in Higher Education*, Routledge, London.

Ramsden, P and Entwistle, N J (1981) Effects of academic departments on students' approaches to studying, *British Journal of Educational Psychology*, **51**, pp 368–83

Rowntree, D (1989) *Assessing Students: How shall we know them?* 2nd rev edn, Kogan Page, London

Rowntree, D (1992) *Exploring Open and Distance Learning*, Kogan Page, London

Rowntree, D (1994) *Preparing Materials for Open, Distance and Flexible Learning*, Kogan Page, London

Rust, R and Wallace, J (1994) *Helping Students to Learn From Each Other*, SEDA Paper 86, SEDA, Birmingham

Saunders, D (ed) (1994) *The Complete Student Handbook*, Blackwell, Oxford

Skinner, B F (1954) The science of learning and the art of teaching, *Harvard Educational Review*, **24**, pp 88–97

Thorley, L and Gregory, R (1994) *Using Group-Based Learning in Higher Education*, Kogan Page, London

Tiberius, R G (1999) *Small Group Teaching: A trouble-shooting guide*, Kogan Page, London

UCoSDA and Loughborough University (1996) *Making the Grade: Achieving high quality assessment profiles*, UCoSDA, Sheffield

Wade, W et al (1994) *Flexible Learning in Higher Education*, Kogan Page, London

Zander, A (1982) *Making Groups Effective*, Jossey-Bass, San Francisco

Index